D1165361

Conversations with Legendary Television Stars

CONVERSATIONS WITH LEGENDARY TELEVISION STARS

Interviews from the First Fifty Years

James Bawden and Ron Miller

UNIVERSITY PRESS OF KENTUCKY

Editorial and Sales Offices: The University Press of Kentucky
663 South Limestone Street, Lexington, Kentucky 40508-4008
www.kentuckypress.com

Library of Congress Cataloging-in-Publication Data

Names: Bawden, James, interviewer editor. | Miller, Ron, 1939– interviewer, editor.
Title: Conversations with legendary television stars : interviews from the first
    fifty years / James Bawden and Ron Miller.
Description: Lexington : The University Press of Kentucky, 2019. |
    Series: Screen classics | Includes index.
Identifiers: LCCN 2019015002| ISBN 9780813177649 (hardcover : alk. paper) |
    ISBN 9780813177663 (pdf) | ISBN 9780813177656 (epub)
Subjects: LCSH: Television broadcasting—United States. | Television actors
    and actresses—United States—Interviews. | Television personalities—United
    States—Interviews.
Classification: LCC PN1992.3.U5 C68 2019 | DDC 791.4502/80922—dc23

This book is printed on acid-free paper meeting
the requirements of the American National Standard
for Permanence in Paper for Printed Library Materials.

Manufactured in the United States of America.

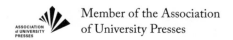

Member of the Association
of University Presses

For my brother, Harry Bawden, and his wife, Martha, for putting up with me all these years.

James Bawden

In memory of four dear departed friends: the novelist Con Sellers, who showed me how to write and market short stories and articles to national magazines while I was still a college student; the great humorist Gerald Nachman, a pal and colleague for half a century; that whimsical wit Murry Frymer, a dear man and brilliant columnist; and the CBS publicist Axel Peterson, who helped me set up many of my interviews in this volume and became a beloved friend along the way.

Ron Miller

Contents

Contents

Introduction

How Television Created Its Legendary Stars

Ron Miller

Since the late 1950s, when virtually every household finally possessed at least one TV set, television has been the dominant North American entertainment medium, replacing radio and severely impacting our moviegoing habits. That's one of the primary reasons James Bawden and I decided early in our separate journalism careers to seek assignments covering the exciting world of television.

Of course, Jim and I were already intense movie fans, so it was a pleasure to discover that so many of the stars who had captivated us in our boyhood years were now working mainly in television—and might actually be available to us for interviews should we wind up on the TV beat. It also was pretty obvious to us that the movie stars of the future were very likely to come from a television background—the great new training ground for the next wave of comedians, action heroes, and musical stars of the big screen. In fact, that trend was already in progress when we started covering TV, and former TV stars like Clint Eastwood, Goldie Hawn, and Annette Funicello were now marquee names at the local bijou. Half a century or so later, it's amazing how many of those stars who started on TV are now considered legendary icons of film.

Many actors who transitioned from movies to television had been big-name stars of the 1930s and 1940s whose box office appeal had faded as they aged, but who still had considerable name value for the TV screen: Lucille Ball, Barbara Stanwyck, Jane Wyman, Loretta Young, Robert Cummings, Robert Young, Ann Sothern, Jane Wyatt, and many more.

Some were veteran performers who had been on stage, screen, or radio before coming to television, but had never become big box office stars. Still, their rich show business experience made them ideal performers for television in those days when the medium was still live, before filmed or videotaped programs. Suddenly, TV was making enormous stars out of them: Jackie Gleason, Sid Caesar, Danny Thomas, Raymond Burr, James Arness, Jack Webb, and the comic who became "Mr. Television" for a whole generation—Milton Berle.

Radio disc jockey Dick Clark became a TV star with his local Philadelphia program *American Bandstand* when it went network and he began to introduce the rock and pop music stars of the 1950s and 1960s to a huge national daytime audience. Meanwhile, the parents of those young viewers were tapping their feet in rhythm with polka king Lawrence Welk, a regional orchestra leader from the "sweet band" era who became a phenomenon when he launched television's *The Lawrence Welk Show*, with its "champagne music" and acts like the comely Lennon Sisters.

Singing cowboys Gene Autry and Roy Rogers had followed the example of William "Hopalong Cassidy" Boyd by shifting from the movie screen to television with great financial success. TV soon had so many westerns—more than thirty in one season—that the genre eventually suffocated itself from overexposure on TV, collapsing on the big screen as well. However, James Arness, who had been an awkward supporting player in movies since *The Farmer's Daughter* in 1947, bloomed into a major TV star as Marshal Matt Dillon on *Gunsmoke*, a show that came over from radio and ran for more than twenty seasons on TV. The TV western genre provided a safe haven for faded movie stars like John Payne (*The Restless Gun*), Dale Robertson (*Tales of Wells Fargo*), Rory Calhoun (*The Texan*), and Ward Bond (*Wagon Train*) while producing new ones like Clint Eastwood (*Rawhide*), Steve McQueen (*Wanted Dead or Alive*), and both James Garner and Roger Moore (*Maverick*). Michael Landon, who had played the title role in the absurdly popular teen drive-in movie *I Was A Teenage Werewolf* in 1957, became one of the most durable of all TV stars in the western *Bonanza*, followed by the frontier saga *Little House on the Prairie*.

More than a few onetime movie stars migrated to TV soap operas, like Macdonald Carey, who became a long-running regular on *Days of Our Lives*. Jack Paar, who had managed only small roles as an actor in movies, became an enormous TV star as the host of *The Tonight Show*. Noel Neill, who had been the big screen's first Lois Lane in the 1940s serials *Superman* (1948) and *Atom Man vs. Superman* (1950), became TV's Lois Lane in the television series version of *Superman*—and the growing juvenile TV audience sustained her. Leonard Nimoy, who had been a bit player in the movie version of the radio show *Queen for a Day* and a zombie in the 1952 movie serial *Zombies of the Stratosphere*, became an iconic TV star as Mr. Spock in the original *Star Trek*. Another interesting thing is that quite a few actors who started out as "second bananas" in some beloved TV shows later rose to full stardom in their own TV series. Consider Harry Morgan, second banana to Spring Byington in *December Bride*, to Jack Webb in *Dragnet*, and to Alan Alda in *M*A*S*H*, who became the top banana in *Pete and Gladys*, the spinoff from *December Bride*, and in *After M*A*S*H*, the sequel series to *M*A*S*H*.

But why do so many of us now consider these performers "legendary" icons of the television medium? I'm guessing there are a couple of obvious reasons. First, the TV medium brought these people right into our homes, often on a regular weekly schedule, and that helped them become much more familiar to us than actors we saw two or three times a year on the movie screen. Familiarity doesn't always breed contempt. More often it makes us feel we know the person better.

Another crucial reason is the fact that the nature of series television requires the creation of likeable characters whose traits we almost immediately start identifying with the actor playing those characters. In other words, Lucille Ball played scores of different characters in the movies, but once she became Lucy Ricardo on *I Love Lucy*, it almost felt like she was the wacky neighbor living next door to us—and we looked forward to seeing her on her regular visits to our living room.

By the same token, a newcomer in movies like James Garner was just another tall, good-looking guy until Warner Bros. found a durable image for him as TV's Bret Maverick, a frontier gambler who would rather fast-talk his way out of a fight, even though he was fully capable of handling himself well enough with his fists or his six-gun. That *Maverick* image fit Garner so perfectly that it stuck with him in his later hit TV detective series, *The Rockford Files*. Jim Rockford was so close to Bret Maverick in nature that one could almost imagine the frontier gambler had been his grandfather. That image was so well liked by his legions of TV fans that it firmly established Garner as a major star who could move back and forth easily between the big and little screens.

TV's uncommon ability to create new images also served someone like Raymond Burr, who had kept busy in movies for years, almost always in smaller roles and more often than not in dark characters of the "heavy" genre, no doubt because Burr was a bulky guy not cut in the traditional heroic mode. He didn't become a genuine star until cast as TV's *Perry Mason*, a role others played before and after him, but never as brilliantly as Burr did. He owned the role forever after.

And though Milton Berle had been in pictures since the silent movie days, he had never become a reliable star who could carry a feature film on his name alone. But in the early days of live television, when the medium desperately needed performers used to holding an audience's attention without the help of film editors, Berle was a godsend. Movie fans had never experienced his uncanny ability to improvise in front of a live audience, which he did regularly with great humor on *The Texaco Star Theatre*, later *The Milton Berle Show*, which delighted viewers from 1948 to 1956.

Like Berle, both Jackie Gleason and Sid Caesar had failed to catch fire as movie stars in the 1940s, but both were experienced live theater and club performers and TV offered them the chance to create their own family of characters, something they'd never been able to do in the movies. And while Red Skelton had managed to reach stardom in the movies, he, too, became even bigger in TV, where his ability to improvise original characters was fully unleashed.

Always regarded as a major Broadway musical star, Mary Martin had indifferent results with her movie career, but her performance as Peter Pan in a series of live television productions gave her the huge national audience that had eluded her for years. Another actress with a solid-gold reputation as a Broadway dramatic star was Julie Harris, who also had failed to light up the movie screen in a number of attempts. The TV medium was ideal for her in the golden age of the late 1940s and early 1950s when live drama was a regular attraction. She dazzled viewers in her many roles on TV's Hallmark Hall of Fame, won two Emmy Awards for dramatic roles, and eventually settled into a comfortable career as a character actress in TV shows like *Knot's Landing*.

The TV medium also has given many actors the chance to move up from "second-banana" status to loftier places at the top of the bunch, often by reinventing themselves in ways that probably wouldn't have been possible under movie studio contracts. Buddy Ebsen, for instance, was an eccentric dancer in an act with his sister in his early movie days at MGM, but when the vogue for that style of dancing wore off in the 1940s, he wound up being a comic sidekick to B-movie western stars at Poverty Row studios in order to pay his rent. When TV gave him the chance to play the rural sidekick to Fess Parker in Walt Disney's *Davy Crockett* programs, that led to his casting as Jed Clampett in CBS's *The Beverly Hillbillies*—and suddenly he was a major star of TV situation comedy. When the networks started dumping their rural comedy shows because not enough younger viewers were watching, Ebsen reinvented himself again as TV sleuth *Barnaby Jones*, once again topping the cast list. What made it possible to extend and enrich Ebsen's acting career was the fact that millions of viewers had come to love the sight and sound of him. He was beloved, a status the actor had earned over many years and never took for granted.

Another good example would be Richard Crenna, who was once the squeaky-voiced student Walter Denton on radio's *Our Miss Brooks* and followed star Eve Arden to television when she took her hit show to the new medium in 1952. Once established as a sitcom star, it was natural for Crenna to stay with the genre, playing the son of grumpy Walter Brennan in TV's *The Real McCoys,* another popular comedy series. But Crenna was a tall, good-looking man who longed to play not only more serious roles but also leading roles. TV gave him the chance to prove he could do it in 1965 in the dramatic series *Slattery's People,* in which he portrayed a US senator and the show's sole leading man. From then on, Crenna had a long and rewarding career as a dramatic actor in films like *The Sand Pebbles* (1966) with Steve McQueen; *Star!* (1968), in which he was leading man to Julie Andrews; and as Sylvester Stallone's mentor in the first Rambo film, *First Blood* (1982), and its first two sequels. Crenna also continued to star in television movies, notably the 1985 miniseries *Doubletake,* in which he created the role of detective Frank Janek, which led to a popular series of Janek movies for television.

Donna Reed and Patty Duke were two Academy Award–winning movie actresses who found new directions for their careers in television, both as stars of situation comedies. Reed, who had won her Oscar playing a prostitute in *From Here to Eternity* (1953), became one of TV's most wholesome sitcom moms in *The Donna Reed Show* (1958–1966), which made her very rich. Duke, the child actress who won her Oscar as Helen Keller in the movie version of *The Miracle Worker* (1962), also became a TV star with a sitcom role, playing twins in *The Patty Duke Show* (1963–1966). After that, she went on to become one of TV's most acclaimed dramatic actresses in movies and miniseries.

In this collection of interviews, James Bawden and I will try to explain what made so many of us embrace these actors and welcome them into our homes each week. We were extremely fortunate to be able to talk with so many of them before they left us for good. We think the stories they have to tell of their struggles to reach stardom and to keep their careers blooming in television are quite fascinating. We hope you will share that feeling with us as you turn the pages of this book and perhaps learn some things you didn't know about TV's greatest stars.

Eddie Albert

Interview by James Bawden

Eddie Albert was already one of the most reliable character actors and occasional leading men in the movies by the late 1940s when he began to seriously consider acting in the new television medium. By the 1950s, he had made a place for himself in TV while still continuing to land strong supporting parts in movies, like his Oscar-nominated role as Gregory Peck's pal in *Roman Holiday* (1953). Then, in the 1960s, Albert landed his first starring role in a TV series, the hit comedy *Green Acres* (1965–1971), following this with his costarring role with Robert Wagner in the mystery series *Switch* (1975–1978). From then on, he continued to work steadily on the small screen.

Albert's success was temporarily slowed during the McCarthy era of the late 1940s and early 1950s when he and his wife, Mexican actress Margo, were both blacklisted for associating with leftist organizations.

With few exceptions, Albert generally played likeable guys, so when he played a nasty character like the vicious prison warden in the 1974 movie *The Longest Yard*, it really shocked his fans.

Albert was the real-life father in a solid show business family, including actress wife Margo, their son actor Edward Albert, who had his own successful career in movies and television, and their adopted daughter Maria, who was active in the management of her father's career.

Setting the Scene

So there I was on a dark and stormy fall night in 1990 at Toronto's lakefront Alliance Studios, weathering a terrific rainstorm and trying to talk to the guest star of the week: Eddie Albert. Albert was the latest American import for *Ray Bradbury Theater* (1985–1887), which used Canadian casts and crews and a US name to boost ratings in American syndication. Albert looked lean and vigor-

6

Eddie Albert with his wife, Margo. James Bawden collection.

ous, hardly anywhere near his age of eighty-one. As the clock struck midnight, he was raring to go in his last scene in the episode, titled "Touch of Petulance."

The Interview

BAWDEN: To begin at the beginning, you were born in 1908 in Rock Island, Illinois.

ALBERT: Not exactly. Mother wasn't married at the time, which was a huge scandal in those days, so she later fudged my birth certificate to read 1908 when the true date was 1906. Dad was Frank Heimburger, who married her the next year. I was the oldest of five kids. When I was one, we moved to Minneapolis and I later studied at Central High School opposite a pert redhead named Harriette Lake, who years later became Ann Sothern and these days insists she was born in 1915. Which would make her about eight when we were classmates together in 1923. I then went to University of Minnesota, where I majored in business. But a little thing called the Crash of 1929 put me on the breadlines.

BAWDEN: So you moved to New York City in 1933 and got some radio gigs.

ALBERT: And changed my name. Too many announcers pronounced it as "hamburger." I became a staple on *The Honeymooners: The Grace and Eddie Show*. I also got roles in such Broadway hits as *Brother Rat* [1936], *Room Service* [1937], and *The Boys from Syracuse* [1938]. In 1936, I was on one of the first live demonstrations of TV, performing with buckets of purple varnish on my face amid the sweltering lights. Then I wrote a play, *The Love Nest*, for TV, which I performed with my acting partner, Grace Brandt. About a hundred TV sets caught that one.

BAWDEN: Then it was off to Hollywood?

ALBERT: Warners bought the film rights to *Brother Rat* and imported me and I was on my way, along with such unknowns as Ronnie Reagan, Jane Wyman, and Wayne Morris. By the time the film had completed shooting, Ronnie became Jane's third husband. All these years later, Janie insisted I be hired for a continuing part on her big hit series *Falcon Crest*—and she also got Eve Arden in another episode. Eve's also from those Warners days. And that's what I call real loyalty.

BAWDEN: Could you have ever imagined Ronald Reagan would one day be president of these United States?

ALBERT [*laughing*]: No! And neither did he! Before the White House, he was the host of TV's *Death Valley Days*.

BAWDEN: How did your Warners contract work out?

ALBERT: It didn't. They rushed me into a Hollywood version of *On Your Toes* [1939], starring Vera Zorina. Ray Enright was the director and he made it in three weeks. The songs were used as background music! No singing at all in a musical! Only the "Slaughter on 10th Avenue" ballet was supercharged and Ray did not direct it. Then I limped into a sequel, *Brother Rat and a Baby*

[1940]. Ouch! I did *Four Wives* [1939], a sequel to *Four Daughters.* Then I made *Four Mothers* [1941]. I was in a very cute Olivia de Havilland picture, *My Love Came Back* [1940]. Jack Warner went into her dressing room one day and there was a shouting match and Jane Wyman, who was also in the picture, said, "Olivia's Olivia-izing again."

BAWDEN: But you made a well-received picture with Humphrey Bogart, *The Wagons Roll at Night* [1941], also with Sylvia Sidney?

ALBERT: Jack Warner realized his studio was stuffed with tough guys and few female stars. So he imported Sylvia, who was no slouch in the shouting department, and she and Bogey went at each other. I was a grocery jerk turned lion tamer. I'm making this one seem actually interesting. Then Sylvia falls for me. Then Joan Leslie, who was only sixteen, falls for me. It was an unscripted remake of *Kid Galahad.* Bogey got first-star billing for the first time, but he was a mean and nasty drunk, I can tell you.

BAWDEN: Then what happened?

ALBERT: I made such stinkers as *Lady Bodyguard* [1943], *Treat 'Em Rough* [1942], *Ladies Day* [1943], and then I headed for the US Army. Anything had to be better than that back-lot trash.

BAWDEN: You served with distinction, receiving a Bronze Star.

ALBERT: The guys who didn't come home deserve the credit. I had to start at the bottom of the barrel again. *Smash-Up: The Story of a Woman* [1947] was the only decent picture I made around then. I also made *Rendezvous with Annie* [1946], *Hit Parade of 1947* [1947], *The Dude Goes West* [1948]. My scenes in *Unconquered* [1947] for Cecil B. DeMille were cut from the picture. I took anything to survive. I was even in a rare Lucille Ball stinker, *The Fuller Brush Girl* [1950].

BAWDEN: But you weren't in losers all the time. You were in *Carrie* [1951] and got your first Oscar nomination for *Roman Holiday* [1953].

ALBERT: *Roman Holiday* was [director] Willie Wyler's love letter to Audrey Hepburn. Willie was ever so patient with her. Besides, he actually liked scenes that took thirty takes. Greg Peck was less enthusiastic as the picture progressed. After all, he was the star, but Audrey got all the attention and finally Paramount asked if she couldn't also be billed above the title. My [character's] name still tickles me: Irving Radovich. People catch it on TV and ask why was it shot in black-and-white? It was Rome in 1953 and the power was iffy and Technicolor used a ton of power and the cameras were far from mobile. So I think they could colorize this one. But you'll notice Greg and Audrey never again worked together.

BAWDEN: What about *I'll Cry Tomorrow* [1955]?

ALBERT: Biographies of singers were popular around then. And Lillian Roth's story was very powerful. Susan Hayward had already impersonated Jane Froman. Here she had a field day, although she was drinking iced tea. But she was a big enough star to demand that. She's one tough cookie and I tried not to get in her way and she got another Oscar nomination.

BAWDEN: I just think *Oklahoma!* [1955] a very weird movie musical.

ALBERT: Oh, you mean Gloria Grahame as Ado Annie? Well, what about Rod Steiger as Jud Fry? I think the leads—Gordon MacRae and Shirley Jones—were fine. But our director, Fred Zinnemann, wasn't suited to something like this. The Agnes De Mille ballets stand up. But nobody has mentioned this one to me recently. I was Ali Hakim, the traveling salesman, and I got a few laughs.

BAWDEN: Some people think you did your best work in *Attack* [1956].

ALBERT: It proved I could do it—play the coward. I mean, I'd been there, I knew war. Same for Jack Palance. His nastiness came from actual combat detail. A recent letter to me said it was the best war movie ever made. And we did it all at California ranches. It all came together because of the intense, fat, creepy Robert Aldrich as director. He knew exactly what he wanted. It was real hell making it, I can tell you. He once told me directing *Baby Jane* was a picnic compared to this one.

BAWDEN: You started doing TV work way back.

ALBERT: Live TV nurtured me. I remember doing a live *Suspense* in 1949, then *Danger, Plymouth Playhouse, Revlon Mirror Theater, Studio One in Hollywood.* My first TV series was *Leave It to Larry* in 1952. We lasted all of eleven episodes. I was a shoe salesman working in the store owned by my father-in-law, played by the marvelous Ed Begley. We started on CBS in October and by the New Year that was it, and Ed was blacklisted around the same time.

BAWDEN: Is it true you turned down *My Three Sons*, which Fred Mac-Murray turned into a monster hit?

ALBERT: Guilty as charged. In 1960, [producer] Don Fedderson then peddled it to MacMurray, who did all his scenes in four months, which left him free for Disney movies the rest of the year. I'd already turned down *Mr. Ed.* Now that one I don't regret.

BAWDEN: How did you get *Green Acres*?

ALBERT: Well, I'd already done twelve episodes of *Petticoat Junction*, starting in 1965, as Oliver Wendell Douglas. Jay Sommars pitched it to CBS as a spin-off and it worked from day one. Of course, it was weird. We filmed it at General Service Studios on North Las Palmas. The problem was to keep a straight face. I told Eva Gabor [his costar] to always stay in character.

Surreal is the right word to describe it. It certainly was not a spin-off as such of either *Petticoat Junction* or *Beverly Hillbillies*. The thing was I farm in a classy suit and tie and Eva wears her finery. And Arnold the Pig was always watching TV on the sofa.

The cast made it: Pat Buttram as Mr. Haney; Tom Lester, who remains my best friend, as Ed Dawson; Frank Cady; Alvy Moore; Hank Patterson—I mean, they became as close as family. I played straight to these characters. We rarely changed a line, it was that well written.

Dick Bare directed 155 of the 170 episodes masterfully. My old pal from WB [Warner Bros.], Vince Sherman, came on board in 1971 for one episode and said all he had to do was bawl, "Action!" We knew our characters that well. We'd normally do an episode every three days. There was no rushing about. Happiest time of my acting life.

I never strained for a laugh. It was all there in the writing and those amazing character actors. The real story was how insane modern society had become. So my character jettisons the rat race and grows carrots. Everyone wanted that same life.

BAWDEN: And then you were canceled.

ALBERT: Made no sense. We remained high in the ratings and young people would stop me everywhere. CBS decided to cancel all its rural shows. Suddenly being number one in the ratings wasn't as important as reaching urban viewers.

BAWDEN: You got a second supporting Oscar nomination for *The Heartbreak Kid* [1972].

ALBERT: It should have been for *The Longest Yard* [1974]. That's all I'm going to say about that.

BAWDEN: But you went back to CBS for *Switch* in 1975.

ALBERT: I was asked by R. J. [Robert Wagner], one of my best friends. It was either work about three days a week on this or die from boredom. It lasted three years. Should have been longer. We had a youngster, Sharon Gless, who since has matured on *Cagney and Lacey*. Glen Larson produced, but he had too many shows running. The quality wasn't always there. I loved the way R. J. knew all the names of the crew and they'd work their butts off for him. In the second year, we became a more traditional detective saga, with the sheen of comedy left behind. Viewers were bewildered. The story lines got dumbed down, I felt. So did R. J. But Glen said he knew best and by the end of the third year the ratings had just dripped away.

Afterword

Albert's last credit was for the TV series *California* in 1997. Albert's wife died in 1985. Eddie Albert suffered from Alzheimer's disease in his later years and died of pneumonia on May 26, 2005. He was ninety-nine. The couple's son, Edward, died in 2006 of lung cancer.

Eve Arden

Interview by James Bawden

When network television finally began to get organized in the late 1940s, one of the supposedly surefire programming moves for the new TV networks was to convert their hit radio programs into TV shows. But it didn't always work out so well.

For instance, radio's longest-running comedy show, *Amos 'n' Andy*, starred two white men, Freeman Gosden and Charles Correll, who played black characters. That could work in radio because you didn't see the actors, but they would have to appear in blackface makeup on-screen. They got away with that in the early 1930s, when they made their only movie appearances, but the practice wasn't acceptable in the late 1940s. African American actors were hired to play the roles when *Amos 'n' Andy* finally came to television in 1951. Though the show was still popular, it drew severe criticism for its image of black culture and finally was taken off the air.

Another hit radio show was *Fibber McGee and Molly*, but radio actors Jim and Marian Jordan both played multiple characters, something that couldn't work on television. When the show finally came to television with different actors, it quickly failed.

But there was no such problem when CBS decided to convert its hit radio comedy series *Our Miss Brooks* into a TV series with its original star— Eve Arden. The seasoned actress already had been in movies for years when *Our Miss Brooks* began on radio in 1948. People knew what she looked like, so they knew what her character, high school teacher Connie Brooks, "looked like" on radio, so it was no surprise to anybody when she brought Miss Brooks to television in 1952.

For Arden, the fact that *Our Miss Brooks* gave her a leading role on both radio and television—the show ran simultaneously on both mediums for several years—was a major career achievement. In her movie years, she appeared

Eve Arden, circa 1939. James Bawden collection.

mostly in supporting parts in comedy and dramatic films, and now she was not only the star of the show, she was playing a beloved character that she was closely identified with for the rest of her life.

She was born in Mill Valley, California, on April 30, 1908, as Eunice Quedens, a name that didn't last long once she decided to become an actress. Tall at five foot seven, she was destined to stand out from the start—and she certainly did.

Setting the Scene

In 1972, Eve Arden's agent was looking for some newspaper space to help publicize the fact that Canada's CBC-TV was programming a festival of twenty-five Eve Arden films. I was happy to talk with her on the phone about the festival—and everything else I could possibly think of at the time. We wound up talking for several hours, despite the pleas from her husband Brooks West that I could hear in the background, imploring her, "Come back to your dinner!"

The following year, we hooked up in person, meeting at the old Brown Derby restaurant at Hollywood Boulevard and Vine Street in Hollywood. Subsequently, we did several more telephone interviews.

The Interview

BAWDEN: I saw you when TV showed *Dancing Lady*, the 1933 musical with Joan Crawford that introduced Fred Astaire to the movies. You were playing a tempestuous southern actress who walked by Crawford in one sequence.

ARDEN: The part was so small I didn't get billing. Two days' work, I think. And I received no further offers, so it was back to Broadway. When I reminded Joan Crawford of that scene twelve years later when we were doing *Mildred Pierce*, she patted me on the shoulder and smiled, "Dear heart." I could tell she remembered zilch!

BAWDEN: So you went back to Broadway?

ARDEN: I'd done the rounds of the movie casting directors. Too tall! Too angular! Not beautiful! So I got a gig in a low-budget show that ran at L.A.'s El Capitaine playhouse. The other unknown kids included Tyrone Power and Kay Thompson. But producer Lee Shubert saw me on a good night and signed me for *Ziegfeld Follies of 1934*. Ziegfeld had just died.

I took the name Eve Arden from a perfume bottle. And I was in the *Follies* with Fanny Brice, Jane Froman, Buddy Ebsen. Then I was in *Parade*, which starred Jimmie Savo. And then came *Ziegfeld Follies of '36* with Fanny Brice, Bob Hope, Judy Canova. When I left that summer, Gypsy Rose Lee was my replacement! But I was back to Hollywood to make a test and then costar in *Oh, Doctor!* with Edward Everett Horton. Eddie gave me a grand bit of advice: "Don't act. Just say the lines with your unique accent and you'll turn out okay."

BAWDEN: What do you remember about *Stage Door* [1937]?

ARDEN: How all these unknowns later became famous: Lucy Ball, Ann Miller, me. And the stars Kate Hepburn and Ginger Rogers were feuding all the way through, particularly "Great Kate." There was a lot of improvisation going on as Lucy and I tried to top each other. Director Greg La Cava liked what we were doing and let us build up our parts, although Great Kate protested. I had to bang out one-liners with a cat wrapped around my shoulders and that cat didn't like me and I had the scratches to show for it! This had been a Broadway hit, but the movie was considered superior. But box office was weak because Hepburn was then considered box office poison. And while the two leads feuded, little Andrea Leeds walked off with the Oscar nomination [in support]. And you know, twenty years later I'm driving through Hollywood and *Stage Door* has been revived. Only the marquee now reads: Lucille Ball and Eve Arden in *Stage Door* with Katharine Hepburn. I should have taken a photo.

BAWDEN: But it made you hot?

ARDEN: As a freelancer. There were no long-term studio offers. Ginger got me hired at RKO for *Having Wonderful Time* [1938], where I met another newcomer—Red Skelton. He just plain liked funny people and recommended me for a job in his comedy *Whistling in the Dark* [1941]. My forte was the one-line. Exit stage right, drop the zinger, exit stage left. Lucy Ball and I competed for the same type parts. I did five of those parts in 1939 and I could do so because my parts were very small. I didn't have to linger. I'd do my scenes and then go onto the next assignment.

BAWDEN: But you had a classic scene in *At the Circus* [1939].

ARDEN: With Groucho Marx. I was Peerless Pauline. The scene people remember is when we're upside down on the ceiling, trading quips. I don't have to tell you the room was specially designed to be completely flipped so that the furniture on the ground could be nailed down. At the end the camera was merely flipped back. I had to wear a sequined cap or my hair would have given it all away, don't you see? And did you know Fred Astaire copied that in one number where he dances on the ceiling? Groucho phoned me and said, "Fred stole our routine." Life on a Marx Brothers set wasn't fun but hard work. Groucho was a deadly serious man who analyzed every joke and rode his brothers to do take after take. But with [Irving] Thalberg [head of MGM production] gone, there was nobody to protect them and this one was rather hurried in production. It was good, but not great like the others.

BAWDEN: You once said you started out wanting to be one of the glamour girls, then slowly changed your mind. What did you think of Hollywood's glamour girls?

ARDEN: I had an Eve Arden bit in *Comrade X* [1940], but Hedy Lamarr was completely frigid off and on camera. And then I was in for a few scenes in *Ziegfeld Girl* [1941], where I got to know Lana Turner a bit. But not Hedy Lamarr, who was completely standoffish. Lana was a complete realist. Knew she was entirely a creation of the studio and she guessed in time audiences would grow tired of her. She played cards with her makeup ladies between scenes and used rough sailor language. But there was no phoniness.

With Rita Hayworth in *Cover Girl* [1944], I saw a very anxious young thing eager to succeed. Both [Lana and Rita] had come up from poverty. Rita started out as a very young dancer in movies. Columbia shaved her hairline back and colored her hair a copper tone. She was given lessons on how to talk and out emerged this very sexy, if insecure, superstar. Directors had to tell her how to do every moment. She was pliable. When she danced, it was magic. But her [singing] voice was always dubbed. I watched both Lana and Rita from afar and figured out it was better to remain just me.

BAWDEN: How did you get to Warners in 1941 for the Marlene Dietrich film *Manpower*?

ARDEN: [Producer] Hal Wallis personally phoned me up and offered it to me. I'd already done a Kay Francis film, *Women in the Wind* [1939] and *A Child Is Born* [1940]. I was dependable and Hal said I could be their next Glenda Farrell, which didn't interest me. Said if I did well I'd be offered a long-term contract, which I definitely did not want. I was too busy freelancing right then. I wasn't too fond of Marlene [Dietrich], who never spoke much to the girls who were her buddies at the club. The director, Raoul Walsh, said she'd wanted only older women so she'd look younger—one of the tricks of the trade. Instead she got me, Lucia Carroll, Lynn Baggott, and Joyce Compton, and she was the oldest one! She kept production on hold for hours while fiddling with her costumes, makeup, and lighting. Once I looked up and she was way up on the gondola, arguing with one of the electricians. Everything was for Marlene. She even provoked a brawl between George Raft and Eddie Robinson. You're right, Raft won.

Wallis told me it was an old favorite story of Jack Warner's that had been used several times since *Tiger Shark* in 1932. Dietrich had a little mirror in her handbag, and just before a shot would check to make sure she had a shadow under her nose. She said [director Josef] von Sternberg had told her to do that. And Hal did come through with a contract offer, which I declined.

BAWDEN: But you returned to Warners in 1944 for *The Doughgirls*, which I've never been able to see.

ARDEN: You haven't missed much. It was a huge Broadway hit, which is where I first saw it. I phoned up producer Mark Hellinger and begged for the role of the Russian sharpshooter. Warners paid a record $250,000 for it and then promptly ruined it by cutting out much of the comedy. Mark said I'd get it if I signed a seven-year contract and I was ready. I had married, I needed stability. I was the celebrated sniper Natalia and I used a very broad accent. The girls were Ann Sheridan, Alexis Smith, and Jane Wyman. Originally Faye Emerson was going to get my part, but comedy wasn't her forte. Wyman and Jack Carson were the scatterbrained couple. The next year Jane made *The Lost Weekend* at Paramount and had a whole new career before her.

BAWDEN: Then you made *Mildred Pierce?*

ARDEN: Not so fast! Next I made *My Reputation* with Barbara Stanwyck and George Brent. We completed it in early 1944, I think, and then it went out to servicemen all over the world. There was such a backlog of product it was on the shelf domestically for two years. This one is Barbara's favorite movie. She was a war widow and it was all very dignified and very, very slow. I was her trusted confidante. George at the end said this was the end of thirteen years at Warners and refused to re-sign. For that offense—disloyalty—Jack [Warner] ordered the credits be reshot and George was denoted to under-title billing. Jack was like that, very vindictive. Then came *Mildred Pierce.*

BAWDEN: And you got your only Oscar nomination for it. What are your memories?

ARDEN: That Barbara [Stanwyck] was first choice, but passed because she didn't want another mother role. Then Bette Davis passed. Joan Crawford was third choice and not wanted by director Mike Curtiz. He'd scream at her to get rid of her shoulder pads. And she was so wound up she'd cry and rage and run off. She knew how much depended on this one being a hit. Curtiz was basically concerned with lighting and shadows. He never gave much direction. Because Joan was so frantic, the set was kept frigid so she wouldn't sweat. Everybody around tested for [the role of] her daughter. I did one test with Joan Leslie and then they got Ann Blyth from Universal. People still quote those lines back to me. Like: "Alligators have the right idea. They eat their young." I thought it might succeed on curiosity value and be a hit. Joan had been away for two years. Then it just grew and grew and became this monster smash. I lost as Best Supporting Actress to Anne Revere [*National Velvet*], and just a few years later she got blacklisted. Joan got her Oscar and a new dressing room at Warners and was now queen of the lot.

BAWDEN: In *Night and Day* [1946] you were a French chanteuse.

ARDEN: I was always asking for a different kind of part. And I got it. Only they added some wisecracks for good measure. I was Gabby and Cary Grant was Cole Porter, and if you believed that, you'd believe anything. I thought I was okay. This was Mary Martin's last movie. She'd done fine here and Jack offered her a contract and she had to decide between *Romance on the High Seas* [on-screen] and *South Pacific* on Broadway. Guess which she chose? Her replacement at Warners was a new girl, name of Doris Day. Jane Wyman was playing a silly showgirl by day [in *Night and Day*] and in the afternoon was over at MGM making *The Yearling*, for which she won her first Oscar nomination.

BAWDEN: What did you think of *The Unfaithful* [1947]?

ARDEN: Director Vince Sherman sent over a script and I read it and telephoned him. "Vince, this is a rewrite of *The Letter*, right?" And he went berserk for a few moments. Because I was right. Look, I have no knowledge why Jack Warner continually saddled Annie [Ann Sheridan] with such heavy melodramatics. Here she was an unfaithful wife, Lew Ayres was the lawyer, and Zachary Scott the husband. We shot a lot of it out on the streets and in a new subdivision where Annie's house was supposed to be. Oh, I was very mean and self-centered there, a new divorcee living high on Wilshire Boulevard in a smart penthouse apartment. The scenic designers outdid themselves and when Zachary, who was my cousin, dropped in on a Saturday night I was lying on the sofa reading a book and drinking white wine! It was a different character for me to explore.

BAWDEN: Then came *Voice of the Turtle* [1947].

ARDEN: Every year I journeyed to New York to catch the new plays and the biggest hit was *Voice of the Turtle* with Maggie Sullavan, Elliott Nugent, and Audrey Christie as an outrageous actress type. When Warners bought it, I was ecstatic and got the part of Olive. Then Irving Rapper was signed to direct. Bad idea. He did well in Bette Davis women's films but wasn't adept in comedy. Warners wooed Sullavan and she even made a test in New York, but Jack wanted her under long-term contract and she hesitated. So he picked Eleanor Parker and in one press release it was mentioned Ellie was a decade younger. Well, Ellie is brilliant in drama but they even made her up to look like Maggie—complete with bangs! And the leading man wasn't Nugent but Ronnie Reagan and he was hopeless at comedy. Plus the script needed rewrites because in the play it's obvious the couple are living together. I got good personal notices. And that's it. It wasn't the anticipated box office hit.

BAWDEN: Around this time you debuted on radio as *Our Miss Brooks*?

Gale Gordon with Eve Arden in *Our Miss Brooks*. Courtesy of the Young and Rubicam agency and CBS.

ARDEN: Well, I'd always been doing radio. I was on *The Ken Murray Show* in 1936 and then I was a regular on *The Danny Kaye Show* on CBS. Then I replaced Joan Davis on Jack Haley's show called *Village Store*. He left and Jack Carson took over and that's when I really got tired of Jack Carson. Verna Felton was on it, too. Then in 1947 CBS sent me the script for *Our Miss Brooks*, written for Shirley Booth, who had passed. It was agreed we'd try it out in summer stock—summer on CBS. A new, unknown actor, Jeff Chandler, was the biology teacher, Phil Boynton, and Gale Gordon was the principal, Mr. Conklin, Gloria McMillan was Harriet, and Dick Crenna was high-pitched Walter Denton. Jane Morgan was my landlady, Mrs. Davis. I was the man-hungry English teacher but I was also a working woman. It just worked and we got a full year's contract. We were on Sundays at 6:30 p.m., which meant we did it in L.A. at 3:30 p.m. Jack Warner couldn't complain. It was my one day off a week.

BAWDEN: By day you toiled at Warners.

ARDEN: In 1949 I was Doris Day's roommate in *My Dream Is Yours* and Jane Wyman's best bud in *The Lady Takes a Sailor*. I didn't want to be a roommate any longer. We were just finished filming with Jane when she got her Oscar [for *Johnny Belinda*] and everybody ran to see it and it was awfully corny. Bette Davis had just left the studio, so Jane got her dressing room and ordered it repainted and fumigated. Bette smoked like crazy, you know.

I told Jack [Warner] formally I was quitting and made my last in 1951, a Joan Crawford comedy called *Goodbye My Fancy*. Joan did not have a funny bone in her body. She loved to suffer. It had been a huge Broadway hit for Madeleine Carroll but the censors cut the red meat out of it.

One day Joan stops me and says, "Eve, they say you are going into television. So sorry." So I read her my contract, which made me very wealthy, and she had bug eyes. She never did get to do a series because, like Bette Davis, she was too big for the small screen. Me, I was sick of wisecracking dames. I craved respectability.

BAWDEN: What happened to Warners? The studio seemed to be sinking like a stone.

ARDEN: You're telling me! As soon as an actor's contract was up, he or she was out. Sheridan, Lupino, Flynn, it happened to them all, and many were at an age they found freelancing tough. The economic model changed. Warners stopped making a movie every week for release. People were moving out to the suburbs where there were no movie theaters. And then TV came along. And it was like a state of panic. I did a terrible movie called *Tea for Two* [1950], a bad remake of *No, No, Nanette,* just because the studio owned the music rights and could make it cheaply. But it did make some money because Doris Day was the big new star.

BAWDEN: How did the TV version of *Our Miss Brooks* differ from the radio version?

ARDEN: Well, we had to ditch Jeff Chandler because he was a red-hot movie star by then. Bob Rockwell replaced him, but for the next year we still did the radio version separately and Jeff stayed on for that. As I recall, we used completely different scripts. After the last radio show, he told me I was something special in his life and he regretted we were married to other people and I never saw him again. It was all so crazy.

A lot of TV hits came from radio: *Father Knows Best, Life of Riley, Burns and Allen*. We'd get the new script on a Friday and do a rough block and on Monday more rehearsals and then do it before a studio audience. Then on Tuesday we'd film touch-ups. So we did two episodes a week, which was heavy. Don't forget, the order was for thirty-nine half hours. Plus the radio show! I always thought the radio shows were better because listeners had to imagine so much. Look, we'd all been doing it on radio except Bob, so we somehow got through it and I got all kinds of awards from teaching associations. In 1953 I did get the Emmy and that was a real thrill.

In 1954 I had my youngest child, Douglas, who was born in September before filming started on a new season. I always thanked him for that.

We ended filming at Desilu in 1957–1958. The show was bad that last year. They moved me to a new school and it didn't take so they brought in all the old gang and we somehow got through it.

BAWDEN: You returned to Warners in 1956 for the movie version of *Our Miss Brooks*.

ARDEN: Definitely a strange experience. Everybody from my era had left except Virginia Mayo, who was doing westerns, and Jane Wyman, whose last WB film [*Miracle in the Rain*] was just going into release. A lot of the crews had been laid off. I don't know why they made this one at the end of the TV series run. It should have been when the series was at its peak. We were all in it—Dick Crenna, Gale Gordon, Bob Rockwell, Jane Morgan—but it wasn't a sitcom at all. It was more of a drama and I had a sort of romance with Don Porter, who was in Ann Sothern's TV series. And I got a note from Jack Warner to have lunch in the studio's executive restaurant. He was one lonely guy, kept complaining there was nobody left to fight with.

BAWDEN: You once told me your favorite series was *The Eve Arden Show* [1957].

ARDEN: CBS threw money at me to immediately return as a book lecturer, and it was so different I took it. But audiences loathed me as a mother and a thoughtful individual. They wanted the wisecracks. We had a good cast, including Allyn Joslyn and Frances Bavier, who then went to *The Andy Griffith Show* as Aunt Bea. Audiences just tuned me out. Bob Young had the same problem. He returned too soon [after *Father Knows Best*] in a stinker called *Window on Main Street,* which also sank like a stone. Also a little show called *Wyatt Earp* was against us. I was wearing all these pretty clothes and nobody wanted me. What a disaster!

BAWDEN: After that series ended you made a dramatic appearance in *Anatomy of a Murder* [1959].

ARDEN: Otto Preminger called me up and offered me the job of Maida, Jimmy Stewart's secretary. The whole shebang was going to be photographed in northern Michigan. I told Otto I wouldn't accept any shouting from him, but I was lucky since all my scenes were with Jimmy. And Otto never yelled at the star. He wouldn't dare. But he did go after others. Like Lana Turner, who had been signed as the murder defendant's wife. He screamed so much at her for wardrobe choices she simply quit and was replaced by Lee Remick, and Otto ordered the press release to mention the fact she was eighteen years younger than Lana.

I spent eight weeks in Ishpeming, Michigan. We were all holed up in the same hotel. Arthur O'Connell was wonderful as the drunken assistant. It was George C. Scott's first movie and Jimmy helped him a lot. And even my husband, Brooks West, had a good part. Jimmy later told me he got so much flak from fans about the adult language, he never again accepted such a daring part, and I think that damaged his later career.

BAWDEN: Then you did *The Dark at the Top of the Stairs* [1960].

ARDEN: [Director] Delbert Mann saw *Anatomy* and offered me the big part of Dorothy McGuire's sister, Lottie, which Eileen Heckart had done on the stage. It was a very depressing story, very true of small-town life in the 1920s. I remember talks with the playwright, Bill Inge. Bob Preston was too hammy in the lead, if you ask me. But I thought Angela Lansbury fine as the blowsy hairdresser who takes him in. I had this delicate balancing act. Lottie is a wisecracker but there's also a sadness. She and her husband, wonderfully played by Frank Overton, are not sexually compatible and she openly talks about that. Not a sympathetic character. She's anti-Semitic in a casual sort of way, as many small-town women were at the time. I knew it would not be popular and it was not. But I'm glad I did it.

BAWDEN: You still did a ton of TV.

ARDEN: It was where I was a star. And I needed big bucks. Still do, by the way. So I did a lot of guest spots. I did a lot of Red Skelton, but you'll notice I never was on Bob Hope. He just never phoned. Heck, I even was in a 1965 Frankie Avalon movie [*Sergeant Deadhead*]. In 1965, I did a CBS pilot where I was a busybody widow constantly visiting relatives and getting them all stirred up. I was grateful it did not sell. The next season CBS asked me to return to series TV in *The Mothers-in-Law*, to be executive-produced by Desi Arnaz. Ann Sothern was to costar until she decided the parts were too similar, so Kaye Ballard came in. We did a pilot and CBS floored Desi by passing. So he shopped the thing to NBC, which bought the show and put us opposite Ed Sullivan at 8:30 on Sunday nights. That was part of the reason we flopped. Another was Desi's temper. He'd rage and the NBC executives had no history with him and they'd shout back. We suddenly got a renewal form but in the second season we switched my husband to Richard Deacon and nobody noticed, which meant nobody was watching.

BAWDEN: But you did another pilot.

ARDEN: You're speaking of the Hildegarde Withers TV movie I made for ABC called *A Very Missing Person* [1972]. You know, the movies starred first Edna May Oliver and then Helen Broderick [as Miss Withers]. But they made her too smart-alecky. I thought it had potential to be part of the Sunday murder mystery wheel. So I just went back to guest work. And all the theater I was doing all along.

BAWDEN: And now what about *Grease* [1979]?

ARDEN: My biggest-ever hit. When they offered me Principal McGee I wondered why. Then I realized it was the Connie Brooks connection. In my mind it was Connie finally getting to occupy the principal's office. And that's the way I did it. Had wonderful scenes with Sid Caesar. Not a funny man off camera. Quiet. Thoughtful. On camera wildly inventive. Just takes one along on a wild ride. And it got me a whole new audience, which was great for me— and Joan Blondell.

Then I did *Dream Merchants* [1980] and the director was old Vincent Sherman, as feisty as ever. So I think I'll go on a bit longer.

Afterword

Our Miss Brooks was a phenomenal success for Eve Arden—a program built around a character based upon her own persona developed over years as a much-loved, wisecracking woman of accomplishment. It ran from 1948 to 1957 on radio and from 1952 to 1956 on television. The 1956 feature film version was literally a coda for the series, ending with Miss Brooks's marriage and a future almost certain to be a good one.

In 1983 Arden costarred in *Grease 2,* and for her final acting gig, in 1987, she was a guest on TV's *Falcon Crest* opposite old pal Jane Wyman.

Arden was married twice—first to Ned Bergen in 1939. They were divorced in 1947. She married actor Brooks West in 1952. He died in 1984. She had four children with West, all but the youngest one, Douglas, adopted. She died on November 12, 1990, of a cardiac arrest. She was eighty-two.

James Arness

Interview by Ron Miller

James Arness embodied one of the most enduring characters in the history of the television medium: frontier marshal Matt Dillon of Dodge City, Kansas, the central persona of *Gunsmoke,* arguably one of the most successful TV dramas of all time.

Arness played other roles before *Gunsmoke* and a precious few after the show ended its incredible twenty-year run, but he'll always be remembered for the role that originated on radio with someone else [William Conrad] playing the part. John Wayne helped him land the role, even appearing on-screen in the first episode of the program to introduce Arness to the television audience. Arness was Wayne's friend and acting protégé; he had appeared in smaller roles in several of the Duke's films, including *Big Jim McLain* (1952), *Island in the Sky* (1953), *Hondo* (1953), and *The Sea Chase* (1955). Wayne had urged him to take the role of Matt Dillon because "you're too big for the movies anyway."

Yes, Arness was pretty big, all right. Some sources say he was six foot seven, but I think I'll go with those sources that say he was six foot six. Anyway, the point is he towered over everybody any time they put him in a scene with other actors. The Duke figured he'd dwarf all comers on the TV screen and that would set him apart from the horde of TV western stars crowding the tube in 1955 when *Gunsmoke* elbowed its way into the prime-time lineup.

The height of Arness wasn't always an asset, though. In the 1940s, when he began to seek roles in pictures, he was so much taller than most leading men on-screen in those days that none of them wanted to be seen standing next to a big, handsome guy like that. One rather famous exception was in *The Farmer's Daughter* (1947) when the film's star, Loretta Young, is shown leaving the farm for the big city, saying good-bye to her three brothers—all huge men of obvious Scandinavian heritage. Arness was one of them and one of the other two was his real-life brother, Peter Graves, who would go on to TV

From left: John Wayne, Ward Bond, and James Arness in the 1953 film *Hondo.* Courtesy of Batjac Productions and MPI.

fame himself in *Mission Impossible* a few years later. (The third brother was played by Keith Andes, who became a leading man for a short time, though his movie career never really flourished.)

Another occasion when his height really counted was when he played the title role in the classic science fiction film of 1951, *The Thing from Another World.* That was Jim Arness playing the giant monster from outer space who scared the dickens out of moviegoers. Arness always seemed a mite embarrassed by that role, but it was certainly a memorable one.

Oddly, both Arness and brother Peter Graves seemed to be offered more roles in science fiction pictures than anything else. Arness played a heroic supporting role in another great sci-fi film of the 1950s—*Them!* (1954), in which he battled giant ants morphed into monsters by nuclear tests. Meanwhile, his brother starred in Poverty Row sci-fi features like *Red Planet Mars* (1952) and *Killers from Space* (1954).

His success on *Gunsmoke* did bring Arness a few offers of leading roles in movies, but he seemed content to stick with the medium that had so warmly

James Arness, circa 1978. Courtesy of MGM Television.

welcomed him in 1955. In 1977, he took the leading role of another frontiers-man, Zeb Macahan, in ABC's *How the West Was Won,* inspired by the epic motion picture of the same name. It became a regular series that ran from 1978 to 1979. He followed that with a real change of pace—a crime drama called *McClain's Law,* which lasted only one season, 1981–1982. He starred in two elaborate TV movies—*The Alamo: Thirteen Days to Glory* (1987), in which he played Jim Bowie, and the remake of *Red River* (1988), in which he took on the leading role that John Wayne had played in the 1948 feature film.

After that, Arness was content to wait for the return of *Gunsmoke* once CBS began to make a series of "reunion" movies that covered the later years of Matt Dillon and some of the other characters from the original series.

Setting the Scene

If you were a TV columnist, as I was from 1977 to 1999, you knew it was a waste of time to ask CBS to arrange an interview with James Arness. He didn't do them—and hadn't done any in a long, long time. In fact, Arness was said to be so anti-publicity that he eventually barred all reporters from the *Gunsmoke* set.

Still, I started asking anyway once Arness agreed to go back to work as Matt Dillon in a series of made-for-TV movies that revisited Dodge City and the characters in *Gunsmoke*. The answer was always "Sorry, but he isn't talking to anyone."

Then, in 1993, I was stunned to get a call from a network publicist who said Arness had agreed to help promote what ultimately turned out to be the final *Gunsmoke* movie. He asked if I wanted to be the lucky guy who got the first of those rare interviews. When I regained consciousness, I locked that interview down as securely as possible.

For me, it was a monumental coup. I loved the "reunion" movies that brought Arness back to his iconic role. The writers had moved the Matt Dillon character on from his old setting and given him new emotional depth. Arness took an eager interest in the reinvention of Marshal Dillon: in those few movies, he reminded me what a fine actor he could be when playing a character he knew intimately, a man who had been tailored over the years to fit him like a glove.

We met for a late breakfast at a restaurant in Beverly Hills. Arness showed up on time and in good spirits and was as friendly and cooperative as if he'd been doing such interviews on a regular schedule for years. I liked him right away and found him to be a thoughtful and considerate man with no trace of superstar ego, even though he was by any measure a genuine TV superstar.

The Interview

MILLER: *Gunsmoke* was planned to be an adult western with a serious character at its center. It had already established that approach on radio. How did you tackle the task of becoming Matt Dillon?

ARNESS: I just stepped into a whole character and tried to stay on my feet and not bump into the furniture. I don't think any series ever got onto television that was that fully evolved. They had fine-tuned this over several seasons [on radio] and had those characters and their relationships down pat.

MILLER: I know you've lavished praise on the writing of the show. Can you talk about that?

ARNESS: It was so strongly written that you could almost bumble your way through it. It would take a really bad actor to screw it up.

MILLER: Do you think the "adult" approach with stories of significance was the reason *Gunsmoke* outlasted every other TV western show?

ARNESS: I think there's a very large element of that in it. How all that worked, I've never known. But I think there's a large group of people out there who have always found a great deal of meaning in it.

MILLER: Nobody ever accused you of being a lightweight in the acting department, but you had little experience playing leading roles. How much did your prior movie work prepare you for being Matt Dillon?

ARNESS: Before *Gunsmoke*, I had small parts, but lots of opportunity to sit around back out of the light and watch really fine actors like John Wayne and Spencer Tracy work. I was not the kind who was really trying to become a skilled craftsman. I wasn't overly tuned to that kind of thing. I was absorbing things, though.

MILLER: Many have assumed John Wayne served as your mentor as an actor.

ARNESS: I didn't sit around discussing the philosophy of acting with other actors and Wayne was like that, too. He was all business on the set and ready to socialize only when the shooting was finished for the day.

MILLER: How about the directors you worked with in pictures before *Gunsmoke*? In 1950, for instance, you worked in John Ford's *Wagon Master*. What was he like?

ARNESS: It was an incredible experience to get on the picture. I just stayed back on the sidelines, which you learned fast to do when you were on one of his sets. Ford had about three hundred to four hundred feet from the camera as a perimeter and when he stepped across that line, you'd better be totally silent. He was a very quiet guy. You could hardly hear him when he was setting something up.

MILLER: How about John Sturges, who gave you the chance to work with Spencer Tracy in *The People against O'Hara* [1951]?

ARNESS: Sturges was a big guy at Metro at the time. I was under contract there for about a year, but I was in six pictures. He was a very professional guy, a good guy to work with.

MILLER: You also were in *Battleground* [1949], which was directed by "Wild" Bill Wellman. Your impression of him?

ARNESS: Wellman was a kind of boisterous character. He told the jokes and, boy, you'd better laugh!

MILLER: And how about settling a big movie mystery for me? Newcomer Christian Nyby directed you in *The Thing from Another World*, but the producer was Howard Hawks, one of the great directors, and many people suspected he must have been doing a lot of the directing himself for the picture to come out so suspenseful and exciting.

ARNESS: He was sort of in the background. Again, he was a sort of quiet guy. He was there, all right, but he wasn't standing behind Nyby for every shot or anything like that.

MILLER: Speaking of influences, I've heard that Milburn Stone, who played Doc from the start of the *Gunsmoke* TV series, was a big influence on you. He was a veteran actor who had been a leading man in B pictures and a seasoned character actor in supporting roles. How influential was he on you?

ARNESS: He was influential on all of us in the ensemble. He was born and raised in Kansas around 1900 on what was then the remnants of the frontier. I remember him so well talking about when he was a young boy, how they'd cruise into town and walk up and down the streets where some of the old guys who had lived at the time of Dodge City were out on the porches, whittling away and telling their stories. Milburn had the highest kind of regard for all that. It was almost sacred to him.

MILLER: You worked so long with Stone and the others that it must have seemed like you were all family members. Was it that way from the start?

ARNESS: Yes it was. Milburn, for example, was such a marvelous guy that you liked him immediately. Yet at the same time, he was very much a disciplinarian dedicated to this project called *Gunsmoke*. In his mind, this was a chance to show that period, that region, and those people in the best way they'd ever been depicted. It was an opportunity he'd waited years for and—*boom*—here it was!

MILLER: The chemistry between you and Amanda Blake was always good and I'm sure most fans of the show assumed Matt and Kitty would someday wind up together. But even though Kitty appeared in the first reunion movie, *Return to Dodge* [1987], and was still devoted to Matt, it must have shocked fans to later discover that Matt had fathered a daughter, but not with Kitty. Would you have gone along with it if they'd had Matt marry Kitty?

ARNESS: Of course, Kitty was the one people used to say you could take further. But I always felt that once you get down that road, it's pretty hard to retreat from it. You could do a story where they get together, but then what do you do next week? Over time, what happened was an intimation of a very close relationship. To a certain degree, people could fill in the blanks if they wanted to.

MILLER: How did fans react when we learned in one of the reunion movies that Matt had a daughter conceived with a character played by Michael Learned in a rather romantic episode back in the original series?

ARNESS: There was kind of a split reaction. Some people felt Matt was out of character, but others felt it showed he was kind of human.

MILLER: Now, Dennis Weaver is one of the original *Gunsmoke* actors who has avoided ever climbing back into his Chester character for the reunion movies or apparently for anything else that would put him back in that character.

ARNESS: He went out and had a very successful career.

MILLER: Did you ever feel like Matt Dillon had limited your career and kept you from being considered for other roles you might have liked to try?

ARNESS: I've never had even the slightest thought of that type. This was as fulfilling as anything I can imagine. I wouldn't trade careers with anyone I can think of, living or dead.

MILLER: Did you realize at the time how big *Gunsmoke* was going to be for you?

ARNESS: At that age, it was fun time for me. I enjoyed it. To me, the whole business was providential, something I fell into.

MILLER: By the second season, you must have realized this thing you'd fallen into was going to be a monster hit.

ARNESS: I couldn't even describe it to you what that felt like. It hit us so big and so fast.

MILLER: Considering how much you loved the show, why did you become so averse to publicity about it?

ARNESS: I didn't always feel that way. When you do the same show, playing the same character six hundred times, you run out of things to say. That's what happened to me after about five years. By nature, to overpublicize things is hard for me to do. Having a show on every Monday night, year after year, is publicity enough. Do more and it starts going against you. Don't stay out there until they start throwing rotten eggs at you.

MILLER: After *Gunsmoke* finished its long run, you tried something quite different as the star of a modern crime show, *McClain's Law.*

ARNESS: That show was such a total switch. Talk about a fish out of water. For twenty years, I'd been out in the boonies with nobody around and suddenly here I was downtown on the streets of San Pedro, waiting to cross on the green light and crowds all around me.

MILLER: Some might think you were too heavily typecast after playing a frontier hero for two decades. Did you ever give any thought to the roads you might have taken beyond *Gunsmoke*?

ARNESS: No director ever sent me a script saying, "Hey, this is the next *Gone with the Wind.*" I never got such a script, never had any remote sort of offer to do something else great. Today they'd offer me *The Thing, Part Two*. And I might even take it.

MILLER: With the success of these new *Gunsmoke* movies, the enormous popularity of Clint Eastwood's *Unforgiven* (1992), and western movies being done for television by Tom Selleck, Sam Elliott, and Kenny Rogers, do you see the western making a big comeback on the screen?

ARNESS: I don't know if that's really happening. To my knowledge, there isn't really a big resurgence of the western. But certainly there's something about the hard-pressed lives of people of the 1990s that might make them see a certain mystique in them and a chance to get away from their present-day concerns.

MILLER: If the *Gunsmoke* movie you just finished turns out to be the final one, will you be out there looking for something else to do?

ARNESS: A paycheck is always nice to have, but I don't have any compulsion to go out and do one more anything.

Afterword

Arness was a rifleman in the US Army in World War II and was severely wounded in the leg during the beach landing at Anzio in 1944. He was plagued with pain from that injury throughout the rest of his life. He also had other problems to cope with that may have contributed to his being publicity shy during his TV fame. He was divorced from his first wife Virginia in 1960 after twelve years of marriage. His daughter from that marriage, Jenny Lee Arness, committed suicide by drug overdose in 1975.

Arness was a surfer, and his son Rolf became world surfing champion in 1970. In 1978 he married his second wife, Janet Surtees, who survived him after his death from natural causes at his home in Brentwood, California, on June 3, 2011. He was eighty-eight.

Bea Arthur

Interview by James Bawden

In the world of 1970s television situation comedy, there was literally nobody like Bea Arthur, who arrived in the middle of CBS's *All in the Family* in 1971 as Edith Bunker's liberal cousin Maude Findlay, and went on to star in two of TV's most successful comedy series—*Maude* and *The Golden Girls*. Tall, imposing, and outspoken, Bea Arthur was the antidote not only to crusty right-winger Archie Bunker but also to a generation of sweet, petite, and occasionally daffy sitcom leading ladies. *Sweet, petite,* and *daffy* definitely were not words ever used to describe either Bea Arthur or the characters she played.

Born Berniece Frankel in New York in 1922, she grew up in Cambridge, Maryland, where her family tried to discourage her stage ambitions. An early, short-lived marriage to producer Robert Alan Aurthur gave her a name change (modified to Arthur).

Arthur was thirty-two when she finally found her first taste of Broadway fame in a 1954 revival of Kurt Weill's *Three Penny Opera* costarring the legendary Lotte Lenya. Then came important parts in *Plain and Fancy* (1955), *Seventh Heaven* (1955), *Nature's Way* (1957), followed by stardom once again in the original 1964 production of *Fiddler on the Roof.* In 1966, she opened with Angela Lansbury in the musical *Mame,* in which their comedy duet "Bosom Buddies" invariably stopped the show. (Arthur reprised her part as sidekick Vera Charles in the truly awful 1974 film version starring Lucille Ball.)

Seasoned by more than two decades of stage experience, Arthur came along at a time when producers like Norman Lear, who first cast her in *All in the Family,* were remaking the image of American women in a new, stronger, more influential model that rapidly altered the way television portrayed them.

Though Arthur had considerable success in theater and made some feature film appearances, television was her domain—and she made a significant mark there, winning two Emmy Awards, and in 2008, a permanent place in the Television Hall of Fame.

34

Setting the Scene

I first met Bea Arthur in a CBS rehearsal hall in June 1972. Her new series *Maude* was due to rev up on CBS in September, and several episodes had already been taped. I was there to interview Bill Macy as part of a series I was writing for the *Spectator* on second bananas, and, after a delightful lunch at a trendy Belgian eatery on the Sunset Strip, he invited me back to CBS to watch a rehearsal. The live taping would take place days later.

I had a jolly talk with Bea Arthur, who assured me she was working well with Macy, joking, "If he interferes with my close-ups I can always sit on him. I'm far taller than he is!" When Macy started teasing her, she snapped at him, "I saw you nude in *Oh, Calcutta*, so there's nothing about you I don't know!"

I conducted a long one-on-one interview with Arthur for her second series, ABC's *Amanda's* (1983), a strangely unfunny US knockoff version of the English series *Fawlty Towers*, which lasted only for thirteen episodes. Arthur welcomed me to her dressing room and said she should have been in bed because she was battling a terrible head cold, but added, "I made this appointment and I'm a pro. So shoot!"

The third time I met with Arthur was in Toronto in 2002 when she was wowing them in a brilliant one-woman show that played to standing-room-only audiences. We went out for dinner afterward. She looked lovely in a sparkly black pants suit, but I noticed she had lost a significant amount of weight. She also knocked back several vodkas in just a few minutes.

The Interview

BAWDEN: When you were a young person just starting to think about an acting career, what kind of future did you see for yourself?

ARTHUR: Look, I had this vision of myself when I was growing up as the next June Allyson. But I sprouted to five feet nine inches and instead of a little tweety voice I could boom like a baritone. So I made adjustments. Another June Allyson I could never be.

BAWDEN: I've heard that you never imagined a career as a TV star.

ARTHUR: Broadway was always my goal. That's as far as I ever wanted to look.

BAWDEN: But instead you started to work in the early days of live television. Was that immediately successful for you?

ARTHUR: Thank God for bits! I worked steadily in small parts on *Kraft Television Theater*, *Studio One*, and on *Caesar's Hour*.

BAWDEN: You became one of Sid Caesar's favorite comedy foils. What did you learn from working with him?

ARTHUR: He taught me to be fearless, to stop quaking if something fell flat. Besides, on live TV it really was all over at the end of the hour. Nobody has dared like Caesar and his talented writers. They included Mel Brooks, Woody Allen, Larry Gelbart—all of them in their twenties.

BAWDEN: You also worked in those [Johnny] Wayne and [Frank] Shuster skits on *The Ed Sullivan Show*.

ARTHUR: These things went on for twenty-two minutes! Without any commercial break! We'd do the Saturday dress rehearsal and normally that was when Ed would start cutting back on material. They never cut one of Wayne and Shuster's routines, as far as I can recall. I can't tell you the nervous state of doing such skits live. My stomach was in knots. What if I forgot a line? I can actually say it never happened.

BAWDEN: Your first real taste of TV stardom came when you first inhabited the character of Maude. How did that happen?

ARTHUR: I was visiting my husband [director Gene Saks] in Hollywood in 1971 and [producer] Norman Lear asked me to do a one shot on *All in the Family* as the liberal cousin of Edith Bunker.

BAWDEN: That character just took off overnight and the episode served as the pilot for a series about Maude. Did you ever imagine you'd star in a spin-off from another series?

ARTHUR: No! I tested on *All in the Family* and that was one episode. But right then spin-offs were all the rage. Norman actually had the idea of spinning off Mrs. Naugatuck, which was crazy. [She was the character played by Hermione Baddeley on *Maude*.]

BAWDEN: I watched tapings of *Maude* and was impressed with how smoothly everything seemed to go. Could you talk about that?

ARTHUR: There was a wonderful cast: Bill Macy, Adrienne Barbeau, Rue McClanahan, Esther Rolle, later Hermione Baddeley. The scripts were about real issues.

BAWDEN: Could you comment on the controversy that erupted when Maude had an abortion?

ARTHUR: The abortion show—I got tons of hate mail on that one. The facelift show was another. We tackled political hot topics and infuriated a lot of viewers. But they still tuned in next week to see what sacred cows we'd tackle next.

Bea Arthur in *Maude*. Courtesy of CBS publicity.

BAWDEN: I heard that your friend Lucille Ball thought some plotlines on *Maude* were too randy for her taste.

ARTHUR: She wanted Maude to do the splits, have pies tossed in her face, the shtick she had done for decades. But that was passé. If Maude were physically abused, it would have stopped the laughter. Ours was a comedy about social conventions. For slapstick or low humor, there was the maid, if you get me.

BAWDEN: When the ratings started to dip in 1977, Norman Lear proposed sending Maude to Congress as a liberal Democrat to give the story a new direction. What about that?

ARTHUR: I turned him down. We'd done everything with that character. I wanted out.

BAWDEN: But after *Maude* ended, you grew tired of staying home and decided to star in *Amanda's*, the American knockoff version of England's *Fawlty Towers*. It turned out to be a disaster and was canceled. What did you think?

ARTHUR: I thought it would turn out to be my final TV series.

BAWDEN: But then producer Susan Harris came along with *The Golden Girls*, which became a huge hit and ran for seven seasons. Of course, you didn't know that was going to happen. So why did you take a chance on it after the debacle of *Amanda's*?

ARTHUR: Because Susan had written the abortion script [for *Maude*] and we taped it without a single change. I needed good scripts. We changed everything on *Amanda's*.

BAWDEN: You were obviously supposed to play Dorothy, but is it true that Betty White was originally supposed to play oversexed Blanche instead of Rue McClanahan?

ARTHUR: She thought it was too much like her Sue Anne character on *The Mary Tyler Moore Show* and asked to play Rose instead.

BAWDEN: Can you explain why *The Golden Girls* became such a quick success?

ARTHUR: The writing was always amazing. Susan Harris wrote 79 [out of 180] scripts. It was pretty racy but it played as funny because, after all, this was a bunch of old seniors. If young women had said such things, there would have been an outcry. I do get bothered when people say Maude and Dorothy were one and the same. I played them supremely differently.

BAWDEN: You didn't take part in the sequel series, *The Golden Palace*, and it lasted only one season with tepid ratings.

ARTHUR: I'd had enough of the part by then.

BAWDEN: Aside from the great success you had in two hit TV series, you also scored big on Broadway in support of Angela Lansbury in the original production of *Mame*. But the reaction to the movie version with you supporting Lucille Ball was terrible. Your feelings about that?

ARTHUR: Hated that! Hated it. Angela should have had it but wasn't considered a [movie] star and Lucy was very big box office. Angela told me to go ahead and do it. She was that much of a pro. But Lucy had experienced a skiing accident and her high kicks were done by a double and the soft focus close-ups of poor Lucy were terrible. She thought it was the greatest thing she'd ever done and the critical reaction, which was all negative, just devastated her.

Afterword

When summing up Bea Arthur's career, it's important to note that she was nearly fifty when *Maude* made her a TV star. She will go down in TV history as one of the greatest of late-blooming stars.

In my notes are several comments about her from people she worked with over the years. I'd like to share some of them with you here. Frank Shuster of the Warne & Shuster comedy team told me: "Bea was irresistible. We always were asking for her. Of course, her height was wonderful for jokes and that deep voice was magnificent, but what startled us was her sheer comic timing. She'd say 'Hello?' in her certain way and the studio audience was in stitches."

Betty White, her *Golden Girls* costar, said: "You'd never think it, but it's Bea who is the nervous Nellie before taping. She's all wound up because she's a perfectionist. But whereas Rue [McClanahan] will sail right through a taping, Bea is just a lump of raw nerves."

When I interviewed Richard Kiley about the 1988 TV movie that he made with Arthur, *My First Love,* he said she was petrified being cast in a stark dramatic part. "She was wonderful but she kept asking if she had dropped all Maude mannerisms. She never really relaxed. It was frightening having to continually placate her. But she got decent reviews."

Arthur did guest parts on other shows after *Golden Girls* ended in 1992 and garnered an Emmy nomination as guest actress in an episode of *Malcolm in the Middle.* She also went back to Broadway in a one-woman show called *Just between Friends.* I caught her in Toronto in 1993 and noticed she was physically diminished. Arthur battled alcoholism.

Bea Arthur was very loyal to old friends. When Toronto TV personality Brian Linehan lost his show, she continued to treat him to weekends at her home. She'd joke she dragged herself up in the morning and put on her dressing gown to find the fastidious Linehan already dressed in his blazer and gray pants, reading *Variety* and *Hollywood Reporter.*

She remained a passionate defender of animal rights all her life; one of her last acts was to send a letter to an Australian chef condemning him for using a recipe made from the livers of geese that had suffered under painful conditions.

Bea Arthur died April 25, 2009, of cancer at her home in the Bel Air section of Los Angeles, surrounded by her sons and grandchildren. She was eighty-six.

Lucille Ball

Interview by James Bawden and Ron Miller

If Milton Berle was the one and only Mr. Television, then Lucille Ball was most definitely the once and forever Ms. Television, not only because of her great success in the medium from the 1950s through the 1980s but because nobody else has come along since to equal the hold she once had on the viewing public.

Though some might suggest that Ball had only a modest career as a movie star from the late 1930s through the early 1950s, the truth is her movie days were her training ground for the television career that was her manifest destiny in show business. Ball was misused by the Hollywood studio system, which never really discovered her true métier as a comic character actress until the new medium had claimed her as its own prize property.

Still, it's possible to see her potential as a dramatic actress in films like *Five Came Back* (1939), *The Big Street* (1942), and *The Dark Corner* (1946) and the belated blossoming of her physical comedy genius in her 1940s comedies like *Miss Grant Takes Richmond* (1949) and *The Fuller Brush Girl* (1950), which showed how much she had learned from the advice of silent comics Harold Lloyd and Buster Keaton and the experience of working with the Marx Brothers, Abbott and Costello, and Bob Hope on her way to the small screen.

But it was her romantic meeting with Cuban bandleader Desi Arnaz while filming *Too Many Girls* (1940) that provided the key to legendary star status for Lucille Ball, a pairing she never denied was the magic push that put her over the top. Arnaz and Ball were an awesome team and together they revolutionized the new medium of television and became rich and powerful, so much so that they wound up buying the RKO studio where Ball had been a chorus girl and bit player in Astaire-Rogers musicals and turning it into their own studio, renamed Desilu.

Ball's legacy in both films and television is one of the richest in show business history. She was the star of several other television comedy series

Lucille Ball as Lucy Ricardo in *I Love Lucy*, circa 1953. Courtesy of CBS publicity.

after *I Love Lucy* (1951–1957), and her films made from 1950 on include such popular hits as *Fancy Pants* (1950), *The Facts of Life* (1960), and *Critic's Choice* (1963) with Bob Hope; *A Guide for the Married Man* (1967) with Walter Matthau; *Yours, Mine, and Ours* (1968) with Henry Fonda; and the 1973 musical *Mame*, as well as her two hits with Desi Arnaz, *The Long, Long Trailer* (1954) and *Forever Darling* (1956).

Setting the Scene

We interviewed Lucille Ball individually on more than one occasion, but we have merged our separate interviews in a combined presentation. However, we offer our own personal account of the circumstances of our interviews.

BAWDEN: I first met Lucille Ball at her Beverly Hills home in 1972. Ball said she never let the press into her spacious mansion, so we talked for hours in her roomy gazebo. I remember she laughed when I said my one-bedroom apartment seemed smaller than her garden feature. At one point, neighbor James Stewart stuck his head over the fence to say hello and she shouted him off: "This is my interview, Jimmy!"

I met her again in 1974 when I happened to be in Los Angeles for the premiere of her musical film *Mame* and we had another get-together in her hotel suite. She was upset that thus far the reviews of *Mame* were stingingly bad.

Later, I did a telephone interview with Ball on the occasion of her 1986 CBS TV movie *Stone Pillow*.

Finally, I visited the set of her 1986 sitcom comeback show *Life with Lucy*, which was a fiasco on all fronts.

MILLER: My first private chat with Lucille Ball was on the telephone in 1977, my first year as a full-time television columnist. She was promoting her latest CBS comedy special. It started out to be a rather embarrassing moment for me because I didn't realize that Lucy had such a deep, husky speaking voice and I assumed her husband Gary Morton had answered my call. I began by saying, "Mr. Morton, I'm Ron Miller and I'm supposed to have an interview with Miss Ball at this time." There was a pause and the deep voice said, "This is Lucy. Let's get going." Well, I regrouped and she turned out to be as nice as she always was in my subsequent chats with her in person.

Our last talk came in 1986 in her dressing room during her lunch break on the day of the taping of her final sitcom, *Life with Lucy*. She was in a very nostalgic mood about returning to the live performance routine in front of a studio audience. I remember it as a poignant, even somewhat sad meeting with a woman I'd always previously found to be lighthearted and cheerful. I suspect it was a period in which she was trying to revive a glorious past but not quite finding conditions right for it.

That night my wife and I attended the performance, which featured John Ritter as her special guest. We both recognized quickly that *Life with Lucy*

Lucille Ball in a glamorous pose from *Ziegfeld Follies* (1946). James Bawden collection.

was not going to work for this beloved lady. The routines seemed dated and her timing was off. She was older and nowhere near as physically flexible as she'd been in the 1950s. The writing was stale and the humor seemed heavily forced. It didn't take long to realize we were witnessing the bittersweet closing of a fabulous career.

The Interview

BAWDEN: You once said people are invariably disappointed when first meeting you?

BALL: Because I'm not a funny person. I couldn't tell a good joke if my life depended on it. To TV viewers I'm Lucy. To friends I'm Lucille. Two separate creations. Lucy is the funny one. Lucille is the one who has been working steadily since she was a teenager.

MILLER: By now, it's obvious that millions of people can say the line "I love Lucy" and really mean it. After so many years in movies from the 1930s through the 1940s, did you ever expect the new medium of television would have such an impact on your career and your life?

BALL: I never thought television would be anything but a fly-by-night thing. Just like everybody else, I expected to work for a year or two and that would be it. I just wanted some fancy home movies to show the kids.

MILLER: Well, even if the television medium didn't look that appealing at first, your attitude must have changed pretty quickly.

BALL: TV had really just begun. CBS got Burns and Allen, Jack Benny, Eve Arden, and us. We all sort of started at the same time. Pioneering was so exciting then. We were making it all up, creating!

BAWDEN: What is the most common misassumption about your career?

BALL: That I bought RKO Studios as revenge for the studio firing me some seventeen years before.

BAWDEN: And the truth?

BALL: My RKO contract was up in 1942. I was offered an extension but chose to sign with MGM, which offered me more money. Biggest mistake of my life. I never really belonged at MGM, which played all kinds of tricks to get me to leave. So I really should have bought MGM if I were looking out for revenge.

MILLER: I've heard there's another misconception about *I Love Lucy:* that you were always ad-libbing your lines.

BALL: I had a woman stand up at a seminar once and say, "Lucy, you and Vivian [Vance] used to ad-lib scenes all the time. Did the writers mind?" I told her there were not many times when Vivian and I ad-libbed. We learned from our writers. We did pretty much word for word what they told us. And the lady said, "I don't believe you and I don't want to!" You know, in the old days at the Emmys there was hardly any mention of the writers. It was as if

Lucille Ball and Desi Arnaz in *I Love Lucy.* Courtesy of CBS and the Ron Miller collection.

Desi and I and Viv made it all up as we went along. I couldn't understand how they could think that.

BAWDEN: When you came to Hollywood, you were hardly an overnight sensation.

BALL: That's putting it mildly. Because I was very tall and all the female stars, in the early '30s at least, were very tiny. I remember once in

1927 I was visiting in New York City and on a double-decker tour bus I watched as Clara Bow came out of a department store with a throng of fans following her. And she was teeny—hardly five feet. And the stars I met when I got to L.A. were all on the small side: Janet Gaynor, Barbara Stanwyck. And then there I was—five feet nine inches. And no studio knew how to deal with that.

BAWDEN: Ann Sothern told me you seemed to follow her from studio to studio.

BALL: Guilty as charged! She started at Columbia. I followed her there. She went to RKO, then I followed. She was signed by MGM in 1939 and I went to Metro in 1942. But I started on TV in 1952, the year before her show [*Private Secretary*] started up, and for her second show [*The Ann Sothern Show*] she worked for my company. So I finally got my revenge.

BAWDEN: You once worked in support in comedies starring Kate Hepburn [*Stage Door*, 1937] and Irene Dunne [*Joy of Living*, 1938]. Did you study their techniques?

BALL: In *Stage Door* Kate played a hoity-toity socialite who wants to become an actress. Call it typecasting. Irene was playing a glamorous movie star with a crazy family in *Joy of Living*. Opposite Doug Fairbanks Jr., *Stage Door* was packed with unknowns who'd soon be famous: Eve Arden, Ann Miller, Jack Carson. Our director, Greg La Cava, was into improvisation. He'd say, "Do it the way you feel," and Ginger Rogers would add something that would make the scene sensational. Great Kate did it the same way, take after take, and then she'd stride back to her dressing room and slam the door shut. Maybe she was a Method actress. She was playing a bitch and being one. But it was Ginger who got the great notices and stole the picture while Kate was declared box office poison the next year. Years later we shared a makeup man at MGM. For *Joy of Living*, Irene would do scenes as many different ways as she could and let Greg pick and choose what he wanted.

MILLER: While you were laboring in the studio system, they pushed you into a number of different kinds of roles, apparently to see what suited you best. One of my favorites was *Five Came Back*, a serious dramatic role for you as a sexy girl who's running away from her sordid life. That part was so far from the Lucy that your fans later came to love that it may shock them to see you as a scarlet woman.

BALL: I was never comfortable being sultry. I don't feel I was cut out for them [sultry characters] and they didn't interest me. I found I could do dramatic parts, but I didn't feel I was learning anything.

BAWDEN: How did you get from Jamestown, New York, to Hollywood anyway?

BALL: I was born in Jamestown, but my dad died of typhoid fever when I was three. We had already moved to Montana and we then [went] back to New York State to the small town of Celoron. And we later moved back to Jamestown when I was a teenager. I later went to the John Murray Anderson School for Dramatic Arts, where I first met a precocious teen named Bette Davis. And she was bossy even then. Then I was hit with rheumatic fever and back in Jamestown for two years, mostly in bed.

BAWDEN: And then?

BALL: I got some work as a print model and then went to Hollywood after a bit of chorus work in Broadway musicals. I think my first movie was *Roman Scandals* in 1933. Paulette Goddard was around and so was a girl we called "Dog Puss." That would be Jane Wyman. There was a brief period at Columbia. I lived in a sleazy rooming house with the other girls, three or four to a room. Over the next two years I had dozens of uncredited bits. I was doing *Roberta* [1935] in another bit when I was befriended by Ginger Rogers. Her mom, Leila, ran a sort of finishing school on the lot to help girls get ahead. Both were wonderful to me. I tried to start such a school when I ran Desilu, but the young kids only wanted to be instant stars. So I had to abandon my school.

BAWDEN: You gradually ascended the ladder of stardom.

BALL: I dated a director, Alexander Hall, whose comedies still shine. He'd take me to one of my flicks and give me a running commentary how I could make each scene funnier. He was at least twenty-five years older, so romance never blossomed. His last-ever film, *Forever Darling* [1956], which Desi and I made at MGM, I insisted Hall direct it.

You see, I never refused a part. I couldn't afford to go on suspension. And I learned by association. I made a disguised B comedy with Jack Oakie [*The Affairs of Annabel,* 1938] plus the sequel [*Annabel Takes a Tour,* 1938], and he showed me how to toss off a line. It takes a lot of patience. The great Harold Lloyd produced another comedy [*A Guy, a Girl, and a Gob,* 1941] and he'd be on the floor every day showing me how to survive a comedic fall, how to do a double take. Great stuff. And I started being real busy in radio. I loved guesting on *Abbott and Costello.* I discovered I could perform better with an audience rooting for me.

MILLER: Hearing that you learned so much about physical comedy from a great silent screen comic like Harold Lloyd makes me wonder how influential Buster Keaton was on your development as a comic actress.

BALL: He was a friend of mine and I learned a lot from him, though I only worked with him once, just before he died.

MILLER: Did you get anything useful from any of the great comic actresses you worked with in pictures?

BALL: Carole Lombard took me aside to talk about dressing and fashions, hairstyles, and how to look.

BAWDEN: Your last batch of RKO films had some strong titles.

BALL: I get notes these days from film scholars because *Dance, Girl, Dance* [1940] was directed by a gal, Dorothy Arzner, although she dressed as a man. I was real nasty to Hank Fonda in *The Big Street* [1942] and then made my last at RKO, *Seven Days Leave* [1942] with that horrible egotist Victor Mature. Then MGM hired me away when my contract was up and that's when my troubles started.

BAWDEN: Explain, please.

BALL: I just wasn't much of a musical comedy star and it showed. I took over in *Du Barry Was a Lady* [1943] when my old pal Ann Sothern got sick and had to go on maternity leave early. *Best Foot Forward* [1943] was a hit, then the decay began. *Meet the People* [1944] was so awful Dick Powell said he'd never again do a musical. It was in black and white, indicating MGM had no enthusiasm from the beginning. I replaced Ann again in *Without Love* [1945], which was a rare Tracy-Hepburn stinker. The script was so bad Keenan Wynn and I would improvise until Great Kate had a shouting match, claiming we were stealing scenes. It lost money. After that MGM started loaning me out. And there was a period I reported for work and was given an office with Buster Keaton while MGM tried to figure out how to fire us.

BAWDEN: I thought you were fine in *The Dark Corner* [1946].

BALL: Directed by Henry Hathaway, who was a shouter. I started stuttering on the set, I was so scared of him. At one point he sent me to my dressing room and locked the door, saying he wasn't going to open it until I knew my lines. I think I might have done the *Abbott and Costello* radio show the night before, so I was tired out. Decades later Hathaway told a newspaper critic he had bumped into me in a café and I thanked him for teaching me professionalism. That's totally bunk! If I ever had seen him again I would have run for the hills.

BAWDEN: When did the Lucy character first appear?

BALL: In an Esther Williams musical, *Easy to Wed* [1946], which was a remake of *Libeled Lady*. I had the Jean Harlow role and Keenan Wynn the [Spencer] Tracy part and he worked with me on making this girl as ditzy as possible. And I tried to be zany in *Her Husband's Affairs* [1947] with Franchot Tone and *Sorrowful Jones* [1949] with Bob Hope, which was Damon Runyonesque stuff. By the time of *The Fuller Brush Girl* [1950], I had my Lucy character down pat.

MILLER: Now that you mention it, many film scholars consider *Easy to Wed* to be your first real showcase for your comedy skills. How did that happen?

BALL: Eddie Buzzell [who directed the picture] was the first director to really take me aside and talk to me about how to do things. I wasn't a big star, so they weren't really working on me or for me that much. I wasn't Greer Garson or Lana Turner or Judy Garland. I was very grateful to be under the umbrella of the studios and be paid as well.

MILLER: Do you think something was lost when the studio system fell apart after the television era came along?

BALL: I feel sorry for people who are starting out now. I really do. There's no creative cocoon around anybody. All the "papas" [studio moguls] died, not that you could ever call Harry Cohn "Papa." [Cohn was the domineering head of Columbia Pictures, where Ball finished her studio days.]

BAWDEN: By the early 1950s, it seemed your movie career was petering out.

BALL: I got a plum part in *The Greatest Show on Earth* [1952] and had to vacate when I found I was pregnant and old Cecil B. DeMille went ballistic when I used the "Force of God" clause in my contract. I can still hear him shouting, "Why would the Lord do this to me? Why?" [Dorothy Lamour took over Lucy's role in the picture.]

BAWDEN: You were already starring in *My Favorite Husband* at the time on radio?

BALL: Started that in 1948 for CBS. It was originally written by Frank Fox and Bill Davenport, who wrote *Ozzie and Harriet*, and after ten episodes it seemed to be over, a ratings flop. NBC tried again with two new writers, Bob Carroll Jr. and Madelyn Pugh, and a new producer, Jess Oppenheimer. Everything was changed, including the names of the main characters. And a bit later we added Gale Gordon and Bea Benaderet. CBS ordered a TV version in 1950, but insisted it had to be produced out of New York because if it were L.A. based, the kinescope [a film version photographed off a TV screen] would have to be used in the East. I said no. I wanted my real-life husband, Desi Arnaz, and not Richard Denning [her husband on the radio show].

BAWDEN: Then what happened?

BALL: Desi just took over. There were no filmed sitcoms or even hour dramas at the time. CBS said we would have to absorb the additional cost, which was formidable. We lost over $1,000 weekly in salary cuts. But in that gamble Desi invented reruns, although nobody knew it at the time. We brought our radio writers with us. It was Jess [Oppenheimer] who insisted we film it with a live audience. Mark Daniels was the first director. He did the first 33 half hours. Bill Asher also started early and directed 101 of them and later we added Jimmy Kern.

There was a huge stink when Desi hired famed cinematographer Karl Freund, who photographed 149 episodes. For Karl, it was the challenge of doing something completely new. The trades [Hollywood trade journals] said Karl must really need the money.

BAWDEN: And then?

BALL: We sold it to CBS as an alternating half hour—like *Burns and Allen* and subsequently *Jack Benny*. Twenty-six new episodes a year with no summer reruns—reruns did not exist as yet. Philip Morris signed on and insisted on thirty-nine half hours a year. Weekly. Don't forget the original pilot was a kinescope because we had to finance it out of our own pockets. I'm not sure it even exists today. It shouldn't! Too pokey and unfunny! We were premiering something completely new. We had to form a new corporation—Desilu. And we initially shot at General Service Studios on Las Palmas, which was empty as movie production was declining. We later moved to 846 Cahuenga and named that lot Desilu.

By the way, *Amos 'n' Andy* was also filmed, but not in front of an audience. Karl had to lease three thirty-five-millimeter cameras and three sets of cameramen. The lighting had to be particularly flat for editing purposes. When I got pregnant and gave birth in the second year, CBS reluctantly substituted reruns from the first year and found ratings were even bigger than the original broadcasts. George Burns watched an early filming and the next year *Burns and Allen* went to film, too. And so did *Ozzie and Harriet,* although it was shot with one camera and no audience—the beginning of canned laughter.

MILLER: Once *I Love Lucy* got going, it was obviously not *My Favorite Husband* from radio, but rather a whole different kind of situation comedy. What was your original concept?

BALL: We didn't want to be a typical Hollywood couple because everybody assumes they have a big house, big car, swimming pool, and no problems.

MILLER: I'm guessing one reason it clicked so well with millions of viewers is the fact that it was about average people struggling to get along, even though Ricky Ricardo was in show business.

BALL: That connected us to every average family in America. If I needed a new sweater or a new coat, we could write a whole show about it. In those days, we didn't have the knowledge of why we were doing any of this. We just wanted it that way.

MILLER: Though you already had a firm grip on the lady we know as Lucy Ricardo, did you keep developing her as you went along?

BALL: I had learned a lot by osmosis until I found my character. Then I learned from my writers.

MILLER: Those writers often had you doing some remarkably strange physical things on camera. How did they know you could do all that stuff?

BALL: They would check with me. Do you mind going in the shower? Do you mind going up on top of the house? Do you think you can parachute out of a plane? Can you work with a bear—or penguins?

MILLER: Do you think you could have such a fabulous career today if you were young and just starting out?

BALL: I think it's much harder for young people to make it today the same way I did. Thank God my kids were able to try their wings and fly away safely. When you're pioneering, when you're crossing the country in a covered wagon, you don't stop to think how you got over that stream. Right now it's too late to even talk about it.

BAWDEN: So with your TV success, you bought RKO?

BALL: Yes, later, in 1957. And to finance that sale, we sold the *I Love Lucy* reruns to CBS, which had fought us bitterly to do the show live!

BAWDEN: What about the cast?

BALL: Desi did it all. He auditioned many guys and got Bill Frawley on condition Bill promised not to drink during production. And only occasionally did he go off the wagon. Vivian Vance became a dear friend, but I'd never met her before her audition. Her contract said she had to be forty pounds heavier than me and wear frumpy clothes. Which she did.

MILLER: Were there any challenges in doing that kind of show on film?

BALL: At first we'd film and film and wind up with over an hour, which had to be cut in half. There was no one to tell us how to do it, you see.

BAWDEN: What are the episodes people tell you they best remember?

BALL: Well, the grape-stomping show and the show that puts Ethel and Lucy on the chocolate assembly line. My favorite is the pantomime with

Harpo [Marx]. We stopped in 1958 because I was so tired and we had run out of story lines. But we did hour-long shows as part of Desilu Playhouse and I think most of these are pretty funny—the one with Tallulah Bankhead is my favorite.

MILLER: In your various comedy shows, you never played the same Lucy, did you?

BALL: My Lucies were all different. I tried to explain that to someone once and it was obvious they didn't know the difference between *I Love Lucy*, *Here's Lucy*, *There Goes Lucy*, or whatever. Everything was always a growing Lucy, taking care of the kids without a husband. I didn't do it to keep up with the times. I never gave it any thought.

BAWDEN: Describe your decision to storm Broadway in 1960 in the musical *Wildcat*.

BALL: I'd describe it as a mistake. We opened on the road in October, hit New York City in December during a blizzard, and I left in May because I had a virus that just would not go away. And I hated doing the same damned thing for eight performances a week. I started dreading going to the theater. You do know Valerie Harper was one of the dancers, don't you? I had toured in *Dream Girl* in 1948 just to prove I could perform live. But I'd never again go to Broadway under any circumstances.

BAWDEN: After *I Love Lucy*, why did you go back to TV in *The Lucy Show*?

BALL: Why not? Vivian Vance was a go. I added Gale Gordon in the second season—finally he was mine. Bob Carroll Jr. and Madelyn [Pugh] Davis were on board. CBS gave us a two-year, no-cut deal. Desi arranged everything, although we were divorced. He used the deal as a springboard for CBS to buy other Desilu shows. I said it had to be shown on Mondays just like *I Love Lucy*. At first I was a widow with two kids and Vivian would be the divorced one. CBS said a lead could never be a divorcée. But I was divorced by that time in real life—go figure. We were down to thirty episodes, which meant two fewer months of shooting—a real blessing. Beginning in the second season I ordered the episodes shot in color because I realized the immense rerun value. CBS did not go to color until 1965. So I had to absorb the additional cost.

BAWDEN: Then Vivian Vance wanted out.

BALL: She had remarried. Her new husband [literary editor John Dodds] wanted her in Connecticut. So she had to fly in and out every weekend and she felt all washed up and finally only agreed to a limited number of guest shots. I begged Ann Sothern to sign up, but she said she'd never be a second banana, so she made guest appearances as Countess Framboise. But without Vi, the show wasn't as funny and I knew it. I tried Joan Blondell, but she lacked "it," To compensate we used a whole truckload of guest stars. I know we were slipping. Desi had been the quality-control guy and he left Desilu and I was now alone. I had to end it all in 1968 when I sold everything to Paramount and that was that.

BAWDEN: You disliked being president of Desilu?

BALL: Very much because the guys were always pushing to see if I faltered. Our stable of TV hits included *Mission: Impossible, Mannix,* and *Star Trek.* That's not bad. But in 1974 I sold Desilu to Paramount TV. I was totally exhausted, I can tell you.

BAWDEN: You started again with *Here's Lucy* in 1968.

BALL: Only to get my kids, Desi Jr. and Lucie, the experience they needed for careers. My new husband Gary Morton executive-produced. We went six more seasons. But I saw CBS was gradually phasing out its old stars like Benny and Skelton. I was by that time an old star. So I voluntarily yanked it in 1974. CBS wanted a Lucie Arnaz spin-off, but I initially said no. She needed to stand on her own, I felt. We ran a back-door pilot as the first episode of the fourth season and, as I suspected, the premise was too weak. It isn't syndicated because the other two series are and how many Lucy shows can a person take? Someday, maybe.

BAWDEN: You got some criticism for doing the movie version of *Mame.*

BALL: I thought it was unfair. Warners offered it to me saying Angela Lansbury [who starred in the Broadway version] wasn't box office. And it did make a pile of dough. The TV fans expected to see Lucy and instead got Lucy-Mame. I'd just suffered a skiing accident, meaning one foot and leg were heavily bandaged. For that showgirl kick in one number they had to use a "kick-in."

BAWDEN: After all that, you did it one more time: *Life with Lucy.* Why the comeback?

BALL: Because I'm bored. I'm sick of those adult shows that portray families in such a bad light. Aaron Spelling offered it to me. I've got Gale Gordon back and Carroll and Davis as writers. Buds like John Ritter are the guest stars. I'm seventy-five so I can't do pratfalls. And I read in the press Brandon Tartikoff at NBC says I'm having a problem with low energy. It's just the opposite—I've got too much. I've got the old team back—my sound-man (Cam McCulloch) has been with me since 1953. I can't call on Viv or Bill Frawley. They've gone to heaven. Maybe I can give hope to oldsters that retirement is hell, so get out there and kick up a storm.

MILLER: And you don't mind playing a grandmother?

BALL: I feel at home with it.

MILLER: The return to a weekly comedy series must feel pretty com-fortable, especially after doing your TV movie *Stone Pillow*, where you played a homeless bag lady. There was nothing very funny about that character. In retrospect, how do you feel about that dark turn to drama?

BALL: CBS wanted me to do something. I'd looked at a lot of scripts and I figured that was far enough away from the Lucy character, so I'll go that far out and see what happens. I found out. The audience was very nice, but they said, "Please don't do that again!" They wrote me letters saying, "You were wonderful, but why?"

MILLER: After all these years, I'm sure you can't go anywhere without being instantly recognized and mobbed by fans who love you. How do you handle that?

BALL: There's a way of parting the waters that I learned from Bob Hope. I don't hesitate. When I want to be noticed, I'm noticed. When I don't want to be noticed, I'm usually pretty successful at it. If you try to hurry, that seems to propel them to stop you. It's like, "We made you! So stop now!" But it's a strange thing: if you just stroll, they stroll with you.

MILLER: I know that your mother always came to the performances of your show. Do you miss not having her out there, watching you when you're taping *Life with Lucy*?

BALL: Oh, but she is out there every time. [Lucy got tears in her eyes at the memory of her late mother.] At the first rehearsal, my daughter sent me a single rose with a card that said, "We're all here in the bleachers, watching every move you make with love and admiration." And it was signed by a whole list of people who are now gone, including my mother.

Afterword

Life with Lucy was canceled after only eight episodes, and Lucille Ball retired to her home life. Producer Aaron Spelling subsequently blamed the fiasco on Ball's desire for full creative control.

Ball died on April 26, 1989, at Cedars-Sinai Hospital in Los Angeles after eight hours of surgery for a ruptured aorta. She was seventy-seven.

News of Lucy's death provoked an enormous wave of national grief and touched off a demand for many books, TV specials, and video releases celebrating her life and career that continues to this day.

Milton Berle

Interview by Ron Miller

It may be impossible for a young television viewer of today to understand why Milton Berle was known through the last fifty years of his life as Mr. Television. If you look at some of the faded kinescopes of his old TV shows from the late 1940s, he doesn't seem all that brilliant, but maybe more like an old burlesque or vaudeville comic cutting loose in a new medium. In truth, Berle actually was a veteran vaudeville comic who was cutting loose in a new medium—and drawing such enormous numbers of viewers that he forced millions of deprived Americans to rush out and buy TV sets so they could watch him every week.

Berle was marginal in terms of reputation when he first started to appear on television. Though he had been in movies since his childhood and was a familiar voice on radio, those mediums never really captured his essence nor displayed his greatest skill, which was working a live audience with rapid-fire jokes, funny faces, wacky costumes, and an aggressive style of humor that almost exhausted you after prolonged exposure.

To fully get Berle, you had to see him work the yokels in person. In TV's early days, it was broadcast live and often looked spontaneous—because much of what you saw really *was* spontaneous. It was as close as you could get to seeing Berle work a crowd up to a lather of laughter. He never lost that skill. I know it because I saw him do it in his eighties during the taping of a *Dean Martin Celebrity Roast* TV special in Las Vegas. Berle had everybody in the bleachers rocking with laughter.

That spontaneity was perfect for the dawn of the TV age. Berle was such an instant success in the new medium that he set the stage for all the comics who followed him, even experienced ones like Bob Hope, Jack Benny, and George Burns. He not only revived his own moribund career, he blazed a trail for the medium with telecasts so infectious that people congregated anyplace where they might find a working TV set, even if it meant visiting a television-owing neighbor they didn't really like or standing on the sidewalk in front of an appliance store to watch Berle on a TV in the window.

At one point, Berle's show was watched by 80 percent of all the households in America that owned TV sets. His show reached number one in the ratings for NBC, and the network did something absolutely unprecedented in show business history: it signed Berle to an exclusive contract for a term of thirty years!

Berle was the first host of NBC's *Texaco Star Theater* in June 1948. It was a live TV show based on the tried-and-true concept of a variety show with a comedian for its master of ceremonies. Others hosted the show, but Berle was the dazzling star who won the hosting job permanently by September of that year. Each episode began with a chorus of four Texaco gas station "servicemen." (In those days, gas stations provided "service" and their employees wore uniforms.) These Texaco guys sang and danced and introduced Berle, who came on in some bizarre outfit and went into his comedy routine before introducing each week's guest performers.

In 1954, the show was renamed *The Milton Berle Show* and continued until 1956. Berle returned in a half-hour format in 1958, but that show lasted only one season. In 1966, a deal was worked out to permit ABC to revive *The Milton Berle Show*, but it, too, lasted only one season.

Though his boom as a TV superstar lasted barely a decade, Berle had by that time become an iconic television star, and he was in steady demand through the years as a guest comic on all kinds of shows and occasionally as a dramatic actor in TV programs and made-for-TV movies.

Berle was born as Mendel Berlinger on July 12, 1908, in New York City. His father was a paint and varnish salesman. He was picked in a talent competition to be a child performer in the famous silent serial *The Perils of Pauline* with Pearl White, filmed in nearby New Jersey. He was shown being thrown from a moving train in one of the episodes. His boyish appeal was enough to get him other work in silent pictures, and when he was sixteen he decided to change his name to Milton Berle. At that young age, he was already working as an emcee in vaudeville shows and had been an actor on Broadway.

Through the 1930s, Berle was always sort of an "emerging" star, never quite becoming a household name. He was featured in an all-star film of 1937 called *New Faces of 1937*, which also included several minor radio comics and one future TV star—singer Harriet Hilliard, who would become the Harriet of the hit show *The Adventures of Ozzie and Harriet*, featuring her husband bandleader Ozzie Nelson and their sons David and Ricky.

Though he headlined a few movies in the 1940s and had his own radio programs on three radio networks—CBS, NBC, and ABC—from 1944 through 1949, it was television that finally made Milton Berle a genuine star and earned him the nickname Mr. Television.

Setting the Scene

Though I saw Milton Berle perform in person on several occasions and met him at press events a few times, I had only one opportunity to chat with him about his career: in 1969 following a hasty press conference for a live performance at the Circle Star Theater-in-the-Round in San Carlos, California. He was warm and friendly enough, but I got the distinct impression he was a supercharged character who seldom slowed down long enough to let his real personality show through the stage persona that seemed always to be "on."

The following piece includes the quotes he gave me during that interview, but it was written after I learned of his death in 2002 as my personal "appreciation" of this great television star.

An Appreciation

Can't you just imagine the crowd that turned out when Milton Berle, television's beloved "Uncle Miltie," showed up at the Pearly Gates and St. Peter handed him a paper to sign, promising he wouldn't smoke any big cigars in the Garden of Tranquility, dress up in any of the lady angels' clothes, or pinch the bottoms of any chorus girls who made it through admissions.

"What is this with all the rules?" I can hear him saying between puffs on his stogie. "I could do all that stuff at the Friars Club. What makes this place so special?"

He'd still sign the papers, of course, because he'd see the people crowding around and he'd do just about anything to please an audience. Besides, the alternative wasn't so great. Who wants to work a room full of people slowly roasting over fires? He stopped playing those joints back in the late 1930s because they wouldn't let him run a tab. And he swore he'd never do his act again where the bouncers carried pitchforks.

Berle in heaven? Boggles the mind, doesn't it? You know he wouldn't even start to relax and enjoy the eternal serenity until somebody booked him for a couple of after-hours shows where he could try out some of that "special cable

Milton Berle, circa 1950. Ron Miller collection.

TV material" he couldn't use before he finally ran out of steam at age ninety-three in 2002 and gave up the ghost, so to speak.

"Say, St. Peter, my good man," he'd finally get around to asking, "do you happen to know where they store the joke files up here?"

Berle was no dummy. He'd figure George Burns, Henny Youngman, and the rest of the comics who got the jump on him would need a place to park their material, figuring at last they'd be safe from Berle stealing it. Well, he wouldn't want to alarm them—or alert them, either. Maybe he'd start by cribbing some stuff from Smith and Dale. They'd never catch on, not the way he'd put it over.

As St. Peter checked him in, you could be sure Berle would be going over all his most reliable material, making a few changes to make it work in the new neighborhood. He couldn't wait for this St. Peter guy to heckle him. Didn't he used to go by the moniker "The Big Fisherman" back on terra firma? If he's that guy, Berle had one for him: "Excuse me, sir," he'd say, "but the last time I saw a mouth like yours it had a hook in it!"

And if one of those angel ladies started giving him the needle, he'd drop back and hit her with an old reliable like "I remember you, madam. You heckled me ten years ago. I never forget a robe."

And speaking of angels, he had something ready if he ever came across one that looked like that Roma Downey dish from *Touched by an Angel* on TV: "Excuse me, miss, but I've never been touched by an angel. Would you mind touching me right here?"

Ah, yes, Berle at the Pearly Gates. What a concept! Except who thought it would ever happen? I was sure he was going to outlive us all and blow cigar smoke over our caskets. The last time I saw him perform in person, he was in his late eighties and he was still a ball of energy. He worked hard for an audience—harder than any performer I've ever seen, not counting the young, chubby, soprano-voiced Wayne Newton, who worked so hard even his shoes sweated. But then Berle had to work hard to put over his material. It was moldy to start, and then it really started to go bad.

I first met Uncle Miltie in 1969. I knew him only from his guest shots on TV and his old movies. We didn't have a TV when he was first earning the title Mr. Television, but I do remember standing on the street watching his show in an appliance store window along with a big crowd of other kids whose folks couldn't afford the new TV sets. They had the sound piped outside, but how long could a kid stand still in one place? I always cut out early, so I never had a feel for his original Texaco show.

But I had seen him in the movies. Two "spooky" comedies—*Over My Dead Body* and *Whispering Ghosts* from 1942—and a wonderful little movie called *Always Leave Them Laughing* in 1949, which Warner Bros. made to cash in on Berle's amazing new popularity as a TV star. It was about a TV comedian's ups and downs and the character was very much like Berle—zany and crass, but a guy who took himself very seriously. Warners gave him Bert

Lahr as a stooge and surrounded him with the studio's most curvaceous young stars—Virginia Mayo and Ruth Roman. In such surroundings, Berle glowed—and I thought he was super.

Berle appeared in lots of other movies over the years, like Stanley Kramer's *It's a Mad, Mad, Mad, Mad World* (1963), but topped the list of stars in few. An exception late in his career: NBC's 1977 TV movie *Have I Got a Christmas for You.*

So I was all cranked up about talking with the legendary Berle, who had come to the San Francisco Bay Area to play one of the great theaters-in-the-round of its day, Circle Star, down the peninsula in San Carlos. At the time, TV's *Laugh-in* was the comedy rage and everybody was talking about Dan Rowan and Dick Martin, who hosted the show.

"Olsen and Johnson did it fifty years ago," Berle sneered when I asked his opinion of the show. "I did it, uh, thirty years ago. New directions in comedy? Naw, there's nothing new. It's like sex. Everybody thinks there's something new going on, but it's all been done before."

I was ready to believe Berle certainly had done everything before at least once. He started in show business as a little kid and was even on-screen with Charlie Chaplin in *Tillie's Punctured Romance* in 1914. "I was even in a kid stage show called *Tidbits of 1918.* That was lovely," Berle said. "But look at the names these teenage bands have today: The Enemas?"

Berle said he was always being busted for violating child labor laws thanks to his mom, who shoved him into show business at age four. "I'm not going to tell you how sad I am I don't have a big college degree," he said. "I'm no child psychologist and I'm not the one to give advice about kids going into show business."

But Berle gave me the impression he'd done a good deal of analyzing himself over the years. For instance, he claimed he went into comedy in his teens because he suddenly grew "gawky and lanky" and looked like such a dork that people wanted to laugh when they first saw him. He also admitted he stole material from *Captain Billy's Whiz Bang* magazine to get started, so I guess the roots of that practice went very deep indeed.

When I talked to him, he was only sixty, but he seemed to have memories that went all the way back to caveman days. He talked in show biz lingo. If I hadn't been weaned on reading *Variety,* the show business trade journal, I'm sure he would have made no sense to me. He also really smoked those big cigars—and kept them going with frequent blasts from a butane lighter that shot up a huge flame and came close to singeing his eyebrows every time.

On that occasion, I didn't exactly form a warm impression of Uncle Miltie. He was so "on" that it was nerve-racking—and I remember he bawled out my photographer for trying to take a picture of him while he was eating a hamburger. He didn't want the public to see a Miltie with his cheeks swollen with burger and strings of onion hanging from his lips.

On later occasions, though, Berle struck me as gentler, warmer, more like a nice old guy who was glad to be remembered. That is—until he got onstage. Once in front of the mike, he was like an ex-soldier who suddenly found himself armed again. He was ready to start mowing people down.

Even to the last, Berle was great with a crowd. He could hammer you into laughing at the most feeble material. I never failed to enjoy one of his live performances.

But how will he do in heaven? Frankly, I don't think it's a Berle crowd. He'll knock 'em dead, so to speak, for awhile, but then he'll start to get on their nerves and they'll take up a petition. Here's hoping he learns to mellow out and makes a few new friends up there, but if they send him somewhere else, I hope it's back home to us. I miss him already, cigar smoke and all.

Afterword

Berle was married four times, twice to his first wife, showgirl Joyce Matthews. He and Matthews were divorced twice. His second wife, publicist Ruth Cosgrove, died in 1989. He married again in 1992 to fashion designer Lorna Adams, who survived him. He had two adopted children with his first two wives and a son whom he fathered out of wedlock but later acknowledged.

My dear friend and colleague the late Murry Frymer interviewed Berle twenty years after I did when the comedian had returned to the Circle Star Theater, this time on a bill with fellow TV comedy pioneers Sid Caesar and Danny Thomas. Frymer remembered that Berle took him up to his hotel room for the interview, but broke down and sobbed when he was unable to open the door with his room key. Berle told Frymer that he was having a terrible time emotionally because his wife, Ruth, had just died. "She was my life," Berle told him, "She held me together."

Frymer told Berle he would go downstairs to the desk and get somebody to open the room for him. When he told the desk clerk what had happened, the man said, "He's locked himself out four times today. He tries to open the door with his car keys."

That night, Frymer attended the show and found Berle lively, funny, and totally himself again. He concluded it was the live audience that really kept the eighty-year-old Berle together.

Berle was diagnosed with colon cancer in 2001 but declined surgery. He died a year later in Los Angeles on March 27, 2002. He was ninety-three.

Mel Blanc

Interview by Ron Miller

It's a cliché in show business to say someone was "one of a kind," particularly in a business where imitation is the sincerest form of flattery. But Mel Blanc was clearly a genuine original when it came to his specialty—voice characterizations. And if you really could somehow successfully imitate him, he was sure to sue you to make sure you didn't ever do it again.

It's hard to imagine any child growing up in America—or anywhere else in the world—without being exposed to the genius of Mel Blanc, who was the original voice of nearly all the Warner Bros. cartoon characters, including Bugs Bunny, Porky Pig, and Daffy Duck. He was also the original voice of Woody Woodpecker and a wide assortment of great TV cartoon characters like Barney Rubble and Dino the Dinosaur from *The Flintstones.*

Yet the parents of those kids watching TV cartoons may remember Blanc most for the characters he played on Jack Benny's radio programs of the 1940s, including Benny's sputtering old Maxwell automobile.

Born Melvin Jerome Blank in San Francisco on May 30, 1908, he changed the spelling of his surname because a teacher once told him he'd wind up a nothing as his last name implied if he didn't apply himself more to his studies. So he changed the name from Blank to Blanc.

Though many voice actors have forged successful careers in recent years, Mel Blanc was the king of the genre during his lifetime. He pioneered the use of screen credits for voice actors—and he zealously protected the voices he created, often taking violators to court if they tried to do any of his patented voices.

Blanc emerged in the 1950s as a very personable actor, too, playing himself as well as his regular radio characters when Jack Benny took his radio show to television. In his later years, with his fame spread nearly everywhere, he became a frequent lecturer. And for years his phonograph records were popular novelty items loved by kids and adults equally.

Because of his prolific work, Blanc's voice is still frequently heard as his movie cartoons and TV programs seem to play on endlessly on television channels and in home video collections.

Setting the Scene

Like every kid of my generation, I grew up with a steady dose of Mel Blanc. I loved trying to do his many cartoon voices and am grateful he never knew about it or he'd have contacted his lawyers. In my early teens, I even did a record pantomime act that made use of Mel Blanc's recorded songs. I took bows that really belonged to him.

In 1984 I had the rare opportunity to go to his home in Beverly Hills and spend an afternoon with him, sitting outside in his beautiful yard, sipping iced tea and talking about his magical world. He was an old man then, but a lively, warm, and generous one who dodged no questions. I had already met some of the greatest animators in American history, including Chuck Jones, Bill Hanna, and Joe Barbera. They all told me that meeting Mel Blanc would be an unforgettable experience. They were absolutely right about that.

The Interview

MILLER: How early did you learn that you had this gift for doing voices?

BLANC: As a kid, when I was about in the fifth grade. I learned all the different dialects. That was actually my start in the business of voices.

MILLER: How did a fifth grader go about learning dialects?

BLANC: For example, I wanted to learn the Japanese dialect, so I went into one of those little produce markets that had fruits and vegetables, pointed at something, and asked the Japanese man who worked there what he called that. And he said, "Well, that's a heddarettus." I wound up buying a head of lettuce from him.

MILLER: Did anybody else in your family have a knack for voices?

BLANC: Nobody in the family before me did voices.

MILLER: Your son Noel does voice characterizations now. So did you train him?

BLANC: Noel is like me. He doesn't like to copy anyone and do impressions. When he was just a little kid, he used to bring the funny papers to me, sit on my lap, and ask me to read them to him. He'd say, "Get ready, Dad!" And

I'd have to read the funnies to him in different voices. When he was just twelve years old, I started talking to him in all these different voices and he answered back in the same voices. That's when I knew he could do such things.

MILLER: Is there something special about your vocal tool kit? I mean, Leonard Maltin once said it was amazing that the same man could do both Tweety Bird and Yosemite Sam. I agree. How special is your vocal equipment?

BLANC: Thirty years ago I went to take out an insurance policy on my voice with Lloyds of London. The policy was to read that I'd get $250 in cash from them every week if I was unable to work with my voice. That was a lot of money back then. But first they said I'd have to have an X-ray of my throat. So I went to a doctor, had my throat X-rayed, and he came in, shaking his head, and said, "This is the first time I've seen the same muscular construction on a throat as Enrico Caruso." And I said, "But I can't sing like that." And he said, "No, but you can lose your voice and in an hour get it back." I guess it's in my genes.

MILLER: Is there anything else you think accounts for your skill?

BLANC: I was in music for several years, so maybe that's why I can get all the sounds, come in on cue and on tempo. That's been very helpful in this cartoon world.

MILLER: Explain what you mean about being "in music."

BLANC: I took violin lessons for eight years and became very knowledgeable about music. My dad was in the ladies' ready-to-wear business, but he also played trumpet. My brother Henry played piano and my mother sang. So we had a regular orchestra at home. But when I went into high school, I wanted to play in the school band, but I thought I'd look pretty silly trying to play the violin while marching with the band, so I took up the tuba.

MILLER: Did this lead you into show business as a career?

BLANC: When I was a kid, I thought I'd go into vaudeville. I used to entertain the school kids at assemblies when I was growing up in Portland, Oregon. I got big laughs from the other kids and even from the teachers, even though they'd still give me bad marks. In 1927, they asked me to do a song on the Hoot Owls, a charitable program in Portland, Oregon. The song was "Juanita." Not the beautiful one you're thinking of but the one that goes, "Wanna eat, wanna eat, Juanita."

[At this point, Blanc got a big smile on his face because he still remembered the lyrics. He sang them to me: "They say that nanny goats eat tomato cans and such, but my girl eats a lot of things that nanny goats won't touch!"]

Anyway, they liked it and so I played with the band there [on the radio in Portland] and when I turned twenty-two, I was made the director of the Orpheum Vaudeville Theater band and conducted the orchestra for Edgar Bergen and Charlie McCarthy when they came to town.

MILLER: What was the next step for you?

BLANC: After that, I had a chance to go into radio in San Francisco as the master of ceremonies on a national program called *Road Show* on NBC. During the hiatus, I went down to Los Angeles. That was in 1932. I married my wife Estelle, and we've been married ever since. But I also started watching the cartoons they were making then and thought what lousy voices the cartoon characters had, so I thought I'd try to go into cartoons.

MILLER: What was your first attempt to join the cartoon world?

BLANC: I went to the man in charge of hiring voices for Schlesinger Cartoons [Leon Schlesinger's company was making cartoons for Warner Bros.] and asked for an audition, but he told me he was sorry, but they had all the voices they needed. So I came back in two weeks and he still said they had all the voices they needed. But I was just as persistent as he was, so I went back every two weeks for a year and a half. Finally, this guy died and I went to the next guy in charge and he said, "Sure. What do you have?"

MILLER: I'm sure you dazzled him with your voices.

BLANC: He asked me if I'd do them again for the cartoon directors and one of them said he had a cartoon coming up with a drunken bull. When I told him I could do a drunken bull, he said, "What are you doing next Tuesday?"

MILLER: Okay, you got in. Did you have any idea how your popularity would take off once you started doing cartoon voices?

BLANC: I wanted to be in the cartoons because I knew I had things I could do that they didn't have. I had the feeling the voices would become popular because I could make them fit the characters so well.

MILLER: How do you start out to create a character's voice?

BLANC: They would show me a picture of the cartoon character and then show me the storyboard. So from just looking at this, I had to create a cartoon voice.

MILLER: Well, the Schlesinger Cartoons introduced Bugs Bunny and you gave him a voice that may be your all-time most famous. Tell me about it.

BLANC: They told me Bugs was a tough little stinker. So I thought to myself, which is the toughest voice—Brooklyn or the Bronx? So I put them

Young Mel Blanc on the radio. Courtesy of Blanc Productions and the American Fine Art collection.

together, Doc! That's how I got the voice for Bugs. ["Heh-heh-heh!" Blanc said, using the famous Bugs dialect.] At first they had big, long teeth sticking out of him. The first couple of pictures I made as Bugs, you couldn't understand what the hell I was talking about. So I told them to take those teeth away and you'd have the regular rabbit voice.

MILLER: How about Porky Pig? How did you get his voice?

BLANC: Funny you should ask. When Mr. Schlesinger asked me to do a pig's voice, I said, "That's a nice thing to ask a nice, clean Jewish boy to do." Porky's stammering came from listening to pig grunts. I saw him as a rather timid fellow.

MILLER: What about Foghorn Leghorn and Yosemite Sam?

BLANC: Foghorn came from a hard-of-hearing sheriff I heard as a kid. And Sam is only two feet tall, but he's a cowboy and he had to have a voice big enough so you'd notice him.

MILLER: Did they do anything to your voice in the editing process for the cartoons?

BLANC: I used the same voice and they'd record it. Let's say the machine worked at twelve hundred revolutions per minute. I'd record the voice at a thousand rpm and they'd play it back at twelve hundred, which raised the voice a little higher [in pitch]. Porky Pig is raised. Daffy Duck is raised. They're all the same voice, but they make them different by playing them back at normal speed.

MILLER: You created all the voices for the major Warner Bros. cartoon characters except for one?

BLANC: Elmer Fudd is the only voice I didn't create. It was created by Arthur O. Bryan, who died about thirty-five years ago. Friz Freleng, one of the directors, came to me and asked me to do Fudd [after Bryan died]. I told him I'd try it, but I didn't like it. [Some sources say Porky Pig also was voiced by another actor before Blanc did the voice.]

MILLER: I guess doing a voice created by someone else is difficult, but I'll bet every school kid in America thinks he can talk like Bugs, Porky, or Daffy.

BLANC: People who try to do my voices are not very successful. They seem to lack something. I don't know whether it's inflection or what it is, but I can tell in a minute if someone is trying to impersonate me because they can't come close to it. The only one who can do it is my son Noel.

MILLER: Did you have trouble when you tried to get screen credit for your voices? It had never been done before.

BLANC: When I went to Mr. Schlesinger and asked him for a raise because I was doing so many characters, he said, "What do you want more money for? You'll just have to pay more taxes." That's the honest to God truth. So I said, "At least give me screen credit for the voice." And he said, "Who ever heard of giving screen credit for a voice?" And I said, "Well, if you don't give me a raise, that's the least you can do."

MILLER: So he gave in and you got screen credit. Would you have rather had the raise?

BLANC: Actually, I'm so happy he didn't give me the raise because when people who had radio shows saw my name on the credits of the cartoons, they called me in to do voices for them. God, I was soon working on maybe twenty transcontinental radio shows a week and getting big pay for it.

MILLER: Did that lead you to the Jack Benny program?

BLANC: Benny was one of the first to call. He had Carmichael the bear who protected his vault. So I went to Jack and did the growl for six months. At the end of six months, I went to him and said, "You know, Jack, I can talk, too!" So Jack had the writers write something in for me. One of the first things for me was the Train Caller: "Train leaving on track 5 for Ana-heim, A-Zu-Za, and Coo-ca-munga!"

MILLER: That one always knocked me out. How inventive did the writers get for you?

BLANC: After awhile, the writers would try to give me something I couldn't do. One of them wrote into a script: "Mel Blanc does a goldfish." He was sure he had me stumped. But I never say no. When I got my cue for the goldfish, I did it. [And he did it again for me: his lips all puckered up like, well, a goldfish! I'd never heard a goldfish, but his impression had a convincing whooshing sort of sound.] They tried various things to throw me. We were visiting Epsom Downs and they put in the script: "Mel Blanc does an English horse whinny." [Blanc did that one for me, too: a snooty-sounding whinny that ends with the sound "a-ho!"]

MILLER: By the 1940s, you began branching out into a field I doubt you'd ever become a star in: musical recordings.

BLANC: First they had me do the cartoon stories [for children's records]. Then I spoke to them about maybe doing novelty records—and they got some writers on it. They sold tremendously. All the Bugs Bunny voices I did were the biggest sellers among children's records.

MILLER: Some of the lines spoken by your cartoon characters are now positively iconic.

BLANC: I gave them a lot of those lines, like "That's all, folks!" They [the studio] had them all copyrighted and trademarked. I never said anything about it because I wanted to keep working for them. So now it's come to the point where we have to ask their permission to use one of the voices.

MILLER: What if they want you to do a voice now?

BLANC: Noel handles all my business. Now when they want me to do a picture, we sock it to them.

MILLER: On January 24, 1961, you were in a terrible auto accident that nearly took your life. Can you talk about that?

BLANC: I had a triple skull fracture along with all the other breaks. I'll tell you something that actually happened. When I was told about it later, I didn't believe it, but my son was there and said the story is true. I was unconscious and the brain specialist came in and said, "How are you doing, Mr. Blanc?" and I didn't even hear him. Then he said, "Bugs, how are you doing today?" and I said, "Just fine, Doc! How are you?" I was as good as dead, but my characters were still alive.

MILLER: Your public must be millions of kids just like me, who grew up loving everything you did. Did you hear from them when you were in the hospital?

BLANC: I received thousands of letters, most of them from kids. They'd say things like, "Dear Bugs Bunny, please don't die! We love you!" Some of them wanted to show how much they loved me by sending me something dear to them—like a penny or a stick of gum. This made me feel like kids of all ages really enjoy my work. That was quite a feeling that went right through me. If they feel that good about me, I've got to recover.

MILLER: How would you sum up your career today?

BLANC: I just love my work and love to do it. I try to bring a little happiness into this world and see people laugh. It's worth a million bucks to me.

Afterword

Mel Blanc did many voices for the Hanna-Barbera television production company, which made some of the most widely seen animated shows on television. His final job was doing voices for *The Jetsons: The Movie* (1990). A lifelong smoker, he was diagnosed with emphysema and admitted to Cedars-Sinai Hospital in Los Angeles in 1989 for treatment. While he was recovering, it was discovered that he had advanced heart disease and he died from it on July 10, 1989. He was eighty-one.

Blanc is interred at the Hollywood Forever Cemetery in Hollywood. His tombstone bears one of the most famous epitaphs of any star: "That's all, folks!"

George Burns

Interview by James Bawden

Some readers may quibble about the use of the word *legendary* in reference to some of the stars covered in this book. Such judgments are always a matter of opinion, but it's unlikely many will quibble over using that word to describe George Burns.

Burns spanned all major entertainment venues for the better part of a century. He and lifelong partner Gracie Allen became stars first in the world of vaudeville. They came to the movies quite early in a series of movie short subjects during the pioneer days of talking pictures. At the same time, around 1930, they began to perform in radio and were legitimate radio stars in the 1930s, which led to starring roles in feature films.

Their fame in radio easily carried them over into the new world of television and *Burns and Allen* became a top-rated TV comedy series. When wife Gracie retired from the act, then died, Burns continued as a single, playing the top clubs in America. Though his TV comedy series without Gracie, such as *Wendy and Me* (1964–1965), were not hits, he had immense success as a guest performer on other comedy shows and as an actor in both TV movies and feature films, most especially *Oh, God!* (1977), in which he played the title role.

Burns even did something no other comedian of his generation had been able to do: he won an Academy Award in the Best Supporting Actor category for his performance in 1975's *The Sunshine Boys*.

Burns continued to perform in clubs and concert engagements right up to the very end of his life, which lasted one hundred years. If that doesn't make a man legendary, what does?

Setting the Scene

I first met George Burns in Hamilton, Ontario, in 1974 as he prepared to perform his one-man show at Hamilton Place. His manager Irving Fein had

George Burns. Courtesy of Charles A. Pomerantz LTD Public Relations.

stipulated a fifteen-minute conversation in Burns's hotel suite, but the grand old trouper insisted on chatting away for several hours.

We met again for a quick lunch in 1985 in Phoenix, where Burns, now a hearty eighty-nine years young, was fronting a new CBS TV comedy series, *George Burns Comedy Week,* produced by Steve Martin. I was totally surprised he remembered me at all!

The Interview

BAWDEN: How did you get started in comedy, and did you ever think you'd last so long at the top?

BURNS: My real name is Nathaniel Birnbaum and I was born in 1896 in New York City. To say we were a poor family is an understatement. I was the ninth of twelve children and my parents came from Galicia, which is now part of Romania. I got my first job aged seven helping make maple syrup candies, and it was so boring all the kids would sing in unison. Soon we were known as the Pee Wee Quartet and I got gigs with the troupe on weekends.

I had a number of early vaudeville partners, all female, but nothing was working until 1923 when I met an Irish Catholic beauty and that was that.

BAWDEN: Who were your heroes in vaudeville?

BURNS: Well, Al Jolson was the greatest entertainer I've ever seen, but a real bastard in real life. Eddie Cantor was somebody I tried to emulate. He had a more wholesome image. I really didn't know Jack Benny in vaudeville much.

BAWDEN: Give me an understanding of what it was like touring in vaudeville.

BURNS: Go read those bound copies of *Variety* from the '20s. They can be found in the public library. Turn to the obituaries, which are littered with horrible death notices—heart attacks, strokes, pneumonia. It meant riding in the sleeper train from city to city, staying in fleabag hotels, and eating cans of beans warmed up on the radiators. It meant fleas, indifferent audiences, washing out underwear in the bathtub. It meant indignity.

But it was also a kind of heaven. I could go on the road with a new sketch, and over forty weeks, hone it to perfection by the time I hit New York City. Today's comics use up all their material in a ten-minute spot on *The Tonight Show* and then they have to start again.

BAWDEN: How often were you in Canada in those years?

BURNS: Oh, practically every season. We'd do a half week in Montreal and then Ottawa, followed by a week in Toronto and then a half week each in Hamilton and London and then be in Detroit the next week. I remember in Hamilton a fellow trouper named Mae West came down with pleurisy and the local doctor came and stayed a week with Mae in her room. Turned out Mae was all better, but she had wasted the good doctor.

BAWDEN: How did you hook up with Gracie Allen?

BURNS: My first partner was Hermosa Jose. We partnered for twenty-six weeks, but nothing jelled. I mean, how could I say, "Say goodnight, Hermosa" and get a laugh? We were never married, so her family refused permission for lengthy tours and so we separated after twenty-six weeks of very few laughs.

BAWDEN: Then you met Gracie Allen?

BURNS: She had started in vaudeville as the Four Colleens with her sisters Hazel, Bessie, and Pearl. We met in vaudeville in Union City and tried a partnership that didn't work at first. She was the straight "man" and I got the laughs, which were few. We were in Hoboken when we changed sides. All I ever had to do was say, "Gracie, how's your brother?" and she'd do ten minutes. You see, she wasn't playing retarded, but innocent. Everything was logical in her scatterbrained world. Throughout 1923 and 1924 we developed our characters. I always wrote for both of us. Gracie wasn't at all like her stage character in real life. That's why she was such a great actress.

BAWDEN: Were you two an overnight sensation?

BURNS: No, it took years to perfect the routine. My brother Will contributed jokes and finally we could afford to hire writers. We finally got to play the Palace Theatre in 1926 and we did some of the first "soundies"—two-reel movie comedies—made in New York's Astoria studios. They were very crude, to put it mildly.

BAWDEN: How did you get into radio?

BURNS: Guy Lombardo hired us as the comics on his radio show in 1930. But his fans wanted only sweet music. Rudy Vallee used us a bit on his show. When Guy switched networks to NBC, we took over for him on CBS. A whole heck of writers were hired because radio eats up material like something else. We had a long-running stunt to help Gracie find her brother that got so big her brother in San Francisco had to go into hiding. There was another time—must have been in 1940—that Gracie launched a presidential campaign on behalf of her Surprise Party and actually got many write-in votes.

BAWDEN: What happened in 1941 when ratings plunged?

BURNS: I simply went on one night and said, "Ladies and gentlemen, Gracie and I are not girlfriend and boyfriend. We're both too old for that. We're married." And we jumped into a sitcom format that lasted right through TV. We used regulars like Mel Blanc, Gale Gordon, Bea Benaderet, and always had a singer like Tony Martin around. You do know, don't you, that Meredith Willson was the music conductor for a long time? We also used Artie Shaw, as I recall. Playing to an audience was always the most important ingredient. And, you know, Gracie always dressed up and wouldn't wear the same dress. She charged them to the sponsor!

BAWDEN: You also began to star in major movies.

BURNS: *International House* [1933] was one of our first comedies for Paramount, an all-star thing; Paramount imported a lot of radio names around that time. Takes were ruined because W. C. Fields couldn't keep a straight face when Gracie was around. He found her screamingly funny. Bela Lugosi was there, too! We'd do two or three of these programmers a year, often with Charlie Ruggles and Mary Boland. In *Six of a Kind* [1934], Fields was back but Gracie was stealing all the laughs in their scenes together.

BAWDEN: How big were you in movies?

BURNS: We were part of a bunch of radio names in *The Big Broadcast* [1932]. Then we did *Big Broadcast of 1936* and that was packed with [Bing] Crosby, [Ethel] Merman, Amos 'n' Andy—you name it. And then we did *Big Broadcast of 1938*. Jack Benny, who also was at the studio, was in this one, but Crosby refused to make any more of these. [Benny eventually bowed out of the movie and was replaced by newcomer Bob Hope.] Paramount used us in a dozen programmers which ran on double bills.

BAWDEN: So you fared best in radio?

BURNS: Our own show was called *Maxwell House Coffee Time* and we could fill that radio auditorium at NBC every week with our fans.

BAWDEN: I saw Gracie on TV recently, dancing in *Damsel in Distress* [1937].

BURNS: She's tapping away on that carny wheel ride. Paramount developed *Road to Singapore* [1940] for us, then we left because MGM offered more dough. So Paramount substituted Bob Hope, Dorothy Lamour, plus Bing Crosby. At MGM, we made *Honolulu* [1939] with Ellie Powell and it wasn't up to scratch. MGM broke up the act and featured Gracie single in *The Gracie Allen Murder Case* [1939] opposite Warren William as Philo Vance. I was paid my standard salary not to appear. And Gracie was alone again in *Mr. and Mrs. North* [1942], and that was about it. She had a gag routine in *Two Girls and a Sailor* [1944]. All that made me mighty unhappy, I can tell you.

BAWDEN: How did you switch to TV?

BURNS: We went live on CBS starting in 1950. Gracie would interpolate material when she had a blackout of lines. It was very scary. And starting in 1953 we filmed it. I visited the set of *I Love Lucy* and saw how creative that process could be. We used our real Beverly Hills house for the establishing shot and brought along much of the cast. Rod Levy started as director, followed by Freddie De Cordova and then Rod Amateau. We got better with every season, I feel. The most important element was the sponsor. Carnation Milk loved our ratings.

Bea Benaderet came along as next-door neighbor Blanche. We started out with Hal March on TV as her husband, but then went with Fred Clark. In 1953, he got a gig in a Betty Grable musical and demanded too much dough, so I hired Larry Keating, who was cheaper and funnier. I just came out onstage and explained Larry would now be playing Harry Morton. Bill Goodwin started out as announcer, but we then got Harry von Zell, who excelled at playing stupid. Harry, on a live radio feed in 1931, said, "Ladies and gentlemen, the president of the United States, Heebert Hoover, I mean Hoovert Heever—oh, ladies and gentlemen, the president."

BAWDEN: Did Gracie have troubles adapting to TV?

BURNS: All she had to do was read the script on radio. On TV, she had to map out her actions in rehearsals and hit those floor marks for the cameras. She had to memorize a large script each week and she couldn't change anything after dress rehearsal. It got her very frazzled. Another thing about Gracie—you couldn't hit her with a pie or expect her to take a pratfall. She was a lady and that might anger the audience. So the TV series isn't as visual as *I Love Lucy* was.

BAWDEN: You also had a number of other TV hits for your company, McCadden Productions.

BURNS: McCadden was the street in Beverly Hills where I still live. We produced *The Bob Cummings Show, Mr. Ed, No Time for Sergeants, Petticoat Junction,* and *The Jack Benny Show* was also under our wing. We were busy.

BAWDEN: I was listening to an old Jack Benny interview where he said you could always make him laugh at the most inauspicious occasions. Do you remember any?

BURNS: Once we were at MGM president Louis Mayer's house for a charity benefit and Jeanette MacDonald got up to warble and I whispered to Jack, who was sitting next to me, "Now, Jack, don't you dare laugh when she sings." And he went under the chair laughing and giggling so much he was asked to leave.

BAWDEN: Were you surprised when Gracie quit in 1958?

BURNS: Saddened, but not surprised. She was experiencing heart problems. She told me over supper one night that at the end of the 1958 season that was it. Leaky valve, just like Jeanette MacDonald. She died in 1964 after a string of heart attacks. One day she just collapsed in a Beverly Hills store. She was in bed one night and was in deep pain, but by the time the fire department arrived she had left us. Years later one of her doctors saw me at an event and said, "With new techniques we could have saved her today." That news made me feel depressed.

BAWDEN: You kept right on going.

BURNS: What was I supposed to do? Retire? No, I did *The George Burns Show* [1958] for CBS but viewers kept asking, "Where's Gracie?" I had Harry von Zell, Bea Benaderet, Larry Keating, but it was Abercrombie without Fitch. Nobody watched. It was dismal. I tried again in 1964 with *Wendy and Me* on ABC with Connie Stevens really up there as our Gracie character. And it lasted a year. So I did Vegas with Carol Channing playing the Gracie character and we toured and toured.

BAWDEN: Then you became a movie superstar.

BURNS: Jack Benny died just as production started on *The Sunshine Boys* with Walter Matthau. I was dubious of standing in for Jack, but I did it as a tribute to Jack, and now I'm an Oscar winner, but there have been no plans as yet to play *Hamlet*. Then I did *Oh, God!* with dear John Denver. Then *Going in Style* [1979] with Art Carney. And finally I'm back in style sixty years after I started. Who knew?

BAWDEN: Future plans?

BURNS: To keep this heart beating until I at least hit one hundred. I still go to Gracie's plot every week to tell her what I'm doing. Sometimes I'd fib a bit if I was at leisure. These days I don't have to make anything up.

Afterword

Burns was married once before he wed Gracie Allen—to Hannah Siegel—from 1917 to 1921. She was the early partner who worked with him under the name Hermosa Jose. The marriage was a token affair to please her parents so they could go on tour together. The marriage was never consummated and they were legally divorced when their stage tour ended.

Burns and Gracie Allen had two children, both adopted—Sandra and Ronnie. Ronnie played himself in their initial TV series.

Though Burns almost always had a lighted cigar in his mouth, he was in remarkably good health most of his life. He died of cardiac arrest at his Beverly Hills home on March 9, 1996. He was one hundred years old.

Raymond Burr

Interview by Ron Miller

Raymond Burr was a Canadian-born actor who learned his craft in theater and radio before coming to Hollywood in the 1940s as a character actor whose specialty was supporting roles as a "heavy," no doubt because of his husky build and his deep, sonorous speaking voice. Burr was soon established as one of the screen's most reliable villains, especially in grim films noir like *Raw Deal* (1948), *Blue Gardenia* (1953), *Gorilla at Large* (1954), and, most memorably, as the wife killer who menaces James Stewart in Alfred Hitchcock's *Rear Window* (1954).

But it may have been his bravura performance as the prosecutor who convicts Montgomery Clift of murder in *A Place in the Sun* (1951) that stuck in the minds of the producers of TV's *Perry Mason* series on CBS in 1957. They first sought him for the role of district attorney Hamilton Burger, but wound up casting him in the show's leading role as defense lawyer Perry Mason. That became the defining role of Burr's career, making him millions as the popular hero of a show that ran for nine seasons, then returned as a series of TV movies, this time on NBC. The TV movies continued even after Burr's death—with other actors playing lawyers who were supposedly filling in for the famous Perry Mason while he was out of town.

Burr's amazing rise as an iconic TV star was not entirely rooted in his Perry Mason role. He also starred in the detective series *Ironside*, which ran six seasons, and played other roles in other series and TV movies, including an acclaimed performance as Pope John XXIII in the 1973 TV movie *A Man Whose Name Was John*.

Burr's popularity was unflagging from the 1950s on, and his work remains in demand in the home video market to this day.

Setting the Scene

My interview with Raymond Burr took place in 1986 when he was happily helping NBC provoke renewed press interest in his string of *Perry Mason* TV movies. He had agreed to do a day of interviews in a classy West Hollywood hotel, lining up back-to-back one-on-one chats with newspaper columnists and TV and radio interviewers. Coming from my home in Sherman Oaks in the San Fernando Valley, I ran into a terrible traffic jam on the mountain pass from the valley and was nearly an hour late for my scheduled interview.

Amazingly, Burr, who was then sixty-eight, immediately made room for me as his next interviewer as soon as I showed up when he learned that I hadn't ditched his interview. I now believe the fact I worked for a San José newspaper helped my cause because it turned out Burr had long ago worked on radio in San José and had taught at a local college. His fondness for those days was obvious once we started talking.

After years of watching Burr be nasty on the big screen and forcefully authoritative on the TV screen, I was surprised to discover he was a genial, good-natured, warm-hearted, and all-around swell guy.

The Interview

MILLER: What's it like sitting down for a bunch of interviews with people who probably were kids when you first started playing Perry Mason?

BURR: Well, I do get tired of answering the same questions I was asked about Perry Mason back in 1957. Some of the new young people are asking me what I did before *Perry Mason* and what I did afterward. They don't even seem to know about the movies or *Ironside*.

MILLER: I've come across some people in the business who refer to your return to the Perry Mason role as a "comeback" for you. I'm told that word irritates you.

BURR: Since *Ironside* ended nine years ago, I've done twelve television specials, eight motion pictures, and a play that ran nearly a whole year. But not one of those was done in Los Angeles. The unfortunate thing is that if you don't live here and you're not in the news locally, you have to explain why you've suddenly come back into the business.

MILLER: Just a quick glance at your professional credits suggests you gained a tremendous amount of experience as an actor before you ever stepped in front of a camera.

Raymond Burr and Barbara Hale in *Perry Mason,* 1962. Courtesy of CBS publicity.

BURR: I did over five thousand radio broadcasts and two hundred plays before I ever got into motion pictures. I started in very small roles in pictures, but they started doing close-ups of me for no reason except the fact you could see I was thinking on camera, which made it look like something was going on in the scene. You don't see that level of experience anymore in young actors.

I've seen young people who, after three years in the business, still have to be told where the lights are and how to hit a mark.

MILLER: Because you weren't an overnight sensation in movies and had to work your way up to featured roles, do you think you learned by watching some of the big-name stars you worked with?

BURR: Oh, yes. I had dinner once with Laurence Olivier, who many regarded as the top of the acting profession, and I asked him how things were going for him and his answer was "I'm still learning."

MILLER: You worked with Clark Gable, the actor they called "the King," in his last years at MGM in the 1950 film *Key to the City*. How was he to work with?

BURR: He was a real pro, never a minute late in the morning. But let me tell you about another old pro from MGM and how he worked: Spencer Tracy. He would come on the set and ask, "Is this the scene we're doing today?" Then he would do the scene perfectly in one take. But one time I was leaving the lot late one night and saw Tracy slipping back onto the soundstage, so I wandered in and watched him. He was all alone, but he had his script in hand and was blocking his scenes for the following day, memorizing all his marks.

MILLER: You work with a lot of young actors today. How often do you see somebody care that much about being prepared?

BURR: The problem with some of our young people today is they become famous overnight because they have a certain personality. They get caught in a web that's very strange. It destroys me to have someone be in a show for two years and still not know where the camera is—or ask, "What lens do you have on?"

MILLER: You were in so many classic films noir, like Anthony Mann's *Raw Deal*, Douglas Sirk's *Sleep My Love* [1948], and Robert Siodmak's *Criss Cross* [1949], but you also worked for perhaps the darkest of noir directors, Fritz Lang, in *Blue Gardenia*. I've heard horror stories about him from such stars as Anna Lee, Henry Fonda, and Glenn Ford. How did it go with him?

BURR: I loved him. He was marvelous to work with.

MILLER: I wouldn't want to leave the impression that all the movies you made in that period were cinema classics. How do you explain your presence in a Poverty Row horror picture called *Bride of the Gorilla* [1951] with Lon Chaney Jr. and the notorious Barbara Payton?

BURR: Well, they promised me the gorilla would be all in my mind. So I finished the show and then they brought in the guy in the gorilla suit and added that to the picture.

MILLER: Before *Perry Mason,* it looked as if you were going to be stuck playing bad guys for the rest of your career.

BURR: I got a lot of attention playing heavies because I never played them all black.

MILLER: I think a prime example of that would be the creepy guy you played in *A Cry in the Night* [1956], where you spied on teenager Natalie Wood, then kidnapped her. There was an element of humanity in that man.

BURR: And working with Natalie Wood, I learned that, even at that young age, she was a real pro. She never stopped learning.

MILLER: But of course, your most unforgettable villain certainly has to be Lars Thorwald in Hitchcock's *Rear Window.* Tell me about that.

BURR: I played him as a man who was pushed beyond his endurance [by his wife]. He was no killer. He was a nice man. And in the picture we don't really know if he killed her or not. I figured he was a plodder through life and so I worked out a plodding kind of walk for him. I used to shock people by saying, "So what if I killed her? It was justifiable homicide!" Hitchcock loved it. We got along very well.

MILLER: But an earlier role turned out to be very crucial in your career—the very tough prosecuting attorney in George Stevens's *A Place in the Sun.*

BURR: The prosecuting attorney was not the one in Theodore Dreiser's novel—a man who used the case to climb very high. In our story, he was a man who walked with a limp, used a cane, and wore a Purple Heart button. He was a very quiet-spoken man, except in the courtroom. He truly believed Montgomery Clift was guilty [of murdering Shelley Winters] and should pay for what he'd done.

MILLER: How did you get along with director Stevens?

BURR: I got to know Mr. Stevens quite well on that picture. Every time I see it, I see things in it I hadn't seen before. He wanted me to test for the role, but I just told him how I wanted to do my scene and he said that was fine. I had this suit of clothes made up for the scene. I couldn't get the clothes to look the way I wanted to look for the picture, so I took the Panama hat and put it into one of those steam presses and held it down until the hat shrank down to almost nothing. Then I had them block it for me. I did the same thing with the suit. It shrunk the shoulder pads, tightened up the threads that made the seams. It looked like it had been worn for forty years. But when I did the scene, Mr. Stevens got up and left. Now that's a terrible thing to happen for a young actor.

Then I didn't hear and I didn't hear about how it went. They had kept the clothes [in the wardrobe department]. Meanwhile, I was offered a couple of other pictures, so I went to the studio to get the clothes back because they were mine. At 7 a.m. the following morning, I got a phone call from Mr. Stevens, who asked me why I took the goddamned clothes home with me. When I told him why, he said, "Of course you're going to do the role. We never tested anyone else. And we'll need the clothes!"

MILLER: It appears that very showy performance in *A Place in the Sun* eventually led you to the *Perry Mason* series. Once you had slimmed down a bit, they decided you were better suited to play Perry Mason rather than the district attorney role they had in mind for you. How did it feel to land a leading man role in a big TV dramatic series?

BURR: I had been trying to transform myself. I was doing a lot of live television in the early 1950s, not playing villains. Of all the movie roles I'd done so far, only about 5 percent were non-heavies. Once TV really got rolling, I decided I'd had enough heavies. I mean, I was running out of ways to play them.

MILLER: Perry Mason had been the lead character in a series of movies in the 1930s that had little to do with the best-selling novels by Erle Stanley Gardner. Now it seems impossible to imagine anyone else in the role.

BURR: While we were doing the show, Erle's novels were being serialized in the *Saturday Evening Post*. I picked up one of the issues, and all the drawings of Perry Mason looked like me. Erle had chosen me for the role, so he couldn't very well react adversely when the illustrations started looking like me.

MILLER: How close did you resemble the Perry Mason in the books?

BURR: You know, he never describes Perry Mason physically in the books. Once I asked Erle why he never described either Perry or Della Street [his secretary], and he said he wanted people to use their imagination. He also feared that making Perry and Della a certain age would date the books, which always remained in print for years. He learned that lesson once when he used the running board of a car as a major plot element—and then cars stopped having running boards!

MILLER: I guess the failure of the 1973 attempt to bring back the series as *The New Perry Mason* with Monte Markham in the title role proved people demanded Raymond Burr and nobody else.

BURR: I wanted that show to be successful. There were reasons why it wasn't. They had to do with the production values of the show. But there would always be comparisons.

MILLER: How do you account for the almost eternal popularity of *Perry Mason* at a time when lawyer shows seems to be popping up everywhere on TV?

BURR: He's a knight in shining armor because he represents the under-dog always. More than that, he represents our system of justice and reaffirms for every generation the fact that our system isn't perfect, but it's still the best system around.

MILLER: Was it a surprise to you that *Perry Mason Returns* [1985], the first two-hour movie that reunited the original TV show cast, was a big hit?

BURR: I expected it to be successful for several reasons. You know, I campaigned hard for CBS to do the original program as two-hour movies so we could do Erle's novels the way they should have been done, but they refused and said it wouldn't work. But I was totally unprepared for *Perry Mason Returns* to be not only the number one program for the week but the highest rated TV movie of that year.

Afterword

Raymond Burr earned acting Emmy Awards for his portrayal of Perry Mason in both 1959 and 1961.

One of Burr's most enduring roles was as the American wire service reporter in the 1955 *Godzilla, King of the Monsters*, a role that wasn't in the original Japanese movie but was added for the American release of the movie. Like Perry Mason, Godzilla has lasted for another generation—and Burr reprised his role in the remake *Godzilla 1985*.

Burr also starred in a reboot of his *Ironside* TV series as a TV movie, but the series itself wasn't revived for another decade. It wasn't successful without Burr.

In real life, Burr was a closeted gay man who had issued false claims of former wives and even a child he never really fathered. He was married once, from 1948 to 1952 to Isabella Ward, but the real love of his life was actor Robert Benevides, who was his life partner from 1960 until Burr's death. He lived on a large ranch with vineyards in Northern California and left all his property and assets to Benevides.

Raymond Burr died from cancer on September 12, 1993, in his ranch home in Healdsburg, California. He was seventy-six.

Glen Campbell

Interview by Ron Miller

If a recording star has the right combination of talent, poise, and personality, the TV medium often has extended a helping hand that has propelled him or her to superstardom. In the 1950s, televised variety shows were grand showcases for recording stars, and their agents labored hard to get them bookings on CBS's *The Ed Sullivan Show* or daytime programs like *The Garry Moore Show* and, of course, the best late-night display case of them all—*The Tonight Show*.

Amiable Glen Campbell had the right combination of talent. He was an accomplished musician whose guitar playing was in steady demand as a backup musician for such multimedia stars as Frank Sinatra, Dean Martin, and Elvis Presley. He was also a good-looking, fresh-faced country boy who appealed to the ladies like catnip to cats—and he was one heck of a fine singer, too.

Born in the tiny community of Billstown, Arkansas, on April 22, 1936, he grew up in the large family of a sharecropper. He picked up a guitar and began playing as a youngster; by his teen years, he was a wicked guitarist. He headed for Los Angeles, where he became a session musician, playing behind dozens of top singers, and ultimately was included in the now legendary "Wrecking Crew" of the very best session musicians in L.A.

In 1964, Campbell made his television debut in the syndicated country music show *Star Route*, which was hosted by former movie cowboy hero Rod Cameron. Slowly, he was gaining a reputation not only as a guitarist but as a very promising country singer. In 1964–1965, he was invited to replace the ailing Brian Wilson as a member of the famous pop group the Beach Boys on their year-long tour.

Soon Campbell's recording career kicked into high gear with a number of mega hits, including "Gentle on My Mind," "By the Time I Get to Phoenix," "Wichita Lineman," "Rhinestone Cowboy," and "Southern Nights." A frequent performer on TV's *The Smothers Brothers Comedy Hour,* he was picked to star in that show's summer replacement series, *The Glen Campbell Goodtime Hour,* which became a hit on its own from 1968 to 1972.

In 1969, Campbell landed a major acting role as the young romantic lead under star John Wayne in the western *True Grit,* which won Wayne the Best Actor Academy Award and got Campbell good reviews and an Oscar nomination for the title tune, which he performed behind the main credits.

Though his movie career never caught fire, Campbell continued to set records as a recording artist and concert performer, creating a lasting musical legacy of seventy albums, twelve of them charting gold, and selling a grand total of 45 million records. In 1967, he won four Grammy Awards in the country and pop categories.

Television remained an essential part of Campbell's career plan, and he was seen regularly over the years in both concerts and guest star appearances.

Setting the Scene

I met Glen Campbell in October 1971 in perhaps his peak years as a performer. He was doing concerts at Circle Star Theater in San Carlos, California, on the San Francisco Peninsula. He was in his midthirties and in robust good health. He was genial and guileless, a regular guy who still seemed a bit dazzled by his enormous success. I'm guessing his problems with alcohol and drugs, which plagued him in later years, were not yet influencing him. We talked during a break in his rehearsal for that night's sold-out performance.

The Interview

MILLER: While I was waiting to talk with you, I met a fan of yours named Roslyn who says she follows you all over the country and has seen you perform more than a thousand times. How do you like that?

CAMPBELL: I guess you could say she's my number one fan. She follows me everywhere I go, never misses a show—even when I'm in Vegas.

MILLER: Some of your people tell me she never really bothers you, but I'm guessing not all your fans are so respectful. They tell me you have hordes of them after you now. What's that like?

CAMPBELL: There are some things I just can't do anymore. I can't take the kids to the park or go to the beach. People crowd around me and it spoils things.

Glen Campbell, circa 1970. Ron Miller collection.

MILLER: Is that the dark side of being a superstar?

CAMPBELL: It's the price you have to pay, I guess. This didn't happen overnight, you know. I used to have to crowd myself into group photos of bands I was playing with just to prove to the folks back home in Arkansas that I really was in show business.

MILLER: Your visits back home must be a little different these days.

CAMPBELL: When I was just a backup musician, I used to go back home and visit Mom and Dad and nobody paid any attention. Now I show up there and half the town is waiting on the front porch.

MILLER: How do you cope with that kind of attention?

CAMPBELL: I don't think I'll ever adjust to being a celebrity. When I get through taping my TV show, there are always people who have been waiting two hours in the cold outside to get my autograph. It wouldn't be right to just walk past them, would it?

MILLER: One of my lady friends wanted me to ask where you get that country boy hairstyle.

CAMPBELL [*laughing*]: Hey, I don't even have a hair stylist. The way I wear my hair—I got the idea myself and that's the way I like it. I go to the same barber all the time. Once I went to a different barber when I was touring with the Beach Boys. It was in Rock Springs, Wyoming. I think the guy made his living shearing sheep. I never did that again.

MILLER: Do you have any idols that you would ask for an autograph?

CAMPBELL: I still have my idols and, yes, I will ask for autographs. I waited for Joe DiMaggio one day when he came off the first tee of the golf course just to get his autograph. I told him it was for my son, but it was really for me.

MILLER: Well, Glen, you starred in a movie with one of my idols—John Wayne. How did that feel?

CAMPBELL: That was any American kid's dream come true. For the first weeks of shooting, I kept saying to myself: "You're riding on a horse beside John Wayne in a movie—and you can't even act!"

MILLER: So I guess you can't really complain when a fan begs you to pose for a picture with her?

CAMPBELL: Heck, no. I never meet somebody I really admire without politely asking them to pose for a photo with their arm around me.

Afterword

I now realize that I was very lucky to meet Glen Campbell at one of the high points of his life. His later years were not always so happy. His follow-up movie to *True Grit*, the 1970 feature *Norwood*, which reteamed him with *True Grit* costar Kim Darby, was a commercial bust and there was no demand for additional Glen Campbell movies. His first three marriages ended in divorce. Along the way he fathered eight children and had a notorious public love affair with country singer Tanya Tucker, who was many years his junior. Their escapades were tabloid fodder, and Campbell's hard drinking and cocaine use even earned him a drunk-driving conviction and a spell in jail.

But Campbell eventually got his life back in order just in time to be diagnosed with Alzheimer's disease in 2010. He bravely struggled on, doing a final concert tour that won him renewed acclaim and a final best-selling album. His fourth wife, Kim, was with him until the end. He died from the disease on August 8, 2017, in Nashville, Tennessee. He was eighty-one.

Macdonald Carey

Interview by James Bawden

Many television "stars of tomorrow" first attracted attention with small roles in daytime serial dramas, then eventually went on to prime-time stardom or leading roles in feature films. But it was always very unusual for a leading player in movies to turn away from the big screen to take a regular role in a daytime soap opera.

The great British-born actress Anna Lee, a leading lady in such films as *King Solomon's Mines* (1937), *How Green Was My Valley* (1941), *Flying Tigers* (1942), and *Bedlam* (1946), is one of the rare examples: she left feature films to star in ABC's *General Hospital* from 1963 through the rest of her life. Leading lady Joan Bennett, a major star in the 1930s and 1940s, gave up the big screen to play the leading role in the *Dark Shadows* TV serial in 1966 and then reprised her role in the 1970 feature film based on the TV series, *House of Dark Shadows*.

But no actor exemplifies that career route more perfectly than Macdonald Carey, a reliable leading man in movies of the 1940s and 1950s, who gave up the big screen to play the leading role in NBC's *Days of Our Lives* soap opera for an epic run of twenty-five years. In the early years of his career, Carey made a name for himself in radio, playing regular roles in such popular daytime shows as *Stella Dallas, Just Plain Bill, Woman in White, John's Other Wife*, and *First Nighter*.

Setting the Scene

I first interviewed Macdonald Carey on the Burbank set of *Days of Our Lives* in 1972. He was then a hale and healthy sixty-seven-year-old. We chatted in his dressing room and later I watched him in rehearsals. We resumed our chat over lunch in the commissary.

He was a delightful man full of stories. When I told him I'd just seen him as Cesare Borgia in the dreadful 1949 *Bride of Vengeance*, Carey winked and said, "I never had the courage to watch that stinker."

In 1988 NBC held an evening event at the Century Plaza Hotel for all its daytime soap stars. When Mac spotted me, he rushed over and sat at my table. I've merged our various chats for this presentation.

The Interview

BAWDEN: How did you get into acting?

CAREY: I started out with a B.A. degree from the University of Iowa—I was born in Cedar City in 1913. But there were no job offers in any profession, so I joined a traveling troupe of actors called the Globe Players and we did pocket versions of Shakespeare in rural Texas. Other unknowns were David Wayne and Martha Scott. Then I did dreary auditions on Broadway until luminary Gertrude Lawrence picked me out of an audition line as her leading man for the new musical *Lady in the Dark* in 1941, and we ran 162 performances to packed houses. Up close she was ugly—big nose, strange brow—but from a distance she gave that light of stardom. Moss Hart directed it and he was very tough on me and got me into dramatic shape. And the biggest star that came out of it was Danny Kaye. Paramount paid a record amount for a Broadway show and signed me, too, but not Gertie and certainly not Danny, who was told to get his nose fixed. Then Paramount went to work on revising everything and by the time production started in 1944 I was in the army and unavailable. Ray Milland took over, which was ironical because I was known around the lot as the second Milland. I got all the parts he turned down.

BAWDEN: But you made your movie debut in Paramount's *Star Spangled Rhythm* [1942]?

CAREY: One of those starry salutes to give our servicemen a lift. I was Louie the Lug in one skit and, since I'd never made a movie, nobody knew who I was. I can't remember what skit it was; I was just background.

BAWDEN: Describe life as a rookie Paramount star.

CAREY: First there was a huge tour of the lot, which took an entire day—the research library, barbershop, makeup, soundstages, furniture warehouse, standing sets. I was bushwhacked at the end of our trek. I met other starlets in photo assignments: Susie Hayward had just defected from Warners, Sonny Tufts was coming on strong, I had a very tiny dressing room at first, whereas Ray Milland had a suite that included a bar and a bedroom. Phony romances with starlets were manufactured for the fan mags and I had to go to every premiere of a Paramount picture in clothes supplied by the studio. When I met the aged Adolph Zukor [head of the studio], he explained, "This is a plant. Ford makes cars, we make pictures. It's assembly line, get it?"

BAWDEN: Then came *Take a Letter, Darling* [1942]?

CAREY: I tested for it with Claudette Colbert. She was rushed into *The Palm Beach Story* [1942] after Carole Lombard died in a plane crash. So Paramount borrowed Rosalind Russell and she was a female executive, and Fred MacMurray was her secretary whose job is to take her around so the wives of her clients won't be suspicious. I was a tobacco heir already married multiple times, and Connie Moore was my sister who takes a shine to Fred. I'd watch Fred mugging and thinking he was so obvious, but when I watched it with an audience, he got big laughs.

BAWDEN: Then came *Dr. Broadway* [1942].

CAREY: And I got first billing as a New York physician, Dr. Timothy Kane, who knows all the theatrical characters. Jean Phillips was my leading lady, and the cast included J. Carrol Naish, Eduardo Ciannelli. Of course it was Damon Runyon territory. It was the directing debut of Anthony Mann, and he already knew how to turn the camera into making memorable shots. Some great character actors mugged all over the place and I'd just stand there and gape. I remember he told Jean to do Ginger Rogers. And yes, it was intended to jump-start another series, but audience reaction was underwhelming and Paramount passed.

BAWDEN: *Wake Island* [1942] was next.

CAREY: A huge box office success. John Farrow [the director] was one of the nastiest guys I ever met, but he really knew how to make actioners. Others in the cast included Brian Donlevy, Bob Preston, and Albert Dekker. Bill Bendix and Walter Abel were around, too. Yes, it was a flag-waver. But it needed to be shown: how a small company held off the Japs for weeks. We shot very quickly. Had to. It came out just six months after the incident and it showed American soldiers at their best. The real guys surrendered just before Christmas 1941 and the survivors were tortured to hell by the enemy. American morale had been sinking fast. We gave movie fans something to cheer about. There were lineups at the theaters to see it.

BAWDEN: What was life like at Paramount for a male starlet?

CAREY: Male starlet? Yes, that's exactly what I was. I remember walking down to wardrobe one day and Claudette Colbert rounds the street shouting, "Hi, Mac!" And I didn't even have a movie under my belt then. In the commissary, Alan Ladd sits down and starts showing me snaps of his kids. All very strange for an anonymous Broadway actor.

BAWDEN: Then came *Shadow of a Doubt* [1943]?

CAREY: I was loaned to Universal because the producer, Jack Skirball, needed somebody cheap and a guy at least as tall as Joe Cotten, who was playing the murderous Uncle Harry. Our star was Teresa Wright and she was red hot. She had two Oscar nominations in the same year. She lost in the main category for *Pride of the Yankees*, but won in support for *Mrs. Miniver*.

I've read Hitch [director Alfred Hitchcock] thinks it's one of his best. Everything was shot on location in sleepy Santa Rosa. I was Teresa's boyfriend and an investigator. Then I showed up one morning after an all-night bender and my hands were shaking badly. Hitch whispered to his secretary, who came back with a flask of bourbon. He poured me a drink and I took it down and ten minutes later did the scene brilliantly. But the humiliation! It was the first indication I was becoming a total alcoholic. Then I made a true B titled *A Salute for Three* and then I went into the army for three years,

BAWDEN: You returned to Hollywood in 1947?

CAREY: Yes. Paramount plopped me into *Suddenly It's Spring* [1946] with Paulette Goddard. This was the fourth time she'd costarred with Fred MacMurray. I asked Mitch Leisen, "What are you doing directing such garbage?" And he said he owed Paulette a favor. She was just awful at matching scenes. She'd do one thing in the close-up and then change everything in the long shot. But it was topical. She was a high-ranking female officer who returns to Fred and he says he wants a divorce. I was the other guy and Arleen Whelan was Fred's other squeeze.

It was a surprise hit and Paramount plopped us both in *Hazard* [1948], directed by George Marshall, which was a sort of comedy about Paulette's gambling addictions. And it really bombed and started a tailspin and Paulette was quickly out of movies.

BAWDEN: I just saw *Bride of Vengeance* with Paulette as Lucrezia Borgia.

CAREY: Poor kid! I was Cesare Borgia. Ray Milland had done the wardrobe tests and then walked. I asked him why and he said, "I only just read the script. I mean, it was a mess." By this time Mitch was only interested in decor—the directing was basically done by his assistant, Phyllis Seaton. Ray Burr was in it, I remember, but so was Billy Gilbert doing his sneezing routines. Paramount never used Paulette again. They paid her off for years not to work for them and her movie career was over.

BAWDEN: Another strange credit is *Dream Girl* [1948] with Betty Hutton.

CAREY: It had been a huge Broadway hit. Betty Hutton was completely miscast. No bellowing here. A complete change of pace and her fans loathed it. I see it as a fascinating failure and I did not need another failure at Paramount.

BAWDEN: How did you get cast in *The Great Gatsby* [1949] remake?

CAREY: Paramount owned the rights and had made a silent in 1926 with Warner Baxter. But Alan Ladd said no, it wasn't his thing. They finally wore him down and what did it was the promise to cast Gene Tierney as Daisy. But Fox finally refused and Paramount used Betty Field from Broadway and frankly, who could see Laddie mooning over Betty Field? I was Nick Carraway, Ruth Hussey was Jordan, and Shelley Winters was Myrtle. Shelley recently told me she has no recollection of making it. Elliott Nugent directed it. He usually did comedies. A hodgepodge. The [F. Scott] Fitzgerald fans didn't come to see it and the Ladd fans avoided it as arty. And the rights subsequently reverted to the Fitzgerald estate, so no one can see it at all.

BAWDEN: What about *Song of Surrender* [1949]?

CAREY: The studio went into a tailspin. Every big star was on the ropes. The only one they tried to salvage was Ladd, but he left knowing he could make more dough freelancing. This one was an attempt to make a star out of Wanda Hendrix, but the public wasn't buying. She was tiny, cute, very sweet. I did a B called *The Lawless* [1950] with poor, lost Gail Russell. There was liquor on her breath at 8 a.m. and I told her I understood, I surely did. Then I supported Ray Milland and Hedy Lamarr in *Copper Canyon* [1950]. Ray loathed Hedy with a passion. But she was red hot after *Samson and Delilah* [1949]. Then my Paramount contract was over and I drifted into the night.

BAWDEN: You landed at Universal-International?

CAREY: At half my old salary. They made programmers—B movies decked out in Technicolor, but shot in three weeks. The first was *Comanche Territory* [1950] with Maureen O'Hara and director George "One Take" Sherman, a tough taskmaster. Then I did *South Sea Sinner* [1950] with Shelley Winters going into her blond bombshell era. When I asked Betty Grable how I became her partner in *Meet Me After the Show* [1951], she said, "You were the cheapest hire." And I stayed at Fox to do *Let's Make It Legal* [1951] with Claudette Colbert. We were a middle-aged couple running around and Claudette told me she had broken her back and had to bow out of *All about Eve* [1950] and this is what Fox gave her in return. There was a cute number named Marilyn Monroe wiggling around. How could we know she'd become the hottest star on the lot within a year? By the way, I was a decade younger than Claudette, but in the movie we're supposed to be the same age.

BAWDEN: Eventually you went into TV.

CAREY: Had to. I had six kids to feed by then. I'd do *Lux Video Theater,* which was live—$650 for two weeks' work and that money was appreciated. In fact, I did a TV version of *Miracle on 34th Street* for *The Twentieth Century-Fox Hour* in 1955 opposite my old pal Teresa Wright and Thomas Mitchell. Little Sandy Descher had the Natalie Wood role. In 1956 I did the TV version of *Dr. Christian,* replacing Jean Hersholt as the kindly doctor. In fact, I played his nephew. We filmed the thirty-nine half hours at ZIV studios on Santa Monica Boulevard. Jean was on his deathbed from cancer, so I don't know how they got him down to film an introduction, welcoming me into the family. A newcomer named Stuart Whitman came in for a few episodes. I remember Whit Bissell being in there, too. Robert Armstrong from *King Kong* [1933]—I remember him there. It ran in syndication and has never been seen again.

BAWDEN: Then came a second series, *Lock Up,* in 1959.

CAREY: Lasted two seasons. I remember Bob Florey was one of the directors. Dane Clark directed three and there was [director] Christian Nyby. Again, a ZIV thingy. I was the defense attorney Herbert Maris and John Doucette was my assistant. By the way, there really was a Maris based in Philadelphia who tried freeing wrongly convicted people.

BAWDEN: Then came your best-ever movie, *These Are the Damned* [1962].

CAREY: It was truncated in the American release, but now the original is out on video. I get letters about it. Joseph Losey was one of those American directors blacklisted. He moved to England and made only classics. The whole idea of a secret government agency manipulating us is more relevant today than it was in 1962. But at the time it didn't give me much of a career lift.

BAWDEN: You've become very open about your battle with alcoholism.

CAREY: I had to confront it or it would have destroyed me. I was ashamed to do anything for years. It's still a battle and always will be for me. Now I work at AA meetings helping others. It's a tough grind. I've got to be there for others. Why did I drink? I'm from an Irish Catholic family. And being an actor is a very unsteady occupation. You're either up or down. You get rejection every day. You're not in charge. The director calls the shots.

On *Days of Our Lives* I started slurring my lines on the set. They wrote in a story where Dr. Horton [his character in the show] had a stroke and then was in bed for a bit. They could have fired me. Instead they encouraged me to seek help. I haven't had a drink in years. But it's a constant battle, I can tell you.

Macdonald Carey in *Days of Our Lives*. James Bawden collection.

BAWDEN: Let's jump back to 1965 when you inaugurated *Days of Our Lives*.

CAREY: I thought, "Oh gosh, now I'm in a daytime soap!" But I'd started in radio serials, and, in fact, playing Dr. Tom Horton made me hot again. I've been doing it seventeen years now. I'll do two to three hours a week. I wondered, "How can I learn so much dialogue?" Easy. I record my lines into a portable tape recorder. Then I play them back as I'm eating dinner. I'll play them again a few hours later and then one last time just before I go to sleep and as soon as I wake up. I've never gone up on my words, but nine days later when the show runs I can't remember a single word if I'm watching.

BAWDEN: How did you get the part?

CAREY: The creators were Ted Corday, Irna Phillips, and Allan Chase. For the first decade it was a half hour and then in 1975 it went to an hour. You know, the Supreme Court judge Thurgood Marshall watched every day. He told me he knew every facet of the story in and out. And it was just about the first soap to come from Los Angeles—all the others were New York based. I could wander in and out of the cast and do other things if I gave the writers ample time. It made me hot again and I guest-starred on *Ben Casey*, *Run for Your Life*, *Owen Marshall*. You name it, I was on it. I was in the miniseries *Roots* [1977]. I knew I'd made it by being in two [episodes] of *Murder, She Wrote*. TV has become my life and I'm grateful for still being able to act at my age.

Afterword

Macdonald Carey continued to devote much of his free time to working with Alcoholics Anonymous. In fact, during one of my interviews with him, he had to break away and rush to offer counsel at an AA meeting in Beverly Hills.

Carey was married to Elizabeth Heckscher from 1948 to 1969. They had six children. After their divorce, Carey was with life partner Lois Kraines until his death. One of Carey's daughters, Lynn Carey, is an actress, singer, and composer whose music was used in two Russ Meyer films—*Beyond the Valley of the Dolls* (1970) and *The Seven Minutes* (1971).

Carey wrote an autobiography—*Days of My Life*—in 1991. He has a star on the Hollywood Walk of Fame for his television work. Carey won two Emmy Awards for his performance in *Days of Our Lives*, in 1974 and 1975. Altogether, he appeared in 561 episodes of the serial drama between 1965 and his death in 1994.

He succumbed to lung cancer on March 21, 1994, in Beverly Hills. He was eighty-one years old.

Dick Clark

Interview by Ron Miller

Once, at a press conference, somebody asked Dick Clark, who was famous for all the talented performers he had introduced to television viewers, exactly what his talent was.

"I have no talent," Clark replied with a big, self-effacing grin. "I just point at talent."

If you first saw Dick Clark with a microphone in his hand, glibly rapping with teenagers on the dance floor of his *American Bandstand* TV series, you could be forgiven for believing that he really thought he had no talent of his own. If you were a latecomer who knew Dick Clark only as a much older host, gabbing furiously as the countdown began on ABC's annual New Year's Eve telecasts, you also could be forgiven for wondering how this guy ever became famous in the first place.

But if you ever spent any time with Dick Clark, as I did on a couple of occasions in the 1980s, when he was arguably at the peak of his Hollywood influence, you surely knew that he was so much more than the slick-talking announcer/disk jockey you saw on TV. And if you ever sat down with him and had a serious conversation, as I also did several times in my years as a syndicated entertainment columnist, you also knew this was one very shrewd and savvy character—a man firmly in control of most of the world around him and the people who inhabited it with him.

Dick Clark's solid position in the history of television has been very well documented. He began in radio, then moved to local television in his youth and began his hosting career on WKTV in Utica, New York, with a country music show called *Cactus Dick and the Santa Fe Riders*. More important, he later took over what amounted to a "record hop" program on a local Philadelphia TV station in the early 1950s and rode the rise of rock and roll to nationwide fame in just a few short years. In August 1957, Dick Clark's *American*

Bandstand moved to the ABC network as a late-afternoon weekday show and quickly became the number one showcase for new rock acts before they were ready to move up to prime-time variety programs like *The Ed Sullivan Show* on CBS.

That same year, ABC became so enthralled with *American Bandstand* that the network gave it a three-month run as a half-hour prime-time series on Mondays from 7:30–8 p.m. (Prime time began earlier back then.) Clark was young, good-looking, and seemed to fit perfectly into any youth-oriented situation. He even got the leading role in a big studio movie—Columbia Pictures' 1960 adaptation of John Farris's best-selling novel *Harrison High*, which was called *Because They're Young*. To make Clark feel right at home, Columbia even added a rock group—Duane Eddy and the Rebels—to the cast.

Clark was a TV institution by the late 1970s. He had begun to spread out into producing his own TV shows—and not just ones that featured him as the host or star. For example, he produced a western series for ABC—*The Guns of Will Sonnett* (1977–1979) starring Walter Brennan and went on to produce many important TV movies, including NBC's *The Man in the Santa Claus Suit* (1979) with Fred Astaire, NBC's *Murder in Texas* (1981), a miniseries starring Katharine Ross, Sam Elliott, Farrah Fawcett, and Andy Griffith, and CBS's *Copacabana* (1985) starring Barry Manilow.

In retrospect, I think Clark may have been a better producer than he was anything else. And in 1979 I think that wasn't an uncommon notion—particularly after ABC let him make a movie about Elvis Presley that forever changed the economics of television.

Until Clark's *Elvis*, directed by John Carpenter (known for *Halloween*, among other works) and starring Kurt Russell as Elvis, the big Sunday-night events on the three commercial TV networks were almost always Hollywood feature films making their TV debut. That year, during the February ratings "sweeps," when the networks programmed the biggest attractions they had, CBS and NBC went with super movie attractions—*Gone with the Wind* (CBS) and *Close Encounters of the Third Kind* (NBC). ABC, which didn't own the rights to anything that big, put on Dick Clark's *Elvis*.

Well, *Elvis* blew the other networks out of the water. It was an enormous hit and a critical success. Believe me, it's still a great movie—and Dick Clark's name is right there on it as executive producer. Its success started the death knell for Hollywood feature films as big commercial TV events. After *Elvis*, the networks learned they could draw bigger viewer numbers with fresh, original made-for-TV movies of their own—and spend less money in the process.

Dick Clark. Courtesy of Dick Clark Productions and The Nashville Network.

Later that year, Clark stumbled a bit when he tried it again with another original TV movie, *The Birth of the Beatles*, which told the story of the Fab Four from their earliest days in Liverpool, when Pete Best and Stu Sutcliffe were with the band. Clark filmed the movie in England, once again hiring a first-rate director—Richard Marquand, who went on to direct *Return of the Jedi* for George Lucas in the *Star Wars* series. But The Beatles didn't like the idea and their company sued Clark, denying him the right to use several of the Beatles songs he wanted for the movie. The movie still got made, but it wasn't well received, and ABC, which showed it on a Friday night, didn't get big ratings for it.

Actually, Clark seldom ran into trouble over rock music that he wanted to use in his various TV shows over the years. The reason was simple: Clark acquired the rights to an awful lot of TV clips of rock stars performing their biggest hits, including virtually everybody who ever appeared on *American Bandstand*. For years I kept running into people who had great ideas for documentaries about famous rock acts but complained loudly that Clark owned the rights to all the footage and wanted a fortune for them to use any of his clips.

Earlier in his career, though, Clark faced serious trouble when the payola scandal rocked the world of disk jockeys and producers of programs featuring pop music acts. Many were indicted for paying off deejays to get exposure for their recordings. Clark was forced to divest his then considerable interests in recording companies and associated businesses.

Clark's influence continued to be felt for years after *American Bandstand* started to fade away in the era of MTV and music videos, even though his familiar show stayed on the air a total of thirty years. His TV "bloopers" specials were big ratings winners. He created the *American Music Awards,* his TV specials intended to rival the Grammys, and did his *Pyramid* game show for years. His *New Year's Rockin' Eve* specials continued after his death.

Setting the Scene

I began to talk with Dick Clark almost as soon as I started my regular television column in 1977. Press-savvy, he did many press conferences and was open to chat with reporters on the phone or in person about his program ventures.

For example, I remember chatting with Clark about the controversy over his movie about the start of the Beatles. He was not a happy camper about the rights dispute he ran into with the band. However, he did a great favor for me. He set me up with an interview with Pete Best, the real "fifth Beatle," who was played by Ryan Michael in Clark's film, *The Birth of the Beatles.* I treasure that bit of insight into rock history.

In 1983, I moved to the Los Angeles area to cover Hollywood close up for my newspaper, the *San José Mercury News,* and the Knight Ridder Syndicate, which served more than one hundred other newspapers with my columns. During that time I made arrangements to spend a morning with Dick

Clark at his office in the San Fernando Valley, talking with him in between whatever else he might be doing and just kind of watching him in action.

It turned out to be a real education for me. First, I should say that Dick Clark was always very cordial with me and never refused to answer any questions, but I don't want to leave the impression that we were all that friendly. Put simply, I felt Clark was aware of the wisdom of cooperating with the press and knew that publicity was good for him and his various projects. But he wasn't somebody who would pat you on the back and tell you what a good job you were doing—and he never sent me any "thank-you" notes for anything I ever wrote about him.

But he did let me watch him do business that day, which was mostly done over the phone, and I was left with the clear impression that here was a guy who was very good at what he was doing—planning shows and issuing orders to his subordinates. One of them was his wife Kari, who in those days functioned pretty much as his personal secretary. I recall him barking orders at her—and not always in soft, dulcet tones. She struck me as extremely efficient—and extraordinarily patient with a man who frequently operated like a whirling dervish.

At one point, I had some time to kill while he was on the phone and wandered around his large office, checking out the many items of memorabilia that reflected the history of rock and roll and, of course, his role in that history.

What follows is my record of the conversations we had during that day I spent with him at his headquarters.

The Interview

MILLER: Just looking around your office, I spotted this poster for a live rock concert featuring an integrated lineup of black and white rock stars scheduled to open in the Deep South. You took many integrated tours into the South when Jim Crow still ruled down there. How did that go?

CLARK: It was difficult. In my business, it was like there were no black people in the 1950s. You weren't supposed to have them mixed in with white people on your show. You weren't supposed to travel with them like we did on our tours. When I went out on the road with rock and roll shows in the South, we had to eat in the Greyhound bus terminal because it was the only place we could eat.

MILLER: But you had black artists on your show from the beginning of *Bandstand*, right?

CLARK: From the day the show went on the air, there were black artists. Dizzy Gillespie was one of the first. Here was a case where black artists were on every day of the week, but there were no black kids in our audience. That had to change.

MILLER: You get lots of credit for the dawn of the rock and roll revolution. Take me back to those early days. How did you get into that music?

CLARK: I was a disk jockey. I wasn't playing middle-of-the-road music, just old-fashioned pop music. But I was a jazz fan. Yet in Philly, the station manager wouldn't let me play the pop music of the day. Management was still hung up on the big-band era and those vocalists. But "Stranded in the Jungle" by the Jayhawks was number one on the charts. That turned their head around real fast. They sent me to Pittsburgh to try to imitate Jay Michaels [a disk jockey], to see what he was doing. What he was doing was what all the young guys were doing—playing black music. But I wasn't even allowed to play Nat King Cole. The guy who ran the station wasn't a racist. He just didn't like Nat's style.

MILLER: But they were smart enough to let you get in on the boom and your audience grew enormously. But did you really like rock and roll best?

CLARK: There's no diplomatic way to answer that. I always avoid answering that question because you're going to look like you're frozen in time. If you rode around with me for a couple of days, you'd find me listening to all kinds of music, from all kinds of periods. I like the good old days of rock and roll because it reminds me of the birth of this whole thing. But the quality was not as sophisticated as it is today, either artistically or technically.

MILLER: Though *Bandstand* has been on for more than a quarter century, there are some acts that never appeared on it. Did you just put the acts on that you personally liked?

CLARK: There isn't anybody who hasn't been on the show because I had any personal preference, one way or another. The usual reason why somebody wasn't on my show is that they were doing too well at the time. Rick Nelson didn't appear because his dad [Ozzie Nelson] didn't want him to compete with his presence on the *Ozzie and Harriet* TV show. Subsequently, he's been on a lot of our shows.

MILLER: Rock music has been through a lot of different periods since it began in the 1950s. Was there ever one of those periods you found distasteful personally?

CLARK: The psychedelic drug-oriented period of San Francisco rock was very difficult for me to get with. First of all, I've never been into drugs.

And I didn't understand the music. It was a little foreign to my ear. That was probably my only dropout period.

MILLER: How do you feel about it when someone uses that famous line, calling you "America's oldest teenager"?

CLARK: It's a funny line. I cherish it. I ask people to use it for introductions because it gives me a jumping-off place. It would be very abnormal for a person my age to try and be a teenager. The side benefit I get from it is that I don't feel my age. I really don't feel like a middle-aged person and that's the biggest perk anybody could get. I mean, I walked into the Hard Rock Café in New York the other night. It was remarkable. Everybody yelled, "Hi, Dick!" It was the nicest thing anybody ever did for me—calling me America's oldest living teenager.

MILLER: Well, you do look and sort of act young. What's your secret?

CLARK: School teachers will tell you this: if you hang around young people a lot, some of it's bound to rub off.

MILLER: But then I've never seen you on the air when you weren't wearing a jacket and a tie. You never dress like a teenager. Is that likely to change?

CLARK: The only thing that changes is the width of my lapels and the ties. Now around here I never wear a tie. Only on television. It's my uniform.

MILLER: You once remarked that you knew the time would come when *Bandstand* would have to be canceled, but others tell me you are so tied to that show that it would be a terrible ordeal for you to see it go. You are now into so many other projects. How important is *Bandstand* to you?

CLARK: I doubt if anything else would ever have happened for me without *Bandstand*. When I made that remark, I didn't know there would be 19 million different kinds of television someday. In that day, we only had network and syndication. We didn't have cable and all the other stuff we have today. That show will never go off the air as long as anybody cares to keep it on. It's a timeless formula, so I retract that original remark.

MILLER: I remember when some folks were ripping into *Bandstand* because you allowed performers to come on the show and lip-synch to their records.

CLARK: I haven't had a nasty remark or a snide comment about lip-synching since the advent of modern music videos. It's a high art form. It's the kind of thing that's been going on in motion pictures since the beginning of soundies. So you don't hear those nasty little barbs thrown our way anymore.

MILLER: But some people say the all-music video channels like MTV have made *Bandstand* obsolete.

CLARK: MTV is the one that may have to look to the future. That has a greater rate of attrition than people watching.

MILLER: Have you ever been close to cancellation of the show? Ratings now are not what they used to be.

CLARK: There was a sales director once at ABC who was concerned about it in the 1960s. It became *The New American Bandstand.* They wanted to call it something else. I can't even remember what they wanted to call it, but it was some god-awful title. I told them that if they changed it, I'd tell them bye-bye and I'd take the show to syndication. That went away very quickly. That's the closest we ever came to cancellation.

MILLER: How do you account for the dip in ratings over the past two years?

CLARK: Of course, its impact on American musical taste diminished quite a bit when it went to once a week. That was twenty years ago. There was a time when it was the only store in town. It still delivers a considerable audience and it's sold out [in terms of advertising] fifty-two weeks a year. It's another indication of the fragmentation of television. If the show were not on the network, it would do better. It would be moved around into better, more logical program areas.

MILLER: Almost everybody I talk with in the business talks about how shrewdly you assembled archives of great rock performers and now dominate the marketplace for such footage.

CLARK: We have the largest pop musical archive in the world. As you will notice from my surroundings, I hardly ever throw anything away. It now has blossomed into one of the fondest dreams I ever had. I started saving old kinescopes and eventually videotapes. It's a losing operation because it costs a great deal of money to preserve all that. But someday I'll take all of that and it will go into a publicly endowed museum of some sort. I've just got to figure out a way for it to pay for itself.

MILLER: How different are the young people who watch *Bandstand* today from the ones who watched it at the beginning?

CLARK: Those original kids were children. These today are young adults. There are no children anymore. That's bad, but there's nothing anybody can do about it. To become so sophisticated so early in your life is the unfortunate penalty we're paying for progress. You'd be abnormal or a liar if you endorsed everything the younger generation does. The fun part for me is this: how many fifty-five-year-old men do you know who could have a conversation with somebody with orange, spiked hair or a woman with her head shaved up the sides in a Mohawk and have it still come off as a conversation?

MILLER: Just being here today and watching you do what you do off camera has been a revelation. This must be the main thing you do and the on-air Dick Clark is the small part.

CLARK: Any hard-working, compulsive person wants to have a hands-on attitude about his or her business. I've always been that way, since I was a child. It's a very small company, but a very active company. I don't know why. It's just the nature of the beast.

MILLER: If something happened to you, who would take over?

CLARK: Hey, I've got a problem right now. The average person has four wisdom teeth. My fourth one is coming in right now—in my fifty-fifth year! I'm teething! Let's assume I'm laid up for some reason like that for four or five weeks. They could find somebody to do the game show [*The $25,000 Pyramid*] very quickly—the announcer could do it. No one is indispensable. You learn that very quickly. There are eight full-time producers here and an equal number of directors. This joint runs when I'm not here. People see me on these shows and think that's my job. Actually, that's about 10 to 15 percent of what I do. We do fifteen *Pyramids* at a time in two days. We do four *American Bandstands* on a Saturday. That puts us ahead. What's interesting is that any one of these shows would be a full-time job for most people.

MILLER: Do you think, when it's all over, that you'll be remembered best for being the host of *American Bandstand*?

CLARK: Yes. It's touched millions of people's lives over three generations. It presented music that wasn't blessed with universal recognition. Rock and roll is now an American contribution to the world. Most important, it showed that people can come together in a social climate and develop an appreciation for one another without killing each other in the process.

Afterword

American Bandstand was finally canceled in 1987. In its final days, it was being taped on Saturdays in a large soundstage on the grounds of ABC's local Los Angeles TV station. I attended one of the final tapings, which featured the rap group Run-D.M.C. The hip-hop era had arrived and I felt Dick Clark and *Bandstand* no longer fit the mood of the youth market in America.

But Clark continued to be a major figure in television after the death of his favorite program. I remember suggesting to Clark on that day I spent with him that he ought to consider doing a movie or TV show about the early days when he toured with rock groups throughout 1950s America. He told me, "I'm thinking about it. We're getting something together."

Sure enough, some twenty years later, he produced the weekly TV drama series *American Dreams* about a 1960s Philadelphia family with a daughter who was a fan of *American Bandstand*. That show gave Clark the chance to reproduce several of the famous rock acts of his early TV days and to get at some of the issues I had in mind when I looked at that vintage poster of his about touring the American South.

Because he was so uniquely poised to be a witness to rock history being made, Clark knew everybody who was any kind of player in the development of that huge musical wave. Not everybody liked him, but he helped so many of them that I'm guessing a majority of the rock stars who came his way were admirers.

I remember asking him how enthused he could be about a new generation of music that was dominated by rap and hip-hop acts like Run-D.M.C. "I don't have to like them all," he told me with a weary grin. "I just have to point at them and say their names."

Dick Clark was married three times and had three children, who all went into one form of show business or another. In 2004, he suffered a mild stroke that left him with impaired speech and yet he came back from that blow to continue to host his *New Year's Rockin' Eve* shows, missing just one before his death from a heart attack in Santa Monica on April 18, 2012. He was eighty-two.

Mike Connors

Interview by James Bawden

Mike Connors was one of a very special group of hunky young potential leading men who surfaced in Hollywood in the 1950s and were given "colorful"
new first names by publicist Henry Willson. Rock Hudson and Tab Hunter
were the most famous and successful of that group, but Touch Connors didn't
become popular in television until he dumped the "cute" first name and became
just plain Mike Connors, star of the long-running private eye series *Mannix*.

Though Connors was in several outstanding films, including *Sudden Fear*
(1952) with Joan Crawford and Jack Palance and *Island in the Sky* (1953) with
John Wayne, his career was heading toward low-budget jobs like *Day the
World Ended* (1955) and *Voodoo Woman* (1957) before he finally became a
leading man in television with the series *Tightrope, Mannix,* and *Today's FBI*.

But *Mannix* was the show that elevated Connors to legendary status as a
TV star. His character, Joe Mannix, was one of the toughest of all TV sleuths
and often wound up in rough-and-tumble brawls with suspects. Radio comics
Bob and Ray did a regular parody of the show on their program and Connors
himself once entertained TV critics by showing them a video parody of his
own show with him imitating Peter Falk's TV sleuth, Columbo, as he might
have appeared as the star of *Mannix*.

Setting the Scene

I first met Mike Connors at the L.A. Aquarium, where he was shooting scenes
for *Mannix* opposite guest star Jack Ging, who once had been a football superstar with the Toronto Argonauts in the Canadian Football League. We later
connected on the set of Connors's next series, *Today's FBI,* in 1981. Later I did
telephone interviews with him on the subject of the 1988 miniseries *War and
Remembrance* and his odd 1993 Quebec-made movie, *Armen and Bullik*.

Julia Adams with Mike Connors in *Mannix*. Courtesy of CBS and the James Bawden collection.

The Interview

BAWDEN: Tell me about your early years.

CONNORS: Well, I'm a proud Armenian and my real name is Krekor Ohanian—same as my father's name. The year was 1925 and I grew up in modest circumstances in Fresno [California] but with two parents who adored all their three kids. Yes, there was discrimination in the schools and yes, I fought back. I had basketball skills honed in high school and after war service in the air force I attended University of California at Los Angeles on a basketball scholarship. My coach was a famous guy: John Wooden. And during one game, movie director William Wellman was in the stands and afterwards arranged a screen test.

BAWDEN: What was your first TV gig?

CONNORS: On *Jukebox Jury* in about 1952 or 1953. It was live, so nothing exists of it today. I was billed as Touch Connors in the Joan Crawford starrer *Sudden Fear* [1953]. That crazy publicist Henry Willson gave me that name alongside Rock Hudson and Tab Hunter and Race Gentry. And yes, Joan did come on to me, but I was born the year she got into pictures. Joan was mad all the time. Warners had just publicly fired her and here she was at RKO. She made life rough for the other female star—Gloria Grahame—and had a running feud with Jack Palance. I guess it was sort of a hit. I was the muscular guy, but luckily had little to say.

BAWDEN: What about your other films at this time?

CONNORS: Wellman got me a bit in *Island in the Sky* [1953]. I'd study John Wayne closely until the big fella yelled at me, "Cut that out!" Ever seen *Swamp Women* [1955]? A gang of busty gals bust out of female penitentiary and get lost in the Louisiana bayou. Roger Corman directed it and we'd shoot a scene until he ran out of film and then go onto the next scene. You mean you've never seen *Swamp Women*? You're really missing something. It took all of ten days to shoot. The script bogged us down more than the bayous. Then I was a "herder" in *The Ten Commandments* [1956]. I can still hear the director, Cecil B. DeMille, shouting, "Tell those villagers to start villaging!"

And I did TV, guesting on *Hey, Jeannie*, *The People's Choice*, and I was on *Wagon Train* and *City Detective* starring Rod Cameron, *Maverick*, *Jefferson Drum*, and *The Californians*.

BAWDEN: Your first series was *Tightrope* in 1959?

CONNORS: Nobody remembers that one at all. The CBS brass were convinced nobody would watch an hour drama. This despite the success over at ABC of series such as *Maverick*. True, *Perry Mason* was an hour and on CBS, but the executives said it only used the basic cast in half of each episode. Even *Gunsmoke* was only a half hour and I've always felt that with an hour we could have told our stories better. Within a few years, half-hour dramas had all but disappeared. You see, it was a cheaper form of TV than two half-hour dramas.

BAWDEN: Those stories about shenanigans on the set of *Where Love Has Gone* [1964]—any truth there?

CONNORS: Oh, it's all true. Susan Hayward came to set with a hardened attitude. She thought the story crap and she'd slam her dressing room shut after every scene. Bette Davis was only ten years Susie's elder and here she's playing the bitchy mom. Bette called her "Little Miss What's Her Name." Susie was more direct: "That dirty old bitch." They should have filmed the behind-the-scenes tantrums rather than the story, which was about the Lana Turner murder. [Turner's daughter had killed Turner's gangster boy friend in defense of her mother. The movie changed the names and fictionalized the actual case.] I just sat there and hoped I'd get out alive. Which I did, but the movie was a big hit for a few weeks at the box office.

BAWDEN: You know, I once had lunch with Bruce Geller, the great producer who created your hit show *Mannix*. But just a few months later he died. Tell me about him.

CONNORS: He died in an airplane crash in 1978. Bruce was a flying nut and he was piloting his Cessna Skymaster and crashed in Buena Vista Canyon in the fog. And we were devastated. We'd lost the pilot of our show, who knew how to revise an inferior script and cast intelligently. The series did go on, but things could never be the same.

BAWDEN: I remember seeing the pilot episode for *Mannix* and thinking it wasn't quite ready. There were too many threads and—

CONNORS: Yes, it was very arty. Bruce streamlined the plotting and his casting decisions were always marvelous. Dick Levinson and Bill Link were co-creators and everything they did was very well thought out. Lucy Ball wrote a personal check for $1 million to bankroll the pilot and she sold it to CBS. They loved most of it, but said they couldn't have Gail Fisher as my secretary. "She's black!" shouted one executive. "She's been black for quite some time," cracked Lucy. They wondered how this would play in CBS's Deep South affiliates but the ratings there were the same as in the North. Score one for Bruce and Lucy.

BAWDEN: You seemed to get the best guest stars perfectly paired with their characters.

CONNORS: Off the top of my head, I remember Diana Muldaur, Dane Clark, Jessica Walter as ones I was thrilled to act with. Paul Krasny directed the most episodes, but would you believe Bill Bixby did four with great style. John Llewelyn Moxey did at least ten. Your Canadian friend Henry Hart did two, Eva Marie Saint's husband Jeffrey Hayden did two, and would you believe it but Mel Tormé even did one in 1974, but the fast pace really got to him.

BAWDEN: Did the series have to end?

CONNORS: It was the last big show made by Desilu, which sold everything to Paramount in 1968. And Paramount was a giant and things we could do at Desilu were no longer possible. Schedules were more restricted. I mean, we did go eight seasons and that means 194 episodes, and what stories were left? And everywhere I go these days people stop and say they're still watching either in reruns or in boxed sets. We never showed blood and corpses like some shows do today. And the location work was always top of the line. If I ever tune in to an old show, sure, I'll watch for a bit.

BAWDEN: Tell me about the craziest-ever cross promotion that CBS devised.

CONNORS: Well, you know that CBS loved these—a story starts on *Barnaby Jones* and ends on *Murder, She Wrote*—that kind of thing. I figured, what the heck? So, as Joe Mannix, I did a 1971 *Here's Lucy*. I didn't want to, but the lady had saved our show. We shot it at Universal as Lucy had left Paramount after selling off Desilu. *Mannix* fans loved it. But never again will I spoof the series that made me.

BAWDEN: What brought you back to series TV and *Today's FBI*?

CONNORS: Boredom. There are only so many guest things I can do. Movie producers see me as a TV actor. Jim Garner, Steve McQueen made the jump. But I'm not so lucky and the same goes for Vince Edwards, Lorne Greene, a lot of us. It's a revamp of the series *The FBI* and I'm Ben Slater, who has been a G-man for like forever. We did a TV movie that fared well and served as the pilot. David Carradine is in for the first episode as a religious fanatic. Don't forget *Mannix* took almost a full season to catch on. I'm not sure networks are willing to wait that long anymore. [*Today's FBI* expired after eighteen episodes.]

BAWDEN: And what about this Quebec-made thriller, *Armen and Bullik*, which stars Quebec pop singer Roch Voisine?

CONNORS (*sighing*): I go where the jobs are. Roch Voisine is the biggest pop star in Quebec. It's doing big business in Montreal. Elsewhere? Who knows? I've also done *Love Boat*. But I'm proudest of *War and Remembrance*. In recent years I'm dancing as fast as I can.

Afterword

Mike Connors married Mary Lou Willey in 1949 and they remained a couple until his death. They had two children, a son and a daughter.

Connors's final screen appearance was in a 2007 episode of the TV sitcom *Two and a Half Men*. He had received a Golden Globe award in 1969 for his performance in *Mannix*.

He died of leukemia on January 26, 2017, in Tarzana, California. He was ninety-one.

William Conrad

Interview by James Bawden

When radio began to fade as the primary home entertainment venue in America in the late 1940s, the new television industry welcomed many well-known radio programs ready to make the transition to a visual medium—and the TV networks also generally welcomed the radio actors who starred in those programs.

Unfortunately, some actors couldn't follow their programs to television because they didn't look the way they sounded on radio. For example, some of the children in radio shows were played by adults and some little boys were even played by grown women. Some actresses who played sexy young characters were much older looking and nowhere near as sexy as they sounded. Worse yet, radio's most popular African American characters—Amos and Andy—were played by white men, not black men. And so on.

Sadly, one of radio's greatest actors, William Conrad, could not follow his character to television. You see, he played heroic frontier marshal Matt Dillon on radio's *Gunsmoke*, but Conrad was an obese fellow the TV producers were afraid would occupy too much of the main street of Dodge City in TV's *Gunsmoke*. Consequently, TV viewers got James Arness, who was tall and lanky, which was the way Conrad made Matt Dillon sound on radio.

Conrad had been quite successful working in movies, mainly because he was almost always cast as a heavy—the imposing bad guy in crime dramas. He was one of the hit men sent to kill Burt Lancaster in the 1946 version of Ernest Hemingway's *The Killers* and the menace coming to murder Barbara Stanwyck in *Sorry, Wrong Number* (1948).

But Conrad wasn't about to give up just because he lost his radio role to a slimmer actor on television. He persisted, ultimately becoming a very busy director of movies and television episodes, and finally the star of not one but several popular television series.

Setting the Scene

I first met William Conrad over a very large lunch in Scarborough, a suburb of Toronto, where he was making the 1982 television movie *Shock Trauma*. Our talk lasted most of the afternoon as technicians tried to fix flaws in the rudimentary HDTV studio. What impressed me that day were his personal warmth as well as his deep knowledge of the TV industry.

We met again in 1989, when he clearly was slowing down and had gained even more poundage. It was at a gathering of CBS stars at a miniature golf course in the Bel Air district of Los Angeles where stars were supposed to play golf with visiting TV critics. Mrs. Conrad had packed a picnic lunch of eight hamburgers, a large carrot salad, and several pies to tide us over the next few hours.

The Interview

BAWDEN: How did you get started?

CONRAD: Well, I was born in Louisville in 1920 and my parents ran a movie theater there. I'd watch all the great films day after day, so I became a silent movie expert at a very young age. Then we moved to Fullerton, California, and at Fullerton College I majored in drama and literature. My first job was at Los Angeles radio station KMPC, and then came a little thing called the war. I was commissioned in 1943 with the air corps, but I also produced radio programs for the Armed Forces Radio Service.

BAWDEN: Do you have any idea how many different roles you played on radio?

CONRAD: By my guesstimate it's around seventy-five hundred, but who's counting? I was in the supporting cast of such radio hits as *The Man Called X* [1944], *Favorite Story* [1946–1949], *Night Beat* [1950–1952], and *Hollywood Star Playhouse* [1953]. On some of these I'd take on five to ten roles per episode and all with different vocal inclinations.

BAWDEN: Your first film was also the first for Burt Lancaster: *The Killers*.

CONRAD: A beautifully made film. The opening scenes at night in the diner are amazing. The photography has never been equaled. Bob Siodmak was one great director, but you critics never seemed to notice him. I was one of the baddies chasing Burt Lancaster. It was Ava Gardner's first big role and here were two of the most beautiful people on earth. And I got noticed, but in a bad way. That's the only type of role I was offered for years.

BAWDEN: Name some other big movies you did around then.

CONRAD: *Body and Soul* [1947] was a huge success for our star, John Garfield. I played a police guy in *Arch of Triumph* [1949], but I never even got billing. In *Sorry, Wrong Number* I watched as Barbara Stanwyck's hair turned gray after weeks screaming in that bed. I guess I just liked meeting Clark Gable in *Any Number Can Play* [1949]. He was my hero as a kid and a lovely gentleman, very reserved. I was a henchman again. I damn near asked for his autograph, but that would have been unprofessional. When I popped up on *Lone Star* in 1952, he came right over and said, "Welcome on board, Bill." Great stars are always that gracious.

BAWDEN: But all this time you were toiling away in radio, too.

CONRAD: It has always been my favorite medium. Because it forces the listener to think, to conjure up the images to suit the dialogue. And my favorite job was as Marshal Matt Dillon, starting on CBS Radio in 1952. Imagine, a radio western! A western is action, fisticuffs, raw energy. And on radio, how can this all be conveyed? Well, we must have been doing something right because we lasted nine seasons through 1961. I even wrote an episode in 1953, just to prove I could do it.

BAWDEN: But—

CONRAD: I know what you're going to say. In 1955 it was transferred to TV. I naïvely thought I'd been partly responsible for its success. Jim Arness was picked and just ran with the part. I was large and portly and definitely not leading man status. And so I tried to understand this, but it was tough.

BAWDEN: Then you segued into directing episodic TV?

CONRAD: Starting with *Highway Patrol,* which consisted of yelling at Broderick Crawford, "No, not that way! Run this way." Then I directed *The Rifleman, Bat Masterson, Route 66, Naked City, Have Gun, Will Travel*—my favorite. Then I even did two episodes of *Gunsmoke.*

BAWDEN: How did you get involved in directing movies for Warners?

CONRAD: Jack Warner saw I could do it fast on several of his TV series. He was looking for a director-producer to make million-dollar movies. It seems like a lot of money, but really wasn't by the '60s. The first was *Two on a Guillotine* [1965], which we shot like a TV episode, using multiple cameras, and it was designed as a Connie Stevens vehicle and it made some money. Critics called *Brainstorm* [1965] with Dana Andrews and Anne Francis a sort of '60s film noir and it made a profit, too.

I packaged Eleanor Parker, Janet Leigh, and Stuart Whitman into a very good version of *An American Dream* [1966], which got critical notices.

Another one I remember is *Chubasco* with Christopher Jones and his wife Susan Strasberg, plus Richard Egan and Ann Sothern. Then Jack sold the studio off and they wanted only expensive movies. But he gave me one of the two statues of the Maltese Falcon—the one slashed by Sydney Greenstreet in the movie—and I treasure it to this day.

BAWDEN: How did you get the plumb role of detective Frank Cannon in 1971?

CONRAD: Westerns were out. It was the era of the private eye, so why not a fat one? Now here's the thing: Quinn Martin had made his TV series for ABC. CBS desperately wanted him and had to be very nice and generous. Quinn was executive producer, but always hands-on. He insisted on multiple days every episode for location shooting. My character has served the LAPD for years, but after the death of his wife and son, he goes private. I learned to shoot a snub-nosed .38, although I could use other weapons. And this necessitated long days at a rifle range as marksmen taught me all this. You know what viewers of reruns noticed? I dropped my pipe after a few seasons and I think this had to do with a change in sponsors.

BAWDEN: Wasn't *Barnaby Jones* sold to CBS as a spin-off of *Cannon*?

CONRAD: It was going to start as an episode of *Cannon* where I'm trying to help Barnaby [Buddy Ebsen] find his long-lost son. But the series got sold before we could film it, so it appears as the first episode of *Barnaby Jones* and I'm in character as Cannon.

BAWDEN: Would you say the success of *Cannon* was due to Quinn Martin?

CONRAD: He leaned heavily on CBS, which gave him the great time slot Tuesdays following *Hawaii Five-0*. And the second year we went Wednesdays at 10, where we mowed down the new Julie Andrews show. And then we pretty much stayed Wednesdays at 9. A good time slot is the most important aspect of an incoming show.

BAWDEN: Was Martin that much a hands-on executive producer?

CONRAD: He read all the scripts, hired the directors and the big cast names. The series was developed by David Moessinger, Steve Kandel, and Earl Booth and they were all fine writers. Arthur Fellows was the supervising producer and a very conscientious guy. Quinn hired only the best directors. Off the top of my head, I can salute Richard Donner, Michael O'Herlihy, Les Martinson, and David Lowell Rich. And it worked wonderfully for five big seasons.

BAWDEN: Ever get the itch to direct the show?

Joan Fontaine with William Conrad in *Cannon,* 1975. Courtesy of CBS publicity.

CONRAD: Hell, no.

BAWDEN: What was the most unusual thing you were asked to do?

CONRAD: When they had me scuba diving. I looked like a gigantic beached sperm whale! Thank goodness the stunt double showed up—nice guy—but he did the underwater stuff.

BAWDEN: Your favorite guest star?

CONRAD: Miss Joan Fontaine. Imagine a chunky guy like me up close with an Oscar winner and a lady to boot.

BAWDEN: Here we are in Toronto at the new HDTV studios in Scarborough as you star in the TV movie *Shock Trauma*. Is it good to be back at work?

CONRAD: There are lots of wonderful scene stealers in this one—all Canadian! But I never retired after *Cannon*. This time I'm playing a real person, Dr. R. Adams Cowley, the Baltimore doctor who founded the first shock trauma unit. This is one of the first shows made in HDTV. Move an inch off your mark and the camera can't pick you up.

Here's a story about the power of TV. I'm walking down a busy Toronto street and a traffic cop says, "Mr. Cannon, what case are you working on today?" As if I'd never left. But with reruns maybe I never have.

BAWDEN: Tell me about your most recent series role as the star of *Jake and the Fatman* [1987–1992].

CONRAD: When CBS pitched me the idea, I said, "Oh, so I'm Jake." The title "Fatman" doesn't really appeal to me, but what can one do? You were just saying you were on the 1977 set of the TV movie *Nero Wolfe*? Well, Thayer David died before it went on the air. They wanted Orson Welles, but he couldn't remember all the lines. I admit I was a bad fit and we only lasted fourteen weeks. This one fits better. There's no straining. Joe Penny [who played Jake] does all the running and jumping this time out. I liked the Hawaii-based shows better, but for economic reasons we had to move back to L.A. Even the dog Max is a good actor, as dogs go.

We used the character first on a *Matlock*. My name then was James "Fatman" McShane. For legal reasons, when we switched webs [networks], it was changed to Jason "Fatman" McShane. I adore working with Penny, but don't tell him that. Freddie Silverman, who helmed all three networks, knows how to create a long-lasting premise. And I hope I never let him—or the fans—down.

Now have a few more hamburgers, and then we'll tackle the pecan pie.

Afterword

Conrad was married three times: to Julie Nelson (1953–1957), Susan Randall (1957–1979), and finally to Lewis Tipton Huntley, the widow of TV newsman

Chet Huntley, from 1980 until his death. Conrad had a son, Christopher, by second wife Susan Randall.

Two years after *Jake and the Fatman* ended its five-season run, William Conrad died from congestive heart failure in Los Angeles on February 11, 1994. He was seventy-three. Conrad was elected to the Radio Hall of Fame after his death.

Robert Cummings

Interview by James Bawden

Robert Cummings was one of many leading actors in films of Hollywood's golden era who managed to reboot their careers by reinventing themselves as television stars.

Cummings had solid credits as a dramatic actor in movies—the hero of Alfred Hitchcock's 1942 *Saboteur*, the lead in *Kings Row* (1942), and Grace Kelly's lover in Hitchcock's 1954 *Dial M for Murder*. But he is mainly remembered as a specialist in romantic light comedy roles, starting with three starring performances opposite Deanna Durbin from 1939 to 1941 and continuing well into the 1950s opposite such stars as Betty Grable, Doris Day, and Shirley MacLaine.

Before his big-screen career had fully faded, Cummings began to work in early television, earning an Emmy for his dramatic performance in the live drama *12 Angry Men* (1954) on *Studio One*. In 1953, he starred in his first situation comedy, *My Hero*, on NBC, playing a real estate salesman with the lovely Julie Bishop as his secretary. It was not a ratings winner, but his second try, *The Bob Cummings Show* (1955–1959), was a big hit. Cummings played a skirt-chasing photographer, supported by Rosemary DeCamp as his sister, Dwayne Hickman as his nephew, and Ann B. Davis as his assistant, who had a crush on him. The show began on NBC, moved to CBS, then returned to NBC before winding up in daytime reruns on ABC. (The series was known as *Love That Bob* during its ABC run and later, when it went into syndication.) A third series, *The New Bob Cummings Show*, cast him as an adventurous charter pilot. It lasted just one season (1961–1962) on CBS. Cummings starred in one more sitcom, *My Living Doll*, playing the mentor to a beautiful girl robot played by the statuesque Julie Newmar. It lasted just the 1964–1965 season on CBS.

Always known for his boyish good looks and seemingly eternal youth, Cummings spent most of his later years as a guru for followers who wanted

Ann B. Davis with Robert Cummings in *The Bob Cummings Show*, circa 1955. Courtesy of NBC publicity.

to stay as young looking as he, publishing books about his health secrets and marketing several products that catered to their needs.

Setting the Scene

In June 1989, TV columnists from all over the United States and Canada were invited by CBS to the Loews Hotel in Redondo Beach to hear pitches for the network's new fall programs. One of the special attractions was a lavish dinner that allowed columnists to chat with classic CBS stars, among them Jane Wyatt, Bob Barker, Buddy Ebsen, Eve Arden, and Andy Griffith. I persuaded a CBS publicist to seat me next to Bob Cummings, a star I'd never met. It turned out to be a delightful evening, and since not many other columnists were eager to meet him, I pretty much had him to myself.

The Interview

BAWDEN: When you were growing up in Joplin, Missouri, were you always determined to be an actor?

CUMMINGS: Oh, no. I always wanted a career in flying. And I had the most important pilot in the world who gave me flying lessons: Orville Wright! I was sixteen to seventeen and he was my godfather. He taught me a love for flying, a true reverence. I still remember the timbre of his voice, so I was under his spell from the first time I met him. He was best friends with my father. My mother was a practicing minister and she married herself to Dad twelve days after I was born. So you see my family was unusual.

BAWDEN: Didn't you want to go to university?

CUMMINGS: I did go to Drury College in Springfield, Missouri, aged seventeen to eighteen. Then an unfunny thing happened—the Great Depression. My father was a physician and all his patients were bankrupt, so he had no cash of his own. He'd played the market and lost all his stocks. So I transferred to the American Academy of Dramatic Arts and they paid first-year students $500 because times were harsh. And that's how I stepped into acting.

BAWDEN: How did that go?

CUMMINGS: I didn't think I'd make it because I was an introvert. I subsequently discovered all the actors I revered were introverts. It's essential to the craft.

BAWDEN: Then you went to Hollywood?

CUMMINGS: Oh, I had a few walk-ons in Broadway plays under the name Blasé Stanhope. And then I accepted a Paramount contract as a male ingénue in the class of 1936. Fellow students included Marsha Hunt and Clara Lou Sheridan, who changed her name to Ann Sheridan and subsequently costarred with me in *Kings Row.*

BAWDEN: Did you get into any big movies?

CUMMINGS: I can barely be seen in *Souls at Sea* [1937]. I didn't care—I was there to study the greatest film actor of them all: Gary Cooper. He seemed to be so still during a take. Then I'd watch the next day in the dailies room and he effortlessly stole that and every other scene. Audiences just bonded with him. Off camera he was shy, stammering, tongue-tied. So I immediately understood: in movies, less means more.

BAWDEN: Eventually you starred in a few Bs?

CUMMINGS: Ever heard of *Desert Gold* [1936] or *Arizona Mahoney* [1936]? Or *Sophie Lang Goes West* [1937]? Did a lot of that grade B stuff.

BAWDEN: Then what happened?

CUMMINGS: When Paramount dropped me in 1938, I jumped to Universal, which was on the upswing. I got into the 1939 sequel *Three Smart Girls Grow Up*, a follow-up to guess what film? [*Three Smart Girls.*] Deanna Durbin was the star and we became fast friends. A grand gal. Had a voice that could have taken her to the Met. Then Universal put me into *The Under-Pup* [1939], which was an attempt to fashion a second Deanna in Gloria Jean just in case Deana ever got uppity. And she was darling in her own way. And later Susannah Foster was imported—another thrilling voice—but Deanna was the only true star. When Universal made the next Durbin film, *Spring Parade* [1940], she asked for me as leading man. I think it's her best film, but it can't be shown today because our director Henry Koster based it on a German film he'd directed in the '30s. And the German writer on that one successfully sued Universal after the war and won a huge settlement.

BAWDEN: You were stepping up in the business?

CUMMINGS: In *One Night in the Tropics* [1940], I was in the first Abbott and Costello feature. And together with Deanna these three saved Universal from bankruptcy. Universal loaned me to MGM for *And One Was Beautiful* [1940] opposite my old Paramount pal Laraine Day, and it was a hit. In 1941 I squired Jean Arthur in *The Devil and Miss Jones*. I was thirty by then but looked nineteen and she was forty looking forty, so a lot of scenes were specially lit for her. Norman Krasna wrote and directed it, and this one really put me over the top. Between scenes Jean was antisocial in terms of small talk, but the public loved her squeaky voice and that wonderful way she had with comedy lines. Her husband Frank Ross produced it. To my regret I never worked with her again. In fact, I may not have ever seen her again. I doubt it!

BAWDEN: Then you went to Fox for *Moon over Miami* [1941].

CUMMINGS: On that one Universal loaned me. I was third-billed after Betty Grable and Don Ameche. Walter Lang directed it, but it was all Betty. She was tiny. Hardly big bosomed compared to such later bombshells as Monroe and Mansfield. It was released in June 1941—but it put Betty across as the darling of servicemen as Pearl Harbor happened a half year later. It was escapism time for movies. I wanted to go into a Saturday matinee at the Westwood Theater and the SRO [standing room only] sign was out front and I couldn't get in!

BAWDEN: I think *It Started with Eve* [1941] is among Durbin's best.

CUMMINGS: She certainly thought so. She was riding high that year. Can somebody explain why she never hit the top ten among box office stars? This one made its costs back and returned huge profits. Charles Laughton [who played her father] was crazy for her, calling Deanna the second greatest actress in Hollywood after Shirley Temple. I mean, their scenes together were splendid. This is the Deanna I want to remember—at the height of her beauty and that voice. It was a huge hit and remade badly with Sandy Dee [1964's *I'd Rather Be Rich*]. Charles saw her years later and he told me he was shocked at her weight gain and her despondency. She sat down with me at a party and said she had to get out of Hollywood before it killed her. She had gone through two quick marriages and she hated the mediocrity of her last movies. And then she vanished forever to France with her third husband, director Charles David. And I lost a great friend.

BAWDEN: Then you were in Alfred Hitchcock's *Saboteur*.

CUMMINGS: Hitch told me the first day I was chosen because I was a Universal contract player and hence cheap and he'd really wanted Gary Cooper. Coop was too expensive and Joel McCrea was busy on something else. Which hardly made me feel great. Priscilla Lane came over from WB and she was hellish to work with. She'd been used to comedy and now she had to do exactly what Hitch ordered. So she got very difficult. The set pieces in this one are terrific. I think I tried hard, but grant I may have been too young for the lead. But we became friends and I'd see the Hitchcocks at various concerts in Hollywood over the years and he was always pleasant. And he must have liked me a bit or why did he hire me again in 1954?

BAWDEN: How did you get the lead in that blockbuster *Kings Row*?

CUMMINGS: I was available. The original choice as Parris was going to be Jeffrey Lynn, who had steadily risen up the ranks at Warners, starting with *Four Sisters* in 1938. But once Sam Wood was hired as director, he began complaining Jeff looked too much like Ronald Reagan [who was also in the film]. Jeffrey took his demotion badly and just walked out of WB and never made another movie until 1948. When I got there, the huge sets were up, covering several large soundstages. Look at the billing. Ann Sheridan is first-billed, but does not appear until halfway through, indicating how big she was at the box office. Ron and I have been close friends ever since. The casting was supreme: Claude Rains, Charles Coburn, Maria Ouspenskaya. As the deranged Cassie, who Parris loves, Bette Davis even made a screen test, but Jack Warner said the role wasn't big enough for one of her stature. He picked Ida Lupino, who flatly refused to do it and went on a long suspension. Betty Field came in, but I don't think she was exactly right.

BAWDEN: You made another WB film around that time, the delightful *Princess O'Rourke* [1943] with Olivia de Havilland.

CUMMINGS: My deal with WB necessitated a second film. This was Livvie's last film under her seven-year contract. And then she thought she'd be free. But Jack insisted she owed him one more film to cover all the time she'd been under suspension. For three years the "de Havilland case" dragged through the courts and Livvie couldn't work for anybody else until she won her case. But *Princess O'Rourke* is delightful. I've always suspected it was the kernel for another princess-in-hiding flick—*Roman Holiday* with Audrey Hepburn, made a decade later.

BAWDEN: Then you went into the air force?

CUMMINGS: As a flight instructor. I never had so much fun working with these young guys. And then at war's end I went back to acting.

BAWDEN: Your first postwar film was *You Came Along* [1945].

CUMMINGS: Hal Wallis's first film after he left Warners the year before. He had a new discovery, Lizabeth Scott, and she was the shyest girl I ever met. Then Hal put her into a few noirs as a hardboiled dame and we never saw the sweet Liz again in films. You've seen it and you know I'm dying of leukemia, hence my forced gaiety, and then the switch to sadness. The script was by Ayn Rand—no, seriously! It was a huge hit with audiences, who were so aware [of] death during the war.

BAWDEN: I think *The Chase* [1946] may be your best-ever film.

CUMMINGS: I think so, too. The story was by Cornell Woolrich. The photography is very moody. We got Michele Morgan on the rebound. This was her last American film. Peter Lorre was terrific. But few people saw it because it didn't have a major distributor. It just died at the box office. Now all these years later and being in public domain people see it on VHS and write me letters about it—all raves.

BAWDEN: You've said the drama behind *The Lost Moment* [1947] was as exciting as the film's story.

CUMMINGS: A very ambitious movie. Based on *The Aspern Papers* by Henry James. It was based on a legend that letters of Percy Shelley were extant. Here the poet is American. I think this change was made for US audiences. The papers are owned by a 105-year-old lady, played brilliantly by Aggie Moorehead. I'm a journalist trying to get the papers and print them. The Venice sets were terrific. Our leading lady was Susan Hayward and to say she loathed director Martin Gabel would be an understatement. Susie had quite a mouth and she used it here. Martin never made another movie. And I'm not sure what fans thought about it. It was an art house movie before there were art houses.

BAWDEN: What do you remember about *Sleep My Love* [1948]?

CUMMINGS: I was partnering Claudette Colbert. She was a gal whose husband [Don Ameche] was trying to kill her. And Don kept kvetching about having to take third billing! Mary Pickford produced it and was often confabbing on set. She called Claudette "one tough cookie." Then Hal Wallis hired me again. I was Loretta Young's costar in *The Accused* [1948]. She was a UCLA professor accused of murdering an amoral student played by Douglas Dick, who I thought would go far. Loretta had just won her Oscar [for *The Farmer's Daughter* in 1947] and was in full dramatic mode. And then came Roz Russell in *Tell It to the Judge* [1949], one of her last films for Columbia. On the first day Roz says the script was a bit thin, so we'd add pratfalls in mud puddles. There was an amorous dog in one scene stopping me from sleeping. And it worked—the receipts were far higher than anticipated.

BAWDEN: Then came your favorite film appearance.

CUMMINGS: I always preferred drama to comedy because comedy was always so much easier for me. I had great expectations for *The Black Book* [1949; also known as *Reign of Terror*], and how many films about the French Revolution have you seen? It was a film noir thingy set way back in the eighteenth century. The budget was limited, so they rejigged some of the sets from *Joan of Arc*. And since it all took place at night, who could see much anyway? Same country, but wrong century! Dick Basehart was terrific as Robespierre and I was the public prosecutor. We needed a few big names but we did have Arlene Dahl, the loveliest leading lady I ever had. Director Anthony Mann shot it at night with shadows everywhere, just like he shot his crime thrillers. People who saw it loved it. But it failed to make back costs.

BAWDEN: Was your age catching up with you?

CUMMINGS: You got it. On the set of *Free for All* [1950], I was thirty-nine and my leading lady, Ann Blyth, was twenty. And with *The Barefoot Mailman* [1951], I was forty-one and my leading lady, Terry Moore, was nineteen. I remember being stuck in this dog-awful Clifton Webb comedy, *For*

Robert Cummings with Grace Kelly in *Dial M for Murder* (1954). Courtesy of Alfred Hitchcock Productions and TV station KBHK (44) in San Francisco.

Heaven's Sake [1950], and I only did it to keep going and I thought there has to be something better out there. And that something was TV.

BAWDEN: So you jumped to TV.

CUMMINGS: *My Hero* in 1952 for NBC. I was a dumb real estate agent. Named Bob Beanbottom. Not funny! And it just got weaker, and after thirty-three episodes I asked NBC to cancel us—a mercy murder. I'd made every mistake, so I could learn from them and try again. But the irony is being on TV made me hot again in movies. I was in demand again, although at budget prices.

BAWDEN: How did you get one of the leads in *Dial M for Murder?*

CUMMINGS: Alfred Hitchcock phoned me at home and he offered me third billing and $25,000 for a month's work. It was all done inside the Warners studio because it was in 3-D and all the effects were mapped up on the floor, which is why you see me looking down quite a bit. I'm not being catty here, but I seemed to be the only one who did not have an affair with Grace Kelly. Certainly Hitch immediately fell for her and Ray Milland pursued her mightily. And she certainly was gorgeous. Hitch dismisses it these days, but he was like a kid in a candy store with all the effects. When the intruder tries to strangle Grace, it was so effective in 3-D. But most cinemas showed it flat because the novelty wore out quickly. And people today ask me why Ray and Grace's apartment was so tiny. But it wasn't in 3-D. On a flat screen, everything got squished up. It was a huge hit and I got many movie offers again.

BAWDEN: Like *Lucky Me* [1954]?

CUMMINGS: I think it was released just a few months after *Dial M.* This was Doris Day's last film at Warners before she left for freelancing. And Jack Warner spent a bucket on it and we filmed it in Miami. Phil Silvers and Nancy Walker were funny, there were a few good tunes, but Doris said she just had to get out of the studio. It made a lot of dough and Doris then gradually became a superstar elsewhere. I felt I might be a bit too old at forty-four, but what did I know?

BAWDEN: You were then in Betty Grable's last film at Fox.

CUMMINGS: *How to Be Very, Very Popular* [1954]. Betty Grable's contract was up and they put her into this silly thing. Nunnally Johnson directed it and Sheree North was her sidekick. Betty couldn't wait to get to the nightclubs and she never again made another movie anywhere. She was a riot, always on the phone to her bookie. But the mantle of blond bombshell had been passed to Marilyn Monroe, no doubt about that. I was told this was a remake of an old Bing Crosby flick with Miriam Hopkins titled *She Loves Me Not,* which I never saw. But the idea it bombed just isn't true. Initial grosses were over $1.6 million, meaning Betty was still pretty popular.

BAWDEN: How did *The Bob Cummings Show* get started?

CUMMINGS: I made every mistake with the first show. So I knew what I wanted and what I didn't want. I played Bob Collins. I stole the name from my old film *You Came Along.* Casting was all-important. I was the lecherous photographer. And Rosemary DeCamp was my older sister Margaret. Dwayne Hickman was my nephew Chuck. And I discovered Ann B. Davis as my assistant Schultzy. I also discovered Nancy Kulp, who later costarred in *The Beverly Hillbillies*. We filmed at General Services Studios right next to George Burns and Gracie Allen. As I always said at the opening, "Hold it! I think you're gonna like this picture!" The comedy here was all in the timing. I could play lecherous, but not overdo it and be dirty. It was insinuations and all the gals were glorious. One of my discoveries, Joi Lansing, was better looking than Monroe! We started in January 1955 on NBC then switched to CBS in September 1955 and went back to NBC in September 1957 and ended in 1959. I think the total was 156 half hours which have been syndicating forever as *Love That Bob*.

Very early on I was doing a scene and George Burns walked in. His show shot next door. And he watched a bit and later came to my dressing room and said, "Bob, why do you have a director? You can do that yourself and pay yourself extra for that service." And since I felt I was doing most of the hard lifting already, I did all the directing for the second season and it worked out fine. We'd shoot a half hour in about three days, using multiple cameras but no audience. And finally I think we just ran out of story ideas.

BAWDEN: You started your third TV series, *The New Bob Cummings Show* in 1961, but it only lasted twenty-two episodes.

CUMMINGS: I was a charter pilot who flew all over the place and did all kinds of other jobs, including solving murders. But it was too expensive for a half-hour show. We didn't use the same sets at all. Costs mounted and I finally had to ask CBS to release me, which the network did because we were being clobbered by NBC's *Dr. Kildare* anyhow.

BAWDEN: You went back to movies.

CUMMINGS: *My Geisha* [1963] was a cute little comedy made by Shirley MacLaine's husband. And I also paired with Shirley and a lot of bigger male stars in *What a Way to Go* [1964]. Can't say I know her very well, but she's a magical comedienne. Then I was in the remake of *Stagecoach* [1966], which wasn't a half-bad western. Our producer, Martin Rackin, is a real card. He told the press, "This time we're going to do this story right!" He was kidding, but all hell broke loose because the original was just about the best western everywhere. I begged him to change the title and I was right. People just ignored it.

BAWDEN: You made yet another TV sitcom.

CUMMINGS: Guilty as charged. *My Living Doll* [1964] was a sort of knockoff of *I Dream of Jeannie*. Julie Newmar was my costar, but the pilot [episode] said it all. In fact a lot of the *Jeannie* crew were with us. I'm a military psychologist and I'm supposed to train this girl robot to be human. [They] wanted to focus on Julie, who was one of the most gorgeous girls I ever met. But every week the premise was the same and there was no comedy at all. Finally, I asked for my release and the show just died.

BAWDEN: Do you have a favorite movie from this era?

CUMMINGS: Oh, yes: *The Carpetbaggers* [1964]. Marvelously shoddy. Based on the Howard Hughes–Jean Harlow romance. Carroll Baker was our blond bombshell, George Peppard our Hughes. Martha Hyer and Elizabeth Ashley were in it. I would sit on the set with Alan Ladd and he'd shake his head at the shenanigans. Laddie died before he could see the warm reception he got when the film previewed. He had a whole new career ahead as a character star. Yes, it's trash. But it's good trash!

BAWDEN: You soldiered on?

CUMMINGS: I did *Bewitched, Here's Lucy, Love, American Style,* even *Love Boat,* where I worked with Ethel Merman. When we moved to Puget Sound, it was a case of out of sight, out of mind. I had to leave L.A. because the air is a killer.

BAWDEN: You were asked recently why you married so often.

CUMMINGS: I claimed I was trying to beat Mickey Rooney's record. Hey, I was only half kidding.

BAWDEN: Do you still travel with large bottles of vitamin pills?

CUMMINGS: No! I carry a whole suitcase of these multivitamins. Hey, it's worked for me so far.

Afterword

Cummings did no more significant acting roles in the year after our interview. Despite his reputation as a health guru, some sources say Cummings was addicted to methamphetamines in his later years, which may have had a negative impact on his career. He was married five times and fathered seven children. One of them, Tony Cummings, was a successful actor who worked in the daytime serial *Another World* in the 1980s. Cummings died on December 2, 1990, from kidney failure and pneumonia at the Motion Picture County Home in Woodland Hills, California. He was eighty.

Susan Douglas

Interview by James Bawden

Susan Douglas was one of the select group of actors who worked steadily in radio soap operas, then made the transition to televised daytime drama. Because of her great experience as a performer in live broadcasting, Douglas continued to work busily in the early days of live television drama once her days as a regular on the hit soap opera *The Guiding Light* came to an end.

Originally from Austria, Douglas came to the United States as a child during the years before World War II. In her early years as a performer, she worked in both radio and as a stage actress in New York. She also appeared in a few offbeat and memorable feature films, including *The Private Affairs of Bel Ami* (1947), the pioneering race relations film *Lost Boundaries* (1949), and the first film to depict America after a nuclear war, the science fiction classic *Five* (1951).

Her marriage to Czech opera star Jan Rubeš, who became a pillar of the Canadian opera scene, brought her to Toronto, where she became a vital supporter of the arts and leader in the creative community.

Setting the Scene

Here's where I must declare my unrequited love for actress Susan Douglas. It all began in 1952 when I was a second grader. I'd leave Toronto's Withrow Avenue Public School and run across the street to my house at noon lunch break. I'd turn on our new TV set and watch Buffalo's WBEN-TV Channel 4. Starting at 12:30 p.m., the CBS affiliate would offer *Search for Tomorrow*, followed at 12:45 by *The Guiding Light*. That's where I first saw the lovely Susan Douglas, who played a young girl named Kathy on *The Guiding Light*. One day Kathy was run over by a bus and was no more. I staggered back to my class that afternoon, utterly desolate.

Susan Douglas. James Bawden collection.

Twenty years later, in 1972, I was visiting the set of a Canadian TV movie and was introduced to a warm, earthy actress with a bright beam of a smile. It was none other than Susan Douglas, who had moved to Toronto, married opera star Jan Rubeš, had children, and was now a mature woman—and still a commanding actress.

We became so close that when I jumped from the *Hamilton Spectator* to the *Toronto Star* in 1980, Douglas furnished a letter of recommendation to the publisher—and I got the job. Later, when movie veteran Laraine Day wasn't sure about granting me an interview, she phoned her friend Susan Douglas, who told Day I was one reporter she might even like.

Susan Douglas and I had many subsequent conversations. I have combined them for this presentation.

The Interview

BAWDEN: I finally get to meet the heroine of *The Guiding Light:* Kathy! Let's start with your background.

DOUGLAS: I was an Austrian refugee, born in Vienna in 1925. My parents bred horses and moved to the new state of Czechoslovakia where they raised racehorses. The '20s and early '30s were a golden time for my family. I thought I'd be a ballerina. I studied hard for many years, but in 1939 when I was fourteen my parents fled to Paris as the rise of Nazism swallowed up first Austria and then Czechoslovakia.

My mother and I took a liner to New York City and three months later the Germans swallowed up France. We barely fit in under the quota regulations. My mother had been born in Italy, so we got in under that quota. We said good-bye to Papa, who went to London as a member of the official Czechoslovakian government in exile.

BAWDEN: But you knew no English?

DOUGLAS: Correct. So I went to three or four movies a day. I'm a fast learner. I'd write down phrases. I didn't know what I was saying, but I got the accent down immediately. My first radio scripts I learned phonetically. I graduated from high school in 1943 and surprised everyone by saying I wanted to be an actress. New York City was supremely crowded, competitive.

Starting in 1945–1946, I did all the radio soaps—about five or six a day. They ran fifteen minutes, required no costumes, just a pre-rehearsal. I got on *The Guiding Light* very quickly as the slightly wayward Kathy.

It was live, but there was no studio audience. Kathy was unmarried and pregnant. I remember the CBS censor running onto the set, beet red with anger. I'd been hired by Irna Phillips and the mere title of the show demonstrated a Christian nature to the storytelling. The soap was never lewd and lascivious.

BAWDEN: You also did theater at that time?

DOUGLAS: I won the Donaldson Award as best newcomer in 1946. At twenty-one! It was for a revival of *He Who Gets Slapped,* which starred Stella Adler and Dennis King. I was Consuelo. We ran forty performances at the Booth. Then the next year came *The Druid Circle* with oldsters Ethel Griffies and Leo G. Carroll and another newcomer, Neva Patterson. That one lasted sixty performances. My farewell was in a 1951 revival of *The Taming of the Shrew.* Other newcomers included Larry Hagman, Thayer David, and Nancy Marchand. We were at City Center for fifteen performances.

BAWDEN: Could you still do theater once you started doing the soap opera on TV?

DOUGLAS: I'd do days on various soaps, but when TV soaps came along I couldn't juggle both. On TV you had to rehearse, be in makeup. It was a different world.

BAWDEN: Can you describe your first day on the TV version of *The Guiding Light* in 1952?

DOUGLAS: We did dry runs for ten days. We had the same cameramen and cameras as *Search for Tomorrow* next door. They'd wheel these huge things across the hall. These same crews also did wrestling at night. A few times a camera would die and we were down to just one. I think there were three basic sets. One was the kitchen, with all new appliances, courtesy of Westinghouse, which was great advertising. One day a buzzer went off and I'm running around and finally I unplugged the damned oven.

BAWDEN: How about dressing rooms?

DOUGLAS: There were two. I shared with the other ladies. I think pay was $125 a day, which was great. At 1 p.m., we were finished for the day. The drama scenes lasted twelve minutes with three minutes for commercials and credits. It was a PG [Procter & Gamble] production, so I got boxes of Ivory soap and cartons of Cheer. The same filmed commercials ran every day. At first we all had flop sweat about hitting our marks and also timing everything down to the last second.

BAWDEN: What did working in a daytime drama mean to you?

DOUGLAS: Honestly, it was just a paycheck. Then the letters started flowing in. I was the so-called bad girl and many unmarried mothers sent me stories about their experiences. I wasn't sure how to respond as I'd just married the tenor Jan Rubeš.

BAWDEN: Who were you close to on the set?

DOUGLAS: Charita Bauer. She lasted there until her death in 1985. Irna Phillips always treated me as a wayward daughter. She wrote my first real pregnancy into the script. I was put in an iron lung so I couldn't show. My second was written into the script as TV's first-ever illegitimate pregnancy, too. When I told her [about her pregnancy] the third time in 1954, she blew up and my character was squished under a bus the very next week. I don't recall ever talking to her again. She was that upset.

BAWDEN: Can you discuss some of your costars?

DOUGLAS: James Lipton was the dark and dashing suitor, later my husband. A dedicated Method actor, he fretted over every line. Now he's a TV interviewer. [Lipton handles the telecasts for the Actors Studio.] My daughter [on the program] was the charming little thing Zena Bethune, who grew into a fine actress and starred in the 1962 series *The Nurses*.

BAWDEN: We haven't talked yet about your short movie career.

DOUGLAS: Short is the word. In 1947, I was whisked to Los Angeles for a very small part in *The Private Affairs of Bel Ami*, made by Albert Lewin, who'd had quite a hit with *The Picture of Dorian Gray* [1945] at MGM. He'd had to leave Metro for this one, which studio head Louis B. Mayer said was too decadent.

I didn't know what to expect. My costar Ann Dvorak warned me our star George Sanders could be quite odious—and he was! It was based on a true tale set in nineteenth-century Paris, but a lot had to be suggested because of the film code of the time. I played a ninny called Suzanne, a teenager, but I don't think I even got mentioned in most reviews. Angela Lansbury was a bud on set, same age as me, but she'd already been Oscar-nominated twice. And she's never asked me to guest on her hit, *Murder, She Wrote*.

BAWDEN: Then came *Lost Boundaries*?

DOUGLAS: I got the part, although my mother said I shouldn't do it. [In the film] I was part of a family of blacks masquerading in New England for decades as whites. Completely true story. Our star Mel Ferrer was only eight years older than I and said he was worried there might be rumors he had black blood. Our producer Louis de Rochemont left Fox to make it—and the irony is we were competing with a similar Fox film called *Pinky*, starring Jeanne

Crain. By the way, the film grossed over $2 million because it was cheaply made but had a titillating subject. Many cinema chains in the South refused to book it. People who watch it these days ask why blacks didn't play the leads. If that had happened, there would have been an even larger boycott.

BAWDEN: Then came the very unusual *Five?*

DOUGLAS: No! I made a Canadian feature, *Forbidden Journey,* before that with my husband and John Colicos. Very few Canadian features had been made by that time. This one got very limited release even in Canada because foreign companies controlled most Canadian theater chains.

Then I made *Five.* To say it was low budgeted would be an understatement. We never did retakes. Not enough money. We'd rehearse and then just did the scenes. Our great director, Arch Oboler, spent a grand total of $75,000. People who saw it were often left crying. People still write me about it. It was the first to tackle the subject of nuclear annihilation. You know that the house on the cliff was a Frank Lloyd Wright creation. One lady said she saw it as a child and became hysterical. This I can believe. I honestly believe the small budget helped. I'd say it took about ten shooting days and we got minimal pay packets. I played Roseanne Rogers, pregnant and scared.

BAWDEN: How many TV episodes do you guesstimate you did in New York City before moving to Toronto in 1959?

DOUGLAS: I'd say about a hundred. That included *Robert Montgomery Presents* multiple times, *Actor's Studio, Suspense,* everything from New York. I was on *Campbell Summer Soundstage* in 1953 in *Something for an Empty Briefcase* opposite a young guy named James Dean, who told me he was off to Hollywood to become a big star. That actually happened. Then three films and two summers later he was dead in a highway crash.

BAWDEN: You kept busy doing live television drama.

DOUGLAS: But the pickings got bare as the decade wore on because production was moving from New York to Hollywood. And then in 1959 I moved to Toronto because Jan's career was flourishing in Canadian opera.

BAWDEN: You acted less once you settled in Toronto.

DOUGLAS: I was tagged an outsider. I got one-shot roles on such series as *Seaway, The Unforeseen, R.C.M.P., The Edison Twins.* The Norman Corwin episode I made for him—*Bingo Twice a Week*—is pretty wonderful. That was one of the first syndicated dramas to be shown on US TV.

BAWDEN: But you were on to other things?

DOUGLAS: I cofounded the Young People's Theatre in 1965. And I was artistic director until 1979.

BAWDEN: I might add that you received the Order of Canada in 1975. I met you again in your office at CBC Radio in 1979 when you were head of radio drama. And you've jumped back into acting with performances in TV's *Haunted by Her Past* [1987] and movies: *Something about Love* [1988] and *The Outside Chance of Maximilian Glick* [1988]. And here it is 1989 and I'm interviewing you again in your office as president of Canadian TV's Family Channel.

DOUGLAS (*laughing*): I'm still kicking. Getting squished under a bus didn't really hurt that much, I guess.

Afterword

Susan Douglas's husband, Jan Rubeš, died in 2009. They'd both been devastated by the death of elder son Dr. Christopher Rubeš from AIDS-related pneumonia in 1996. Douglas established the Christopher J. Rubeš Center for EMS Studies. They had two other sons.

Susan Douglas Rubeš died in Toronto on January 23, 2013. She was eighty-seven.

Buddy Ebsen

Interview by James Bawden and Ron Miller

Few actors in show business history were as adept at reinventing themselves as the amazing Buddy Ebsen, who managed to create new screen personas for himself in just about every decade of his long and fruitful career.

In the late 1920s, he was half of a brother/sister dance act that made him and sister Vilma stars in the vaudeville world, then on the Broadway stage, even including a turn in the legendary *Ziegfeld Follies*. In the 1930s, after one movie with his sister, Ebsen went ahead as a single dancer whose specialty was the "eccentric" novelty style that saw him perform on-screen with such unusual partners as Shirley Temple and Judy Garland. Walt Disney even hired him to provide the style for animators to copy, via the rotoscope process, so they could turn Mickey Mouse into an Ebsen-like dancer in cartoons.

After he served in the Coast Guard during World War II, Ebsen's career as a musical movie dancing star was pretty much over, and he slipped into a new role in the 1950s as a comic sidekick to singing cowboy Rex Allen in a series of B westerns. That led to his casting as the frontier sidekick to Fess Parker's Davy Crockett in the phenomenally popular Walt Disney TV programs that subsequently were reedited and released as two hit feature films, *Davy Crockett, King of the Wild Frontier* (1955) and *Davy Crockett and the River Pirates* (1956).

In the 1960s, Ebsen once again found an all-new wave of popularity when he was cast as Jed Clampett, the country hick who strikes it rich and moves his entire family to California in the CBS situation comedy *The Beverly Hillbillies*, which ran for a decade and was at one time the most-watched TV show in America.

Ebsen once again needed to reinvent himself after CBS cancelled *The Beverly Hillbillies*, despite high ratings, during its infamous purge of rural programs to satisfy advertisers who wanted to appeal to younger viewers. This time

Buddy Ebsen as Barnaby Jones, circa 1973. Courtesy of CBS publicity.

Ebsen became an elderly private detective in CBS's *Barnaby Jones* (1973–1980), a weekly mystery series that also became a long-running hit for the network.

Still later, in the 1980s, Ebsen slipped into a new phase as a character actor in supporting roles, joining the cast of the mystery series *Matt Houston* (1984–1985). Finally, Ebsen did it again in the 1990s, turning himself into a touring one-man-show star, doing a little comedy, a little dancing, and even playing the saxophone.

Buddy Ebsen and Donna Douglas in *The Beverly Hillbillies.* Courtesy of CBS publicity.

Setting the Scene

Each of us interviewed Buddy Ebsen independently on multiple occasions. We have merged our separate interviews for this presentation, but in this section we each discuss the circumstances of our meetings with Ebsen.

BAWDEN: I well remember the first time I met Buddy Ebsen. I'd motored with a photographer for Canada's *Hamilton Spectator* from Hamilton to Upper Canada Pioneer Village in November 1971. It was just outside

Cornwall, Ontario. The meticulous reconstruction of colonial life had been redressed by CBS for a new TV version of *Tom Sawyer*. Over the first few hours we were there, I met Vic Morrow, Jane Wyatt, John McGiver, and finally Ebsen, who greeted me with "Brrrr! It's cold here!" Indeed, an early snowstorm had blanketed the village with a few feet of heavy snow—and poor Tom Sawyer (Jeff Tyler) had to run barefoot down a winding lane in one scene. At lunch that day Ebsen regaled us with anecdotes of an already full career, Jane Wyatt compared Cary Grant and Ronnie Colman as screen kissers, and McGiver snoozed in the cafeteria before an open fire.

I met Ebsen again a few years later when he was making yet another comeback as TV's Barnaby Jones and was surprised he actually remembered me. We sat together for dinner, and he told me a series of new anecdotes.

Still later, we had a reunion over the phone when Ebsen, aged seventy-six, joined the cast of *Matt Houston* in 1984.

MILLER: My first chat with Buddy Ebsen came in 1973 at a small gathering of columnists at CBS Television City in Hollywood to promote his debut as the star of *Barnaby Jones*. We met again for a talk in 1979 during the run of that show and finally talked a third time over the telephone in advance of a CBS *Beverly Hillbillies* reunion special in 1993, the same year he made a cameo appearance—as Barnaby Jones—in *The Beverly Hillbillies* feature film.

I remember Ebsen as a warm and genial guy who sent me a personal letter after our first interview, thanking me and inviting me to join him during the summer for a cruise on his catamaran, *The Polynesian Concept*.

The Interview

BAWDEN: How did you get into show biz?

EBSEN: Well, son, it was a long and winding road, and it all started in 1908 in Belleville, Illinois—my birth name is Christian Ludolf Ebsen Jr. My dad, Christian Ludolf Ebsen Sr., was from that part of Denmark seized by the Germans in the war for Schleswig-Holstein. He started by opening a dance studio and then he had a fitness shop and then he operated a natatorium, which was the then fancy term for an indoor swimming pool. But the weathers were brutal for Mother's health, so when I was ten, the family moved to Palm Beach [Florida]. I graduated from Orlando High School in 1926, aged eighteen, and then entered the University of Florida, where I hoped to become a doctor. But right then there was a vast collapse in Florida real estate and I had to leave school, aged twenty.

BAWDEN: Then came show biz?

EBSEN: I went to New York City as a soda jerk. My sister Vilma joined me and we did a vaudeville act titled the Baby Astaires. We were also in the choruses of such Broadway hits as *Whoopee* [1928] and *Ziegfeld Follies of 1934*. Walter Winchell caught us on tour in Atlantic City and he was so powerful at the time with his column in the *New York Mirror* that mention got us to the Palace in New York City. We carried that rave column around until it was in tatters. There were no copy machines back then. And by this time an MGM scout came backstage and offered us a short-term deal. I insisted Vilma be included as well because I needed the company. We took a dual silent screen test in New York. I think it must have been a silent test because, let's face it, we didn't have perfect features.

BAWDEN: Do you remember what they offered you?

EBSEN: It was for two years, ending at $1,500 a week for each of us. But Vilma hated the talkies. Everything was done over and over for different camera angles. So, she was with me in *Broadway Melody of 1936* [1935] and then begged off. She opened her own Hollywood dance studio and do you know she's still at it? [Vilma Ebsen lived to be ninety-six, but never made another movie.]

BAWDEN: What do you remember about that first movie?

EBSEN: How very nice our star Eleanor Powell was. Also Jack Benny, who was the master of ceremonies. Vilma and I had to warble "Sing Before Breakfast" while Ellie rat-tapped. She was her own choreographer. No one could tap like her. But she was fascinated with our loosey-goosey style. She came to all our rehearsals. Bob Taylor [the film's romantic leading man] was better looking than any of us. Such a shy guy. But it was a huge hit. And she [Powell] asked for me again in *Born to Dance* [1936].

BAWDEN: That's a favorite musical of mine.

EBSEN: You know, when *Born to Dance* came on TV in 1958 people everywhere were saying to me, "Buddy, I didn't know you could dance." But I still list "dancer" as my profession. Sure, I've watched it and honestly I don't remember looking so young. When Jimmy Stewart starts warblin', it just cracks me up. [Stewart sings the classic "Easy to Love" in the film.] But I still wonder why Virginia Bruce got to sing "I've Got You under My Skin" and not the magical Frances Langford. My favorite was "Swinging the Jinx Away." It was such a huge hit and Louis B. Mayer offered me a long-term contract and I refused and I saw how angry he became when stymied.

BAWDEN: Then you were loaned to Fox for *Captain January* [1936] with Shirley Temple?

Buddy Ebsen dances with Shirley Temple in *Captain January* (1936). Courtesy of TV station KBHK (44) in San Francisco and Twentieth Century-Fox.

EBSEN: I just loved getting out of the Metro fishbowl. David Butler was a kind, unassuming director. Shirley Temple was a superstar right then. But she was an eight-year-old kid. Everything had to be presented to her as fun or she wouldn't do it. At a certain time each afternoon Mrs. Temple would say, "It's time for us to leave." She really protected Shirley, as opposed to Judy Garland's mother, who let her daughter work morning, noon, and night. I'd do a step and Shirley could ape it. She was a very quick study. Our best routine? "At the Codfish Ball." When it was released to TV, I started getting printed fan letters from her new generation of fans.

BAWDEN: Then came Judy Garland in *Broadway Melody of 1938* [1937].

EBSEN: A darling. So talented. Every once in a while the producer, Irvin Cummings, would ask if anyone needed a stimulant and the MGM nurse would administer what I think was Benzedrine and it screwed with Judy's sleep patterns. She'd be up all night trying to work off all that stimulation. Remember, she was just a kid of sixteen, but we all knew her mother drove her to breakdowns. And I saw that same desperation on the set of *The Wizard of Oz* [1939]. By contrast, Shirley's family were completely protective.

BAWDEN: Didn't Walt Disney pay you to come over and dance all over the place for the next Mickey Mouse short?

EBSEN: Then he had his animators draw the way I was dancing. Easiest money I ever made. Don't forget, I wore a Mickey Mouse T-shirt in *Broadway Melody of 1936* and then a Donald Duck one in 1938. I asked Walt and he said it was great free advertisement.

BAWDEN: When you recently watched *The Wizard of Oz* on TV, did you see somebody awfully familiar?

EBSEN: In a long shot I saw me! Me! I was originally cast as the Scarecrow, but Ray Bolger hated being the Tin Man so we swapped after conferring with [director] Victor Fleming. They used paint and aluminum dust in the wardrobe tests but within a week I was coughing and gasping for air. It was the dust, the hospital ER staff told me, and I decided to leave—and live. MGM said I was malingering and they refused to use me again, although I still was on contract. When Margaret Hamilton as the Wicked Witch was severely burned and hospitalized, she was similarly roughed up, but she had virtually completed her part and couldn't be replaced. And I'm told one of my recorded songs is on one MGM album. Talking about it is very hurtful, let me tell you.

MILLER: Well, Jack Haley wasn't a dancer. Did they make use of any of the dancing you did on camera before you left the role to him?

EBSEN: I think some of the leg shots are mine.

MILLER: How did you part company with MGM studio boss Louis B. Mayer, who was so enthusiastic about signing you in the first place?

EBSEN: I always thought he was honest, but I left when he said something to me I just couldn't buy. He told me I'd never get the parts I wanted unless he could tie me up so tight in a contract that they'd own me.

MILLER: Your reaction to that?

EBSEN: I told him, "The sound of that coming out of your mouth is like a boat running aground. I couldn't be a piece of goods on your counter!"

BAWDEN: Right after you left MGM, America went to war. What did you do in the years of World War II?

EBSEN: I was in the US Coast Guard and I was discharged as a lieutenant in 1946.

BAWDEN: Then what happened?

EBSEN: I did grade C westerns to keep going.

MILLER: In 1950–1951, you made five westerns at Republic Pictures as the sidekick to singing cowboy Rex Allen in movies with titles like *Rodeo*

King and the Senorita [1951] and *Utah Wagon Train* [1951]. I heard you even tried song writing to make ends meet. How did that work out?

EBSEN: Well, one of my songs was called "I Own a Palomino and He's a Pal-o-Mine."

MILLER: I guess that's why we're not humming too many Ebsen tunes these days. During that lean period, you also went on the road with your sister again. Any memories of that time in your life?

EBSEN: I remember one night when we were motoring across country, doing a series of one-night stands. It began to snow heavily and the car had no heater. I had to stop every few miles to scrape ice off the windshield with my pocket comb. My sister was bundled up in all her costumes to keep from freezing. Suddenly, I started laughing out loud and my sister asked me what I could possibly find to laugh about. And I said, "L. B. Mayer certainly isn't telling me what to do!"

BAWDEN: You also started to work in the new medium of television, didn't you?

EBSEN: I made my first live TV acting on the *Chevrolet Tele-Theatre*. I did a lot of live TV in those years. I remember a live production of *Seven Keys to Baldpate* in 1952. I didn't get another A movie until *Night People* in 1954. A lot of it was shot in Berlin, which was then a divided city. Greg Peck was a huge star at the time, very nice, no pretensions. I suppose people have forgotten it because the Cold War is over.

MILLER: In those early TV days, you played all kinds of parts, including bad guys in TV westerns. By then I guess you had become quite an expert at reinventing yourself. Was that part of your master plan to remain a star?

EBSEN: In order to survive, you can't just do one thing. Well, I guess some people can, but I can't.

BAWDEN: Then Walt Disney made you're a star all over again on TV in 1954.

EBSEN: He personally phoned me and pitched *Davy Crockett* and I said, "Can I play Davy?" Walt laughed and said, "Buddy, you're too old." Well, that floored me, but probably Walt was correct. So I was George Russell. [Fess Parker was cast as Davy.] Later, Walt told me he made several millions on the paraphernalia over the next ten years. What kid didn't have a coonskin hat? I mean, Walt tried and tried to replicate the [success of Davy Crockett] with such miniseries as *Andy Burnett, Elfego Baca, Texas John Slaughter,* but it never happened. Walt ordered everything shot in color although ABC and all the webs were only black and white. He said when color came this one would do well in reruns. The first three episodes were strung together as the 1955 feature *Davy Crockett, King of the Wild Frontier*. We filmed at Great Smoky Mountains National Park and the final two episodes were theatrically released as *Davy Crockett and the River Pirates*, filmed at Cave-in-Rock, Illinois. I still get fan mail. But people remember it as a very long-running series, which it wasn't.

BAWDEN: There was some irony in costarring in NBC's *North West Passage* in 1958–1959.

EBSEN: Yes, back at MGM. All my old adversaries, including Mayer, were gone. My personal blacklist was over. We filmed a lot on the old back lot and even out on the old wilderness set. We made twenty-six episodes, but couldn't gain traction in the ratings. NBC put us on Sunday nights at 7:30 up against *Jack Benny* on CBS and *Maverick* on ABC, which was an hour show. I told Jack, "You had *Lassie* as lead-in while we had *Saber of London*" [a.k.a. *Mark Saber*]. Guess which show lasted only twenty-six episodes!

BAWDEN: You seemed to guest on all the TV westerns.

EBSEN: They loved me on *Maverick, Bronco, Have Gun, Will Travel, Rawhide*, but I also did *Barbara Stanwyck, Twilight Zone*. Heck, I even did *Playhouse 90* live.

BAWDEN: How were you cast as Audrey Hepburn's aged vet husband in *Breakfast at Tiffany's* [1961]?

EBSEN: I thought it unusual when director Blake Edwards called me in for a talk. He'd seen me in a *Playhouse 90* and said he always favored unusual casting. I said maybe it was a bit too weird and Blake said, "Oh, no, I'm casting Mickey Rooney as Audrey's upstairs neighbor, who is Japanese. Now, that's weird!" Audrey was a dear to work with, although she adored her multiple takes. I'm a one-take man himself. I still say the sexiest gal on that one was Pat Neal.

BAWDEN: And the next year you started *Beverly Hillbillies*.

EBSEN: The producer, Paul Henning, said I was always the number one choice. He said to play it completely straight—no mugging—to give the character humanity because there'd be crazies all around him. And I first appeared on *Green Acres* as a test run, but *Beverly Hillbillies* was definitely not a spin-off. We clicked from the get-go. I mean we made 274 episodes and we really had to stretch it near the end. We were number one the first season. And the second. We fell to number twelve in the third and eighth in the fourth. In 1969, we were still eighteenth. I think the second season we averaged a 30 share. [The share measures the percentage of all TV sets that were tuned to a show at the time of broadcast. The 30 share was very good for that period.] I'm not kidding. We were all the rage. Our ratings can never be equaled because the three-network TV universe has gone.

BAWDEN: You finally were hailed as a great comic actor because of your performance as Jed Clampett.

EBSEN: I'm glad I finally got recognition. But what about Irene Ryan as Granny? She'd been toiling in Hollywood for decades with little recognition. I first met Max Baer Jr. [who played Jethro] at the fights at Madison Square Garden when he was a little niblet. His dad was fighting that night. [Max Baer Sr. was a heavyweight boxing champ in the 1930s and later became a successful actor.] Jed was honest and smarter than any city slicker, but he was out of his environment. I played him as a naïf. Jethro was the imbecile, Elly Mae [Donna Douglas] the kittenish gal who looked amazing.

Paul Henning wrote parts of 274 episodes and Joe Depew helmed 145 episodes, followed by Richard Whorf, who did over 60. We filmed at Film-ways on Wilshire Boulevard and generally did an episode in three to four days. As we got to understand the material, we could do three in two weeks.

BAWDEN: Didn't you feature some heavy-duty guest stars now and then?

EBSEN: I think Sharon Tate made one of her first appearances and she was glorious. John Wayne loved the show so much he asked to do an unbilled cameo in 1967.

MILLER: I know quite a few of us television critics were unkind to *Beverly Hillbillies*. Did your huge ratings success make you immune to those reviews?

EBSEN: There was one critic—I forget his name—who said it was a one-joke show that wouldn't last. Ten years later, when he came to interview me on the set of *Barnaby Jones*, I told him, "You were *so* right!"

MILLER: Why do you think fans of the show still look back at it with so much fondness?

EBSEN: They see the direction in which we're moving, so they try to pull back from the present. We're making progress, but towards what? We forget about the bad parts of the good old days. That's why we try to remember the good parts and cling to them.

BAWDEN: Did the cancellation in 1971 sting?

EBSEN: Very much. But CBS was hearing from high-end sponsors that the network had too many rural shows. So we went, *Green Acres* went a year earlier, *Petticoat Junction* also died in 1971. All Henning shows.

MILLER: Did you hold a grudge against CBS's head programmer, Fred Silverman, for killing your hit show?

EBSEN: I didn't like him for a while, but when he picked up *Barnaby Jones*, I changed my mind about him. [Ebsen's percentage profit deal on *Hillbillies* also made him a millionaire many times over. What's more, he took pride in the fact that *Barnaby Jones* consistently beat the programs that Silverman put up against the show once Silverman became chief programmer at ABC, then became NBC's president.]

BAWDEN: You once went on the road in a play with your daughter Bonnie to introduce her to acting. How did that go?

EBSEN: We got raves everywhere. And lost a packet. I'll give you an example: we got raves in Detroit, but only filled the seats on matinees. Why? The Fisher Theater is located downtown and many older playgoers wouldn't go down there after dark because it's so dangerous. And it was the same in every major city where we played. So I was almost relieved to close the tour early.

BAWDEN: You speak so fondly of your *Hillbillies* costar Irene Ryan. After the show was canceled, I remember seeing her get huge applause in the Broadway musical *Pippin*.

EBSEN: I saw her, too. There she was at age seventy making her Broadway debut, getting raves. I noticed the oxygen canisters in the wings. She could barely breathe. But she was determined to go on and finish her career on the highest of notes. She never told me at the time, but she had an inoperable brain tumor and died the next year. I still miss her.

BAWDEN: Then came another TV comeback for you as *Barnaby Jones*.

EBSEN: Producer Edward Hume came to my sailboat and said, "TV has a fat detective, a blind detective, so why not a white old guy detective?" I told him, "Look, I'm your man. I'm sixty-seven." And I thought it would never sell, but it did and then I thought it might last a year, and we were around for eight years and by then I was a really old detective. In fact, in the third year CBS added Mark Shera to do all the heavy lifting and the running up hills. And I specifically asked for Lee Meriwether, who I already knew, as my daughter-in-law.

Edward had created *Cannon*, *Streets of San Francisco*, and *Toma*. Who was I to argue? I told him to assemble a crack crew. We had some fine directors, including Walter Grauman, Les Martinson, Alf Kjellin. Costars? We had Dabney Coleman come and go, Bradford Dillman, my daughter Bonnie Ebsen, Susan Sullivan, Bob Webber. Edward went after quality guest stars and we paid very well. And for the pilot, he craftily plopped us on *Cannon*, thus guaranteeing a big audience.

MILLER: Was it a relief to play a sophisticated man so far from the country hicks you'd been playing for years?

EBSEN: He's the kind of man who would be comfortable in any surroundings. I was happy to get the chance to show I can do that sort of thing, too.

BAWDEN: So why come back to play a supporting role in another TV series—*Matt Houston*?

EBSEN: I'm the geezer who offers Matt experience. A few days every episode is all that I can do at this stage. I'm seventy-six and I have to do something. And I'm guessing I'll do a bit of tap dancing, if asked. I don't think TV can get rid of me. I'm the late bloomer who just won't go away.

MILLER: You're now doing a one-man show in clubs. How are you keeping fit and, because you're always trying something new, what new challenges are you taking on in your senior years?

EBSEN: I do a routine of kung fu exercises to stay fit and still hoof a little. I also paint in oils and right now I'm catching up on something I started sixty-seven years ago when I played the saxophone in the high school band. A few months ago I saw President Clinton playing the saxophone [on television], so I went out and bought one. I'm playing different things in my act I'd never thought of playing before. It kind of renews my zest for life.

Afterword

Buddy Ebsen was married three times, first to Ruth Cambridge (1936–1942), then to Nancy Wolcott (1945–1985), and finally to Dorothy Knott in 1985; she remained his wife until his death from complications of pneumonia in Torrance, California, on July 6, 2003. He was ninety-five. He was the author of several books, including an autobiography, a nonfiction book about sailing, and two novels.

John Forsythe

Interview by James Bawden and Ron Miller

John Forsythe had a modest success as a leading man in films, especially in the 1950s and 1960s, when he was leading man to Loretta Young in *It Happens Every Thursday* (1953), the star of two lesser Alfred Hitchcock films—*The Trouble with Harry* (1955) and *Topaz* (1969)—and the stalwart detective of *In Cold Blood* (1967).

But Forsythe is best remembered for his TV work as the star of three memorable series—the situation comedy *Bachelor Father* (1957–1962), which appeared on all three broadcast networks during its prime-time run; *Charlie's Angels* (1976–1981), the action series in which he played the heard but never seen man in charge of the show's three female stars; and the serial drama *Dynasty* (1981–1989), which reached the exalted status of TV's most-watched program at one point during its original run on ABC.

Forsythe began his professional career in show business as a baseball commentator for the Brooklyn Dodgers and went on to do lots of acting roles on both radio and the stage, where he soon established himself as a solid performer in Broadway shows. That led him to live TV drama in the late 1940s.

Though he continued to get roles in feature films—a great example was the corrupt judge he played in . . . *And Justice for All* (1979)—Forsythe quickly learned TV was his most rewarding venue, and the lifestyle it permitted appealed to him so much that he eventually made the medium his permanent home, finally starring in a great many made-for-television movies.

Throughout his career, Forsythe displayed great versatility, able to shift from broad comedy to serious drama with apparent ease. He almost always played upper-class men of dignity and was, both in person and on the screen, a stylish, well-groomed, and distinguished-looking man.

Setting the Scene

We both conducted separate interviews with John Forsythe at different times, but we have merged them for this presentation. However, here are our individual reports on the circumstances of our talks with him.

BAWDEN: I first interviewed John Forsythe on the set of his new series *Dynasty* in early January 1981 at the Spelling studios in downtown Hollywood. The location was the sprawling living room set for the Carrington clan. Creator Esther Shapiro arranged the hour-long confab because she needed to make a sale to Canadian TV for the ABC series to go into profit. Forsythe was delightful and humorous in relating a career that had already spanned four decades. First impression: Forsythe at sixty-three was devilishly handsome and tanned, looking as if he were in his forties. I arranged years later to be at his table at an ABC salute to producer Aaron Spelling at the Century Plaza Hotel in which stars from all his series, past and present, would be seated at different tables. Forsythe recognized me and talked about his post-*Dynasty* career, which was booming.

MILLER: My first private conversation with Forsythe was in 1980, between scenes he was filming for the opening episode of *Dynasty*, which was filmed on location at the Filoli Estate in rural San Mateo County, in Northern California. I had seen Forsythe last in his 1979 feature film . . . *And Justice for All* with Al Pacino. His performance in a rather nasty role in the movie was widely praised. The real John Forsythe turned out to be the complete flip side of that character. He was a convivial, good-natured, and instantly likeable man. After our chat, to my surprise he invited me to join the filming of his wedding to costar Linda Evans. I was herded into the rear echelon of a vast sea of extras—but to this day, I can't spot myself anywhere in the scene, although I've checked the DVD. Still, I have fond memories of being an eyewitness to the nuptials of two legendary TV characters, Blake and Krystle Carrington.

Several years later, I had lunch with Forsythe after *Dynasty* had ended its initial run and found him to be just as down to earth and likeable as before. The occasion this time was the starring role he was playing in the 1987 ABC made-for-television movie *On Fire*.

The Interview

MILLER: As I understand it, you came from a conservative family with a father who was an executive at a brokerage firm. How did he react when you let him know you wanted to become an actor?

FORSYTHE: There was a long pause and then he said, "You know, I don't worry about you. I always think you're going to land on your feet. But what makes you think you can become an actor? You don't look like an actor. You don't dress like an actor, sound like an actor, nor have the things an actor seems to have."

MILLER: So how did that turn out? Did he ever come around to appreciating your choice of a career?

FORSYTHE: Happily, he lived long enough to see me do quite well, so I think he was proud of me.

BAWDEN: I had no idea until you told me that you were once a "male starlet" at Warner Bros.

FORSYTHE (*laughing*): All true. I had bits so tiny in early 1942–1943 that even I can't remember them. I was unbilled many times in crowd scenes. I remember playing an RCMP [Canadian Mountie] type in *Northern Pursuit* [1943], a hoot of an Errol Flynn vehicle about Nazis infiltrating the Canadian Arctic. Then I played a guy called Sparks in the Cary Grant war epic *Destination Tokyo* [1943] and then I went into the real war. When I came out the other end my WB contract was over and I had to start all over again.

BAWDEN: People always say what an Establishment type you are both on and off screen.

FORSYTHE (*laughing*): Well, my real name is Jacob Freund and I'm Polish and Russian Jewish stock. I did grow up in a tony neighborhood of Philadelphia. I started out as a student at the University of North Carolina, then switched to become a baseball announcer for the Brooklyn Dodgers. After war work I went to the Actors Studio and by 1948 I was getting bits on live TV in New York. One of my first live gigs was on *Kraft Theatre* in—would you believe it—*Wuthering Heights* [1948]. Then, get this, I had the effrontery of replacing Hank Fonda in the original production of *Mister Roberts* [1950]. Then I starred in a stage hit, *Teahouse of the August Moon* [1953], but Glenn Ford took over in the movie.

BAWDEN: Then you went Hollywood again?

FORSYTHE: Had to. Needed the dough. I had small kids. Needed steady emolument. Started out as Loretta Young's hubby in *It Happens Every Thursday*, her last-ever movie before ditching movies for TV. My first as a movie star. Then I went to MGM for a darned good western, *Escape from Fort Bravo* [1953], starring Bill Holden and Eleanor Parker and I was Ellie's Confederate lover. In *The Glass Web* [1953] Eddie Robinson gave me acting lessons—like, "Go for it, kid! Just try to steal this scene from me." But

I couldn't, of course. Then I was in *The Trouble with Harry,* Alfred Hitchcock's weird comedy, only nobody in the audience was laughing. Confusion reigned and it was a singular flop. And yes, he did tell me to try a TV series because I told him with a young family I needed a steady income. He also thought that my style of acting was better suited to TV because movie production was way down.

BAWDEN: You had a lot to do with the storyline for the series you did: *Bachelor Father?*

FORSYTHE: I picked the character's name. It was based on two bon vivant lawyers who lived in Beverly Hills. What little girl wouldn't love to live in Beverly Hills, I ask you? Harry Ackerman was the first producer. He had each show shot in three to four days. Remember my costar Noreen Corcoran had to have four hours of schoolwork every week. She came from a show biz family, so her dad or mom were always on set and we closed at 5:30 p.m. no matter what. A sort of pilot ran on *General Electric Theatre* before CBS picked us up for a September debut. We alternated with *Jack Benny* Sunday nights at 7:30, hammocked between *Lassie* and *Ed Sullivan,* but CBS was never satisfied with the ratings. We did twenty-six episodes [for each of the] first two seasons, with no repeats, and then CBS brutally canceled us. Revue Studios brought in a new producer, Everett Freeman, and resold us to NBC for two more seasons. Then we went to ABC for the final season. We were on all three networks for a grand total of five seasons and 157 episodes.

BAWDEN: Nobody seems to remember it much these days.

FORSYTHE: It ran for years in syndication, but I agree it's not up there with *Leave It to Beaver.* There were some big-name guest stars like Edgar Bergen, Gisele Mackenzie. My future *Dynasty* wife, Linda Evans, was fifteen when she guested. George Burns's son Ronnie did a couple, Jack Benny did one. Our first producer, Harry Ackerman, later told me he learned a lot—and went on to produce *Bewitched* and *I Dream of Jeannie.* And when it was all over in 1962 I was, well, *depleted* is the word I'm searching for.

MILLER: Did your success as a sitcom star in *Bachelor Father* push you toward more "loveable dad"–type comedy roles?

FORSYTHE: I never wanted to be just a light comedian on television. When you make your first success on TV that's immediately how you get categorized, so I was considered a light comedian. That was even though I'd been a founding member of the Actors Studio and was in the original cast of Arthur Miller's first play, *All My Sons.* So what I did was try to break away.

BAWDEN: You tried movies again.

FORSYTHE: I can see that grin on your face. *Kitten with a Whip* [1964] is the masterpiece you are thinking about. I saw it on TV recently, or should I say a bit of it, and it's not really that bad. Ann-Margret is a bipolar delinquent, as far as I recall, and I was a very repressed middle classer. Boy, did we get mauled by the critics! And you know, it might have worked as a TV flick if made a few years later. That awful hippie dialogue made me laugh. Perhaps it was a comedy all along,

Next I did *Madame X* [1966] with Lana Turner and this one made a bucket of dough. They asked Myrna Loy to play my mother and she wired, "I know I'm old, but I'm not that old!" Then [producer] Ross Hunter tried to get oldster Kay Francis interested and she declined. Connie Bennett took it and went right after Lana. Then she died just as the picture was released. Then Lana said she was leaving the picture because Keir Dullea, playing her son, looked too old for the part!

BAWDEN: Why go back to series TV with *The John Forsythe Show* [1965–1966]?

FORSYTHE: I've asked that question myself. I was a wealthy bachelor, a retired US Air Force major who inherits an exclusive girls' school. It was a sort of extension of the first show! My own company, Forsythe Productions, ran it and I hired Ann B. Davis and Elsa Lanchester for the laughs. I hired my own daughters, Brooke, eleven, and Page, fourteen, and there was another real doll—Peggy Lipton—who would find fame on *The Mod Squad*. It got mediocre ratings, so NBC had me change the plot to become a master spy using the school as a secret base of operations. Viewers thought: "What?" And it sank like a stone, twenty-two episodes, and I begged NBC to please not renew us and they obliged.

BAWDEN: But you then did *To Rome with Love* [1969–1971].

FORSYTHE: I was a teacher who loses his wife and to escape I go to Rome with my three daughters and an aunt [Kay Medford], and we had such guests as Geraldine Brooks, John Howard, and to pep up ratings we added Walter Brennan, the greatest scene stealer I have ever met. We had directors like Freddie De Cordova and Charles Barton, who directed Abbott and Costello movies. Did we go to Rome? Not! Don Fedderson [*My Three Sons*] did it, but people just wouldn't watch. CBS gave us three time slots in two years and nothing worked. I think the time for this kind of sitcom had truly passed.

MILLER: Some actors have told me they found it risky to stray too far from the kind of roles their fans wanted to see them play. I think, for example, fans rebelled when Cary Grant played a genuine heel in *None but the Lonely Heart* [1944], even though critics praised his daring change of pace.

FORSYTHE: Cary Grant was a good friend of mine and a wonderful guy. But the audience didn't buy him that way and he didn't buy himself that way. He wanted to do what he did best and not stray away from that. In our business, a lot of it is governed by commercial boundaries. I think it's particularly dangerous in television, where the connection between actor and audience is so intimate. If they expect you to give them Quick Quaker Oats and you suddenly switch to All-Bran, they may not want that at all.

BAWDEN: You've been in a ton of TV movies over the years.

FORSYTHE: The one I made in 1964, *See How They Run*, started the whole genre. It costarred Jane Wyatt plus Leslie Nielsen before he became funny, and dear old Franchot Tone. Then I did *Murder Once Removed* [1971], *The Letters* [1973], *The Deadly Tower* [1975]. I was always careful not to price myself out of the market.

MILLER: One of your most image-shattering may have been *On Fire* [1987], in which you played a character who can't cope with his retirement from a long career as a firefighter. You got into that character so deeply that I wondered if it resonated in some way with your own life.

FORSYTHE: My father was a very vital, bright, and active man who died two years after he was forced to retire [because of a maximum age requirement]. The way it affected my family is pretty much what that picture is all about.

MILLER: There was a strong message in that film, as I recall, about the issue of mandatory retirement.

FORSYTHE: It's so much a part of the whole tapestry of the country today—people who spend their lives concentrating almost solely on work, then when it's ripped away from them, it causes devastation.

MILLER: Well, you don't have mandatory retirement in your business, so have you given much thought to retirement in your future?

FORSYTHE: We should all be preparing for the time when we have to taper off, and your work is not the most compelling thing in your life. You have to build outside interests, which my father didn't have. [Forsythe took his own advice and became deeply involved in ownership of Thoroughbred racehorses. He was quite successful at it and was at one point on the board of directors of the Hollywood Park racetrack.] On the other hand, most people of my age would be retired by now, but I'm still playing love scenes with Linda Evans.

BAWDEN: How did you get the plum lead as the unseen boss of *Charlie's Angels*?

FORSYTHE: Producer Aaron Spelling pitched it as a case of simply coming in and reading lines. No makeup! Ann Sothern got there first in *My*

John Forsythe as Blake Carrington in *Dynasty* with TV wife Linda Evans, circa 1981. Courtesy of ABC publicity.

Mother the Car. But I thought it was a great, if outrageous, idea. I'd amble in every few weeks and read the lines. Mostly I'd prerecord the lines because that was the easiest way. And you do know Aaron tried to copy the format? He used the premise in a pilot that ran on *Charlie's Angels* called *Jo's Boys* with the great Barbara Stanwyck unseen but heard distinctly, and she had three hunks as the detectives. ABC said, "No, thanks!"

BAWDEN: Now we're up to *Dynasty*.

FORSYTHE: I'm not proud. I seized the part of Blake Carrington after George Peppard walked out after a week of arguing with the producers. Actually, it was creator Esther Shapiro who thought of me and wondered if I could be tough enough. I told her to check out my performance as Judge Henry Fielding in . . . *And Justice for All.* Which she did and I was hired. We ran for eight seasons and 217 hour episodes and there was the inevitable spin-off, *The Colbys,* which only lasted 1985–1986. I was reunited with Pamela Franklin, Linda Evans, and even Joan Collins, who I'd taught drama in New York, way back in the early '50s.

BAWDEN: I remember you talking about the internecine warfare raging behind the scenes on *Dynasty.*

FORSYTHE (*chuckling*): That was inevitable. Esther Shapiro is a tough, resilient cookie. Multitalented, creative, always brimming with story ideas. And Aaron Spelling's no wilting wallflower. They had dueling ideas of how the show should proceed. And there was a lot of conflict. I once asked Esther if she sympathized with Alexis [Joan Collins's character] or Krystle [Linda Evans]. And she threw me by saying she's more like my character, Blake. And she was foremost in the licensing agreements that really sold the show. Of course, people ask me all that time about a family that's so rich—why do all these people live under the same roof? and I say, "Because there would be no story if they were all scattered about."

MILLER: I believe one of the marvelous side effects of *Dynasty* has been your influence on making men with gray hair seem like sex symbols on TV.

FORSYTHE: Some years ago, it was taboo for a guy to have gray hair. It immediately branded him as old and decrepit. But it has something of an allure now. Look at the male models today and you'll see a few guys with gray hair. I think the perception of being old has altered somewhat. Age is a relative thing. I know a lot of people who are sixty and have vitality and energy and the keenness of thirty-year-olds. And I know some thirty-year-olds who are goddamned old. Our business is so dependent on talent and individuality that age is totally irrelevant today. I'm sixty-eight years old. It's not that I look young. I think I'm younger than my years. There's no secret about my age. I've never denied it—and the audience accepts me on that basis.

MILLER: So how do you explain the mass appeal of the Blake Carrington character?

FORSYTHE: I think part of it is the country's always looking for a father image of one kind or another. He used power, but he always used it well.

MILLER: So he never became as dark a character as his counterpart in *Dallas*, J. R. Ewing. Were you in any way responsible for the mellower image of Blake?

FORSYTHE: It came from me because I wasn't interested [in playing a villain]. They got me at the beginning with the prospect of playing a dimensional character. Then I discovered the writing was not what they'd promised. They had me doing some very bad things, like setting dogs on people. I went to the producers and said, "I don't want to be J. R. I don't want to be namby-pamby, but I don't want to be Larry Hagman either. [Hagman played J. R. Ewing in *Dallas*.] He does that already and he does it very well. I told them Blake is tough, hard, and a consummate businessman. He can be fairly ruthless in some of his dealings, but if that's the kind of man you want, I don't want to be in the part. I'll get the hell out right now.

BAWDEN: Any idea why you've lasted so long in such a cutthroat business?

FORSYTHE: Having triple bypass surgery in 1979. I'm not kidding. An actor must be healthy and resilient. Saved my life. I had the surgery and three months later I was back on the tennis courts. Seriously, luck has a bit to do with it. I think it's also lack of temperament. I always preferred TV to movies. I like to sleep in my own bed at night and take long vacations. My dad once told me when I was fifteen: "I never worry about you like the other two children. You go with the punches. You never complain when something doesn't go right. This is a trait you were born with because I'm nothing like that at all."

Afterword

After our interviews with John Forsythe, he starred in yet another TV comedy series, *The Powers That Be* (1992–1993), and served as host of the TV series *I Witness Video* (1993–1994). He also did *Dynasty* reunion specials in 1991 and 2006. He also reprised his role as Charlie in the feature films *Charlie's Angels* (2000) and *Charlie's Angels: Full Throttle* (2003).

Forsythe was married three times, first to Parker Worthington McCormick in 1939 (divorced in 1943), then to Julie Warren from 1943 until her death in 1994. In 2002, he married Nicole Carter, who died a few months after his death. He had three children.

After successfully battling colon cancer, Forsythe died from pneumonia on April 1, 2010, in Santa Ynez, California. He was ninety-two.

Annette Funicello

Interview by James Bawden

Annette Funicello was the most famous of the original Walt Disney Mouseke-teers, the group of talented youngsters who starred in Walt Disney's *The Mickey Mouse Club* from 1955 to 1959, first on ABC and then in syndication to local TV stations. She was the only one of the original group to become a full-fledged star in her grown-up years, and she will always be remembered as the most beloved of all the child stars launched by that memorable series.

Born on October 22, 1942, she began to sing, dance, and act in her juve-nile years and was signed by Walt Disney himself at the age of twelve. Annette, as she was known to her millions of fans, became a popular recording star and played one other significant role in the television of that era—as Italian exchange student Gina Minelli, who came to live with the Danny Williams family in the 1959 season of Danny Thomas's *Make Room for Daddy*, one of the era's top situation comedy hits.

Funicello blossomed into a genuine beauty in her late teen years and in 1963 she was cast in the leading role of the feature film *Beach Party* opposite pop music star Frankie Avalon. It was an enormous hit and the first in a long series of teen-oriented musical comedy films now considered to be the build-ing blocks of the 1960s "beach party" genre.

She temporarily retired to marry and start a family, then her career came to a premature close when she was diagnosed with multiple sclerosis and had to withdraw from performing as her physical condition sharply declined.

Setting the Scene

In 1971 I was seated next to Funicello at an evening event hosted by NBC at Disneyland, which was for years her professional headquarters. By that time

Frankie Avalon with Annette Funicello. Courtesy of the Shefrin Company.

she had virtually retired from show business, but was still treasured as a member of the Disney family.

A lot of ex-Mouseketeers were there that night to greet visiting TV critics, but Funicello was the one everybody wanted to meet and pose with for a picture. I found her to be very friendly but a little distant in manner. However, when other Mouseketeers from the past came by her table, she'd wave energetically. For me, it was like being a witness to someone's cheerful high school reunion.

The Interview

BAWDEN: Tell me about how it all started for you.

FUNICELLO: I had a stage mom and I started singing and dancing when I was four.

BAWDEN: You were one of hundreds of kids who auditioned for *The Mickey Mouse Club* in 1955. When Walt Disney signed you, is it true you thought of changing your last name?

FUNICELLO: Uncle Walt was horrified. I was his idea of ethnic on the show and he told me to keep my name. He said the name Disney was his original name and people never forgot that.

BAWDEN: Did he kind of design an image for you?

FUNICELLO: He was a Puritan. As I grew older, he supervised my wardrobe, forbade smoking. I was his definition of a good girl. And that's what he wanted.

BAWDEN: What was it like to work as a Mouseketeer, then have it all come to an end when the original series was canceled?

FUNICELLO: It was a tough life. Legally we had to have a certain number of hours of schooling a day. The musical numbers required a lot of preparation. Then the show got killed and I lost some good friends and I cried a bit.

BAWDEN: Disney gave you lots of roles in the serials like *The Further Adventures of Spin and Marty* [1956], and he even gave you your own story called *Annette* [1958]. But he also put you into some of his biggest movies, like *The Shaggy Dog* [1959] starring Fred MacMurray. How did you like him?

FUNICELLO: He was pleasant but distant.

BAWDEN: How much control did Mr. Disney exert over your life?

FUNICELLO: He even supervised my dates. He never wanted to see me at a nightclub. Every date had to be chaperoned. And usually there'd be a Disney photographer along to turn it all into a photo shoot. And a makeup artist, so I always looked my best. Uncle Walt believed young people should be deferential and never talk back.

BAWDEN: One of the legendary stories about you is that you once had a crush on Guy Williams, who played Zorro in the famous Disney series, so Mr. Disney cast you in a guest role on the show.

FUNICELLO: I was in seventh heaven that week!

BAWDEN: Once your appeal as a star was obvious, Disney loaned you out for roles outside his realm, like your time as a semi-regular on *Make Room for Daddy* in 1959 and roles on the TV series *Wagon Train* and *Burke's Law* in 1963 and *The Greatest Show on Earth* in 1964. But your biggest Disney movie was the musical remake of *Babes in Toyland* [1961] with pop singer Tommy Sands. Tell me about that one.

FUNICELLO: There were months of rehearsals, huge sets, many takes. All the musical numbers were prerecorded. And it laid a big egg. Teenagers didn't want to see that sort of thing. I think because of the huge cost, it barely made back its costs.

BAWDEN: You were still under contract to Walt Disney when American-International Pictures [AIP] offered you the leading female role in *Beach Party*. Didn't that rattle the Disney image a bit?

FUNICELLO: Uncle Walt had final say. He fretted a bit and then told me it was okay provided I did not wear a two-piece swimsuit. I remember he said, "You must never show your belly button!" and I never have.

BAWDEN: From today's perspective, that movie seems pretty innocent, but I remember seeing one of the ads that showed you in a two-piece bathing suit that the studio apparently painted on your image. How did that go over with Disney?

FUNICELLO: Uncle Walt went berserk and phoned up AIP head Sam Arkoff to shout, "How dare you put Annette in a bikini!" But technically it wasn't a bikini and Uncle Walt could do nothing about it.

BAWDEN: The enormous success of that picture led to *Muscle Beach Party* [1964], *Bikini Beach* [1964], *Pajama Party* [1964], *Beach Blanket Bingo* [1965], *How to Stuff a Wild Bikini* [1965], and *Dr. Goldfoot and the Bikini Machine* [1965]. What brought an end to that great run of hit movies?

FUNICELLO: I made *Fireball 500* [1966] with Frankie Avalon and Fabian, then *Thunder Alley* [1966] with Fabian. They were beach movies without the beach. Our days of glory went *poof* very fast!

Afterword

By that time in her life, Funicello could not have cared less. She married agent Jack Gilardi in 1965 and retired to have three children. Divorced in 1983, she married horse breeder Glen Holt. She became a homebody, devoted to family. Occasionally she'd slip out of retirement for a gig on TV's *Love, American Style* or *Fantasy Island*. But mostly she was seen on TV in commercials as spokesperson for Skippy peanut butter.

In 1987 she began experiencing symptoms of multiple sclerosis while filming the comeback film *Back to the Beach* opposite her old costar Frankie Avalon. She went public about her illness in 1992, then made the TV movie *A Dream Is a Wish Your Heart Makes: The Annette Funicello Story* with Avalon and Dick Clark playing themselves.

I still fondly remember the lovely girl who sat with the TV critics in the dark as the fireworks blazed in the sky that night in 1971. Then she shook hands and said she had to get back to her kids. That was the way Funicello always behaved, thoroughly professional to the end.

Though her valiant struggle with MS continued for two decades after she was first diagnosed, her life became more and more that of a shut-in as she lost her ability to walk and finally to speak. She died from complications of the illness in Bakersfield, California, on April 8, 2013. She was seventy.

James Garner

Interview by James Bawden and Ron Miller

In the 1950s, three really outstanding leading male movie actors emerged from the popular genre of television westerns: Clint Eastwood (*Rawhide*), Steve McQueen (*Wanted, Dead or Alive*), and James Garner (*Maverick*). Though Eastwood and McQueen had substantially more successful careers in feature films and never went back to the small screen, Garner certainly had a meaningful movie career, also remaining an enormously popular TV star in both subsequent nonwestern series and made-for-television movies.

As a movie star, Garner had several notable achievements. He was the leading man to some of Hollywood's top female stars, including Natalie Wood in *Cash McCall* (1959), Audrey Hepburn in *The Children's Hour* (1961), Doris Day in both *Move Over, Darling* (1963) and *The Thrill of It All* (1963), Lee Remick in *The Wheeler Dealers* (1963), Julie Andrews in both *The Americanization of Emily* (1964) and *Victor/Victoria* (1982), and Sally Field in *Murphy's Romance* (1985), a performance that earned him a Best Actor Oscar nomination.

Those roles mostly displayed Garner's appeal as a romantic leading man, but he also established himself as an action hero in such male-oriented films as *The Great Escape* (1963), *Grand Prix* (1966), *Marlowe* (1969), and numerous big-screen westerns, including *Duel at Diablo* (1966), *Skin Game* (1971), and his two comic westerns: *Support Your Local Sheriff* (1969) and *Support Your Local Gunfighter* (1971).

But it was television where Garner made his most significant mark as an actor. He was the main star of several weekly series, among them *Maverick* (1957–1962), *Nichols* (1971–1972), *Bret Maverick* (1981–1982), *The Rockford Files* (1974–1980), *Man of the People* (1991), and *First Monday* (2002). In addition, Garner played recurring roles in *Chicago Hope* and *Eight Simple Rules* (2003) and made token appearances in the series *Young Maverick* (1979)

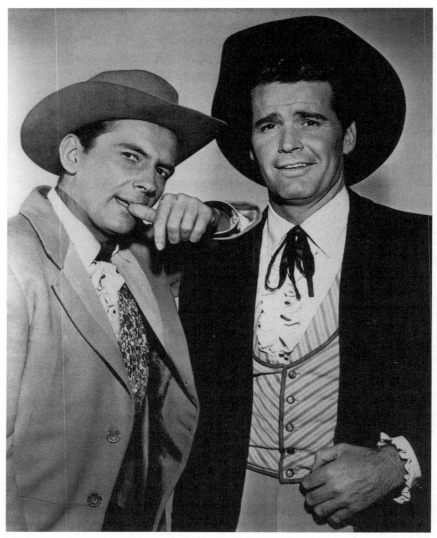

Jack Kelly (*left*) as Bart and James Garner as brother Bret in *Maverick,* circa 1957. Courtesy of ABC publicity.

and in the 1994 feature film *Maverick* starring Mel Gibson as Bret Maverick.

Garner's work in television movies and miniseries was generally acclaimed by critics, especially his performance in the 1980 *Heartsounds,* in which he played a physician facing severe heart problems; his work as the caring brother of schizophrenic James Woods in *Promise* (1986); and his leading role in

HBO's 1993 *Barbarians at the Gate.* Garner also played the leading role in the 1995 miniseries *Streets of Laredo,* a sequel to *Lonesome Dove.*

Like *Maverick,* Garner's hit detective series, *The Rockford Files,* seemed to have an eternal life, and Garner made eight TV movies reprising his Jim Rockford character in the 1990s.

Setting the Scene

Each of us interviewed James Garner separately on different occasions. We have merged our interviews for this presentation, but in this section we offer our personal memories of the circumstances of our separate chats with the star.

BAWDEN: My first interview with James Garner was in 1978 over lunch in his mobile home dressing room on the Universal lot, right beside the soundstages containing the standing sets for his current hit *The Rockford Files.* We dined on stale ham and cheese sandwiches and soda water. Executive producer Meta Rosenberg was present for part of our chat. It was supposed to last an hour, but Garner asked me to linger while a construction flaw was fixed for the next scene.

We also had a grand reunion in the *Toronto Star* newsroom in 1984 when he was appearing in the acclaimed TV movie *Heartsounds* opposite Mary Tyler Moore, who was also present, along with executive producer Fay Kanin. I later interviewed Garner at the gala wrap party for the TV miniseries *Space* in 1985.

MILLER: I spoke with Garner briefly on a number of occasions in the 1980s, usually before or after press conferences, and had a long, leisurely lunch with him in Los Angeles when he was promoting his 1989 TV movie *My Name Is Bill W.* The last time we talked was at a panel celebration of the career of TV writer-producer Roy Huggins at the Los Angeles County Museum in the late 1990s

My impression of Jim Garner never changed through all of our meetings. He was a witty, candid, and genial guy, and every time we got together was a memorable occasion for me.

The Interview

BAWDEN: I always like to ask actors how they got into the business.

GARNER: In my case I was driving around Beverly Hills and saw a lady driver who was vacating a parking spot, so I took it. It was outside the offices of a press agent and casting director named Paul Gregory. I'd met him at

Hollywood High School, recognized the name. And we had a warm reunion and he said he was casting for extras in the Broadway-bound drama *The Caine Mutiny Court Martial* [1954], and I did a test and had the job. I was unemployed at the time, so I didn't care how low the pay was.

I always say I learned how to act watching the back of Henry Fonda's head for 199 performances. [Fonda was starring in the play.] We did get to Broadway and it was a big hit with superb direction from Charles Laughton. In fact, for years afterwards I basically gave my interpretation of Fonda. Maybe I'm still doing it.

BAWDEN: Did you always want to act?

GARNER: Heck, no! I was born in Norman, Oklahoma, in 1928, the youngest of three boys. Acting wasn't something we considered. It was mainly a question of survival of the fittest. I had several step-mamas. The last, Grace, was a darling. I joined the United States Merchant Marine, aged sixteen, and later was in the California Army National Guard. I was in Korea for more than a year and I was wounded several times.

MILLER: I heard you were offered a screen test at Fox while you were doing the Broadway show.

GARNER: They wanted to screen test me in New York City, but I had heard through the grapevine that the Hollywood set didn't like actors who were tested in New York. So I told them I was leaving New York for Hollywood and would test for them there, but not in New York. That was total bullshit since I'd never even had a speaking role anywhere at all before. So they agreed and I came out and did a screen test with Rita Moreno. But [Daryl] Zanuck [head of production at Fox] was off in Europe chasing Bella Darvi [a Fox starlet] and never saw it, so the option on me ran out.

MILLER: Well, you were in Hollywood, so what else did you try?

GARNER: I went to Warners and did a couple of jobs for them and went into their acting school for about twelve minutes. Me and Dennis Hopper and Jimmy Dean.

BAWDEN: At Warners you got your first experience with television?

GARNER: I got commercial work first. In 1955 I tested for the lead in *Cheyenne*, Warners' first TV western, but they chose Clint Walker.

MILLER: Did Warners have other plans for you?

GARNER: Even though I'd already done five things for them, they wanted me to do a screen test. I said, "What's this?" But I agreed and they optioned me for a month. I told them I'd give them two weeks to pick up my option. They were testing fourteen actors a day. I remember telling them,

"I don't care if you sign me, but don't miss out on this kid Michael Landon. He's good!"

MILLER: That doesn't sound like it was calculated to endear you to the studio. Was that an honest expression of your attitude about stardom?

GARNER: I was always that way. If you don't know any different, what the hell? I wanted to do what I wanted to do, and if they didn't like it, I could always go back to pumping gas or laying carpets. So they asked me for another week to make up their minds and I said no, so they signed me that night.

MILLER: Wasn't that taking quite a gamble?

GARNER: If you're already there at the studio, you have a better chance they'll use you than if you're an actor from the outside.

MILLER: Once they signed you, did the studio have a master plan for you?

GARNER: No, they didn't have a master plan for me. I was doing *Sayonara* [1957] in Japan when they were getting ready to do *Maverick*. They were testing every guy in town and had run out of guys to test.

BAWDEN: So how did they come to cast you as Bret Maverick?

GARNER: I had a supporting part in a 1957 TV drama starring Charlie Ruggles, and producer Roy Huggins liked my comedic take and invited me in to read for *Maverick*. The first thing he did was shorten my name from Bumgarner to Garner, for obvious reasons. ABC picked us up and said we'd go against *Ed Sullivan* and *Steve Allen* [on the Sunday night lineup], but ABC was the third-place network and only interested in getting young viewers to attack the advertisers. I thought we'd last a year, but people started talking about us.

MILLER: Did Huggins have any trouble convincing the studio you were the right guy?

GARNER: I don't think so. They were looking at the dailies coming back from Japan on *Sayonara,* so they said, "Shoot, we have this guy under contract already, so we might as well use him."

BAWDEN: That didn't exactly propel you into the financial big leagues, did it?

GARNER: I think I started at around $450 an episode. I had to fight for every increase, Jack Warner [head of production] was that kind of guy. He once threatened to fire me, but that would have destroyed the series.

We needed a six- to seven-day shoot. There were standing sets at the studio, plus we'd shoot out at Warners' ranch for more actionful scenes. The idea was to do everything on the first take and then we could go home after twelve hours. So Roy had two episodes being shot by different crews—TV series ran thirty-nine episodes in those days. I'd make a guest appearance in every other episode that starred Jack Kelly as my brother. And later, when we got really behind, they hired Roger Moore as the British cousin [to star in other episodes].

BAWDEN: What did daily TV acting teach you?

GARNER: Professionalism. You worked no matter what. On Friday nights we'd toil away until dawn broke on Saturday. Six-day shooting was abolished by the Actors Guild in 1955, much to the disgust of Jack Warner. We had some pretty fair directors, you know, including Budd Boetticher, George Waggner, Abner Biberman. One could learn a lot of technical things from such guys.

MILLER: You mentioned Budd Boetticher. Wasn't he influential in not only helping set the image of Bret Maverick but in setting your own image as an actor?

GARNER: That character was originally a kind of Errol Flynn type, but Boetticher and I looked at the script, which had him saying things like "He went thataway," and decided to have him put his tongue in his cheek and play it that way. Roy Huggins said, "Hey, this works!" Boetticher directed the first three episodes and it set a pattern. They say the first role you play that's successful usually sticks with you. It was something I fell into and it turned out to be something I could do pretty well and liked it. So I used it. Boy, did I use it!

MILLER: That laidback, tongue-in-cheek kind of character fit you so well. Did you learn anything about how to develop a screen image from any of the big-name actors you worked with?

GARNER: Spencer Tracy always said he never wanted to be caught acting. I feel that way, too. If you're acting up a storm, the audience notices that and it takes them out of the story. I've made a pretty good career out of it and so far nobody's ever accused me of acting. Henry Fonda and Johnny Hodiak both told me the same thing: be on-screen the same way you are off-screen and people can't help but like you. So I've always tried to be natural, as much like me as I could be.

BAWDEN: During your summer vacation, you made inexpensive movies for WB.

GARNER: We called them programmers. I did *Darby's Rangers* [1958] opposite Etchika Choureau, who was Jack's latest discovery. He said she'd be the next Sophia Loren. The next summer I starred in *Up Periscope* opposite Eddie O'Brien, one of the best actors I'd ever meet. Then in 1960 it was *Cash*

McCall starring Natalie Wood, who was on the cusp of superstardom. I was trying to prove I was more than another TV cowboy, you see.

MILLER: On *Darby's Rangers*, you worked with an old veteran action picture director, "Wild Bill" Wellman. How did you get along?

GARNER: Charlton Heston was supposed to do it, but he got in an argument with Warners and suddenly he was out and I was in. Wellman really didn't want me as the star of the picture, but he had to accept me. At the end of the picture, he said, "Jim, I have to tell you, you did a hell of a job." We became friends, but I was too young for that picture—and too inexperienced.

MILLER: You didn't always behave like a happy camper, even back in those days, did you?

GARNER: I fought them over things I didn't want to do. For example, they wanted me to play a character role in *Up Periscope*. I didn't want to do it and when Tab Hunter decided he didn't want to be in the picture at all, they gave me the starring role.

BAWDEN: Why did the *Maverick* series end in 1962?

GARNER: We just ran out of steam, that's all. My contract was up and I was getting movie offers. I'd done sixty hours. Enough is enough.

BAWDEN: You started in bigger movies with *The Children's Hour* in 1961.

GARNER: I was embarrassed by the content. [Lesbianism was a rare issue for movies then.] Willie Wyler directed the original version in 1935 as *These Three*. Now he wanted to open up the lesbian theme. Audrey Hepburn felt she owed him one for *Roman Holiday* [the 1953 Wyler film that earned her the Best Actress Oscar], Shirley MacLaine wanted to prove she was fearless. Me? I just moped around and the movie wasn't half as interesting as the original. Go figure that out.

BAWDEN: But you did make a big jump into box office movie stardom and some other TV names just couldn't do it.

GARNER: Vince Edwards [from TV's *Ben Casey*] was the first to try and he didn't make it. Dick Chamberlain [TV's *Dr. Kildare*] tried, but he's a very good classical actor. I guess Steve McQueen was the first to vault that barrier. I worked with Steve on *The Great Escape*—a great box office hit—and he was always a minimalist and he showed one the way. Then I made *The Thrill of It All* with Doris Day, who is great at physical comedy, and that one was a huge hit. Doris and I took over for Marilyn Monroe and Dean Martin after Marilyn died and her last movie was only half made, so we redid everything as *Move Over, Darling* and that was another hit. And I wish I'd done more with Doris. And then a bit later she jumped into TV and her series ran for five years.

BAWDEN: Then you made your favorite film, *The Americanization of Emily.*

GARNER: Made before Julie Andrews did *The Sound of Music.* And she's sexier here than she was later allowed to be. I was hired by director Willie Wyler, who was then fired by the producer [Martin Ransohoff] because Willie wanted Paddy Chayefsky's script rewritten! These days I get letters from college kids who study the script in English classes and I agree it's one of the best ever. Arthur Hiller stepped in and his direction is impeccable. It's the best movie I ever made—and I wound up making some dandies.

MILLER: Wasn't that like the *Up Periscope* deal all over again? You weren't the original choice for the leading male role, were you?

GARNER: It was the same thing. Bill Holden was going to play that part, but his agent got in a fight with the producer and Bill dropped out. I was going to play the James Coburn part, but wound up playing the Holden part.

BAWDEN: And your worst picture was made just a few years later.

GARNER: *The Pink Jungle,* made in 1968. It was supposed to be a parody of jungle flicks. But we never went anywhere near South America. A real stinker.

BAWDEN: Why jump back to TV with the NBC series *Nichols?*

GARNER: Producer Frank Pierson pitched it to me and said my company, Cherokee, could produce it. It meant going back to Warners, but Jack Warner was no longer around and I never retain grudges. John Badham was one of the directors and Peter Tewskbury another. The scripts were better written than any movie except for the Paddy Chayefsky one. And we had top guest stars: Jack Elam, Scatman Crothers, Ricardo Montalban. Margot Kidder became a star off it. But NBC was still operating in a three-network universe and they had other product on the shelf ready to test, so they canceled us after twenty-four episodes. But it remains my favorite series by far.

BAWDEN: But you went back at it for the same network five years later. Explain!

GARNER: I never keep a grudge. Roy Huggins, who gave me my career, came up with *The Rockford Files,* tailored exactly to my personality. Stephen Cannell was just beginning his brilliant writing career and he wrote an amazing number of them. Cherokee Productions signed up and I installed Meta Rosenberg as executive producer. Mike Post did the catchy theme. We debuted in September 1976 and remained a top-twenty show [for years].

James Garner with guest star Rita Moreno in *The Rockford Files*, 1978. Courtesy of NBC publicity.

MILLER: Jim Rockford seemed so much like Bret Maverick that many fans wondered if they were blood relatives.

GARNER: Roy always thought of Rockford as Maverick in modern clothes. We even reworked some of the original Maverick scripts for *Rockford Files*.

BAWDEN: You also enticed some big-name guest stars.

GARNER: Like Lauren Bacall? She owed me after I did that awful horror film just to please her [1981's *The Fan*]. And Rita Moreno, Lou Gossett, Isaac Hayes, and others kept coming back as repeat characters because we treated them right. A lot was due to the time slot—Friday night at 9. In series TV the time slot means everything.

MILLER: Tom Selleck has always said he owed you big-time for the break you gave him by putting him into *The Rockford Files* as rival detective Lance White, which led to his being cast as the star of *Magnum, P.I.*

GARNER: The first time he walked on the set I said, "My God! This guy has to be a big star!" We talked a lot about it. I told him, "You're a really nice guy, a good actor, and you've got these looks. You can't help but be a star, so handle yourself accordingly and do the things you feel good about."

BAWDEN: I noticed you were being treated by the studio nurse before our interview. Did you suffer an injury today?

GARNER: I guess I need a stuntman—or a new knee. [In 1979, doctors advised him to take time off to heal and he decided to end the show. NBC and Universal claimed the series was in deficit because of the high-priced guest stars. Garner complained the studio wasted money in production overhead. Garner later instituted a lawsuit but settled out of court, and the settlement prohibited discussion of the final terms or other details.]

BAWDEN: It's now 1984 and you're getting some of the best reviews of your career for your performances in made-for-television movies.

GARNER: I'm still at it. I'll next be doing a theatrical opposite Sally Field titled *Murphy's Romance.*

MILLER: In my opinion, you were never better than you were in *Promise,* the Hallmark movie you produced for CBS in which you were cast against your usual type as a bachelor playboy who suddenly has to take responsibility for his schizophrenic brother. This wasn't your traditional leading man role.

GARNER: I'm in the position now to do what I want to do and not what they expect of me. I'm a little older now. How long can you be the hero? As an actor, I want to do a few different things. I never wanted to be typed. I could do comedy well, even black comedy, and people recognized that. But I grew tired of doing that same role. I wasn't going to do *Promise.* We had it written for other people. That was really a project for Jimmy Woods and I wasn't going to play the other part. I promised him an Emmy and he got it. Hallmark wanted me to do it, so I did it.

BAWDEN: All the reviews you get basically say the same thing.

GARNER: Yeah. How I'm "surprisingly effective." As if I haven't learned my craft after thirty-five years of doing it. I think it's great I'm still wanted. I don't get the girl, but even when I was young I rarely got her. Just say I'm a bub who knew his limitations and went from there. And if nothing else works in a scene, I can go back to imitating Hank Fonda. Deep, deep down I'm still Jimmy Bumgarner, hoping nobody will notice.

MILLER: I gather you have no regrets that you've spent the best years of your career doing television and never were tempted to leave the medium for good?

GARNER: I think the best writing today is being done for television. I really do. Look at the movies today—animals coming out of people's bellies, blowing up worlds? Dealing with the human condition isn't done so much in the movies anymore.

MILLER: So what do you think your legacy as an actor will be?

GARNER: I'm not concerned about legacy. When I die, I want to be cremated and don't want anybody to cry. If they want to have a drink over it, that's fine. But I don't want 'em getting upset over it. I don't have any feelings of immortality.

Afterword

After our respective interviews with James Garner, he continued to work in both television and the occasional movie, like the nostalgic *Space Cowboys* (2000), in which he played an aging astronaut. It reunited him with Clint Eastwood, who had appeared in support of Garner in an early episode of *Maverick*. In 1996, he had costarred with Jack Lemmon in *My Fellow Americans*, both of them playing former US presidents. In 2011, his autobiography, *The Garner Files: A Memoir*, was published.

Garner won the Emmy Award for Dramatic Actor in a Series for *The Rockford Files* in the 1976–1977 TV season.

Garner was married only once. Lois and he were wed in 1956. After a separation, the two were reconciled and stayed together until his death in Los Angeles on July 19, 2014, from a massive heart attack. He was eighty-six. He had two daughters, Kim and Gigi.

Peter Graves

Interview by James Bawden

Along with older brother James Arness, Peter Graves was half of perhaps the most successful brother act in television history. While his brother starred in *Gunsmoke*, the longest-running dramatic series of TV's first seventy years, and two other series, Peter Graves starred in the major hit *Mission: Impossible*, two other weekly series (*Court Martial, Whiplash*), and *Fury*, a long-running Saturday morning children's series. He also served as host of the popular documentary series *Biography* and the PBS series *Discover: The World of Science*.

With his brother, Graves made his screen debut unbilled as one of the brothers of Loretta Young in 1947's *The Farmer's Daughter*. He went on to star in the science fiction films *Red Planet Mars* (1952), *Killers from Space* (1954), and *It Conquered the World* (1956), as well as appearing in a few more prestigious roles in films like *Night of the Hunter* (1955) and *The Long Gray Line* (1956) before turning to full-time television work. In his later years, he returned to starring roles in movies like the hit comedy *Airplane!* (1980) and *Airplane! II: The Sequel* (1982).

Graves had a long and busy career, including many starring roles in made-for-television movies.

Setting the Scene

My first interview with Peter Graves was on the busy set of *Mission: Impossible* in June 1972. The CBS press representative said he wanted to start me off with an amiable TV star with no pretensions—and that would be Graves.

I watched the director setting up a tightly controlled scene that had Graves and his team lifting up an ancient Egyptian sarcophagus and prying it open. This was done on cue, but out walked Ann B. Davis from the series shooting next door: *The Partridge Family*, spoiling the scene. For a brief moment, Graves lost his legendary cool as Davis sprinted from the scene.

However, over a light lunch, he was back to his amiable self, reminiscing and teasing his cast mates.

I also did a phone interview with Graves in 1983 when he was promoting his fine guest status on the acclaimed miniseries *The Winds of War*.

The Interview

BAWDEN: How did you wind up an actor?

GRAVES: Well, it sort of runs in the family. I was born Peter Duesler Aurness. Dad was a businessman from Norway—the family name was Aursnes but when Dad immigrated to New York City in 1887, the official at the gate spelled it a different way and it stuck. He spent his life selling medical supplies.

BAWDEN: Then what happened?

GRAVES: I graduated from Southwest High School in 1944 and was in the army for two years. I then went to the University of Minnesota on the G.I. Bill and picked drama as my major.

BAWDEN: Why turn to acting?

GRAVES: Well, I played the sax in the school orchestra. Does that count? Then at U.M. I thought I'd try drama. My brother Jim was already in L.A. by that time. Then, after graduating, I thought I'd try acting professionally. So I went to L.A. and I got discovered.

BAWDEN: What was your first credit?

GRAVES: I played Rory Calhoun's younger brother in an oater titled *Rogue River* in 1951. The director, John Rawlins, took a shine to me and immediately used me again in *Fort Defiance* starring Dane Clark and Ben Johnson. These were filmed in color in about two weeks for a little company titled Ventura Productions. They ran on the bottom of double bills. Then I had a small part in *Stalag 17* [1953], which starred Bill Holden. It was quite an experience and I saw how much work I'd need to put in to be on that level with Holden. Director Billy Wilder was gruff at times, but he'd do take after take to get what he wanted.

BAWDEN: You also did a whole lot of TV?

GRAVES: It paid the bills and my agent said what I needed most was experience. So I was on *Schlitz Playhouse, Chevron Theatre, Pepsi-Cola Playhouse, Gruen Green* Playhouse—now there's a credit—and *TV Reader's Digest*.

My movies were getting better: *Black Tuesday* [1954], where I watched Vic Mature stumble around, and John Ford's *The Long Gray Line* [1954].

BAWDEN: By then you also had a famous brother—Jim Arness of *Gunsmoke*. Did that ever give you problems with casting directors?

GRAVES: No, because we never worked together—and that was a deliberate decision on my part. So few people recognized the connection. We're both tall, but the resemblance ends there. We keep in touch mostly by phone. We've never been up for the same role, I think, and Jim loves doing his westerns. I'm hoping Dad would be proud of both of us.

BAWDEN: I used to watch *Fury* on NBC every Saturday morning, beginning in 1955.

GRAVES: A fine kids' show. NBC put a lot of dough into it for a Saturday morning show and we wound up making 116 episodes over six seasons. We only went off because costs increased every year. But the audience grew every season. The best actor was Highland Dale, who played Fury. What an actor, although he did have a bevy of stand-ins for action shots. He always did the close-ups. Leon Fromkess and Irving Cummings Jr. were the producers. They hired a lot of old familiar faces: Tom Keene, Addison Richards, Dabbs Greer, Slim Pickens. Big-name TV directors like Lesley Selander and Earl Bellamy were used. Bobby Diamond was our star and when he grew up he became a lawyer and a darned good one, with a rather theatrical approach to courtroom affairs. My one caveat: if only they had shot in color it might be seen more these days.

BAWDEN: How did you get on *Mission: Impossible* in 1967?

GRAVES: I had what they wanted. I was a TV name by that time and reliable. Steven Hill was the star the first year, but not available after 4 p.m. Fridays because of his Orthodox Jewish faith. And Steve also balked at some of the action bits he was required to do. There were five remaining episodes and his character was gradually written out. I came on in 1968 and I said I'd work around the clock if need be. And by season two the unit was using virtually the same agents in every episode: Barbara Bain as Cinnamon, Greg Morris as Barnaby, Peter Lupus as Willy, and Martin Landau as Rollin—although I do remember some guest stars as agents, too. Landau had been a guest star in the first season, but became a regular in the second and he added that touch of class. Lee Meriwether joined us in the fourth year and Lesley Anne Warren came in the fifth year.

BAWDEN: Why did the show become such a hit?

GRAVES: It was well made. [Bruce] Geller was a hands-on producer who liked everything to be top notch. We were on Sundays at 10—one of the

Peter Graves (*center*) with the cast of *Mission: Impossible,* circa 1970. James Bawden collection.

most-watched hours on network TV—so we had better be good. The Cold War was still raging. That made it relevant and many of the episodes were partly based on factual cases. I'm told that employees of the CIA were told to watch every episode so they could learn something. And we certainly did other stories, including fighting third world baddies. There were stories about trying to infiltrate a neo-Nazi revival in Germany. Somebody later noticed there were few gun incidents and that was deliberate. There are better ways to snuff out the enemy.

BAWDEN: Why do you think it faltered in the fifth season?

GRAVES: Our new producer, Bruce Lansbury, was aware we were running out of new story material. People still watched because they expected certain things. Locations in Los Angeles were hardly conducive to the mainly European locales. We used campuses in Pasadena a lot and the Brentwood campus of Mount St. Mary's, and we once used discarded sets from *Hogan's Heroes*. Yes, that's true. Geller wasn't around anymore and Paramount was complaining about the rising costs. A lot of expensive sets were built, only to be blown up in the story lines. Producer Bruce Lansbury had a problem in getting fresh story lines but also keeping the personality of the series. We lasted seven seasons, which says a lot.

BAWDEN: There was a revival of the show, but in Australia? Explain, please.

GRAVES: I was the only cast regular to return in 1988 in Australia. But we got Greg Morris and Lynda Day George back as guest stars. And don't forget Bob Johnson, who voiced the Tape! The time was fifteen years after the original and I resumed my performance as Jim Phelps. There was a writers' strike in L.A. so ABC decided to revive it far from US shores. Scripts [from the original series] were used, but updated to more modern realities. When the strike ended, they were able to use originals. Yes, there was an establishing shot of San Francisco and the Aussie accents of some cast members were disconcerting. But it could have lasted longer with a better time slot. [The revived version ran from 1988 to 1990.]

BAWDEN: I like your portrayal of Palmer Kirby in *The Winds of War* [1983]. You are still keeping busy.

GRAVES: That was a fascinatingly flawed character and most scenes were with Polly Bergen in brave dramatic form. I do *Fantasy Island* every year, *Love Boat, Murder, She Wrote*. I even did a *Lucy*. I've narrated sixteen episodes of *Biography*. I'm a TV star and not a movie star, so I can work in my chosen medium as often as I'm asked.

Afterword

Peter Graves's last professional work was as a commercial spokesman in TV ads and as the narrator of video games. He was married only once, to Joan

Endress, from 1950 to his death. They had three daughters. Graves won a Golden Globe Award in 1971 for his performance in *Mission: Impossible* and a prime-time Emmy Award in 1997 for his hosting work on *Biography*. He has a star on the Hollywood Walk of Fame.

Graves suffered a heart attack and died on March 14, 2010, four days before his birthday. He was eighty-three.

Lorne Greene

Interview by James Bawden

Though Canada has generated some truly great films and TV programs over the past century, it has always had to deal with the problem of Hollywood draining off the Canadian talent pool and turning Canadian actors into American movie and TV stars.

It's been happening ever since Canada's Mary Pickford became "America's Sweetheart" in the silent days. It's easy to understand why Canadians do so well in America: there isn't much physical difference between a Canadian and an American. Nobody questioned the fact that Canada's Raymond Massey was so convincing playing American president Abraham Lincoln that he almost always was up for the role anytime anyone needed another Abe Lincoln. Did anybody question the presence of Canadian-born Glenn Ford on the faculty of an urban American high school in 1955's *The Blackboard Jungle*?

In television, Canadians have always made a big impact, from Massey as the mentor of Richard Chamberlain in *Dr. Kildare* to Michael J. Fox as the quintessential right-wing American teen boy in *Family Ties*.

Certainly among the most beloved of all Canadian-born TV stars was Lorne Greene, the leading player in one of the most successful TV westerns of all time—*Bonanza*. From that long-running series, Greene went on to play the leading role in *Griff*, a modern detective series that lasted only one season, and then returned in the original *Battlestar Galactica*, the expensive science fiction series in which he leaped from the boss man of a huge frontier ranch to the boss man of a fantastic spacecraft of the future. That show ran a few seasons, became a cult favorite, and finally was brought back to life on cable television with an all-new cast.

Greene's story of success is an unusual and fascinating one: he emerged from radio, where he was best known for his work in news and documentaries, and had a brief run as a player in feature films before TV beckoned.

Setting the Scene

I first met and interviewed Lorne Greene when I was a newly installed summer student at the *Toronto Globe and Mail* in 1971. Greene and his wife were being feted at a lavish ball at Toronto's Four Seasons Hotel by the Canadian Jewish Congress. The event turned into a night of anecdotes and reminiscences by old pals from past decades.

Greene was jovial, and he invited me onto the set of *Bonanza* the next time I was in L.A. That was in June 1972 on the old Paramount lot as he prepared to shoot a scene on the western street originally built for Alan Ladd's movies.

We met again in Pebble Beach in Northern California in June 1973 when he spent a day chatting up visiting TV critics for his short-lived cop series *Griff.* I interviewed him again on the set of *Battlestar Galactica* in 1978.

We talked later on the set of his next short-run series, *Code Red,* in 1979. Finally, we met in a Toronto dubbing studio in 1982 where he was recording narration for a nature series, *Lorne Greene's New Wilderness.*

The Interview

BAWDEN: Tell me how you got started.

GREENE: I was born in 1915 in Ottawa. My birth name is Lyon Chaim Green and dad Daniel was a shoemaker and a damn fine one. My parents were Russian Jewish immigrants to this great capital city. My parents called me Chaim and I switched to Lorne in public school because it seemed more Anglo. I was the drama teacher at Camp Arowhon in Algonquin Park for several summers and I started on radio at Queen's University in Kingston on our radio station CFRC. I graduated in chemical engineering, but various teachers said how deep and powerful my voice was for a kid of twenty. I then had my first paid job as an announcer at CBC Radio before joining the Royal Canadian Air Force as a flier.

BAWDEN: My parents remembered hearing you announce the CBC Radio evening news and they remembered your nickname: the Voice of Doom.

GREENE (*laughing*): That's because every night there seemed to be another disaster. I mean, Canadians were expiring daily so one had to be extremely sympathetic—and authoritative. Remember, I only was the announcer. A staff of writers presented me with a finished script. I'd read once for time and

185

Lorne Greene with Richard Hatch in *Battlestar Galactica*. Courtesy of ABC publicity.

they'd change stuff. I was not allowed to change a word. The worst part was the ending: the list of Canadians killed that day.

BAWDEN: The bios of you say you invented a stopwatch that ran backwards.

GREENE: I needed it because every second of unused airtime was precious. No pre-taping! We'd get war reports from CBC's Matthew Halton in the field sent via short wave and these went onto huge acetate records. One night a record broke and I had to ad-lib until the next one could be plopped on. There were no commercials. It was like flying blind in a snowstorm. Not for the faint of heart!

BAWDEN: You also narrated documentaries.

GREENE: The most famous was the National Film Board of Canada documentary *Fighting Norway* in 1943.

BAWDEN: After the war?

GREENE: I set up my own school for announcers in Toronto. TV stations needed them, radio stations were growing. Several hundred young guys went through. I don't remember any women. It was that kind of a world. The most famous grad I guess was Leslie Nielsen.

BAWDEN: You started acting on live CBC Radio dramas?

GREENE. Yes—and then I auditioned for Katharine Cornell in 1953. She hired me for *The Prescott Proposals,* which ran at the Broadhurst Theatre, which was set at the United Nations and had the wonderful British character star Felix Aylmer in tow. Kath played a U.N. delegate—I'm not sure we learned her name. In one scene I have to grab her and take her around the waist. Couldn't do it. She was that stout by this time. And she laughed merrily and said, "Okay, no more cheesecake!" Her husband Guthrie McClintic wasn't directing her, but Howard Lindsay, who cowrote with Russell Crouse, and she seemed out of sorts.

In 1955, I went to Canada's Stratford and was Brutus in *Julius Caesar* and Morocco in *The Merchant of Venice*. In 1957, I tried again on Broadway with *Speaking of Murder* with Brenda de Banzie, Neva Patterson, and Estelle Winwood. We lasted twenty-seven performances. The very next year José Ferrer chose me as costar in the play *Edwin Booth*. Robert Carroll was John Wilkes Booth and other Canadians in the cast included Lois Smith and Anne Helm. We went twenty-four performances. I have so far declined any more Broadway offers. Or maybe it's because there were none!

BAWDEN: Your first movie part was in *The Silver Chalice* [1954]?

GREENE: That's the one where Paul Newman took out newspaper ads of apology when it first ran on TV. And yes, it is that bad. Then I was in a dandy little policier—*Tight Spot* [1955], one of Ginger Rogers's last flicks. But Eddie Robinson stole every scene he was in, much to Ginger's dismay.

In 1956, I was the nasty daddy in *Autumn Leaves*. Joan Crawford is in love with the much younger Cliff Robertson and I'm trying to drive him crazy. One day we were on location and Joan had a memory block. She ran sobbing to her portable dressing room, claiming a front tooth had become loose. Director Bob Aldrich assigned me to get her. We sat in that little van for what seemed hours as Joan seethed away. Finally she asked me if I thought she should do Broadway. I could have told the truth and flatly said no, but I said I thought it would be a grand idea and she liked it and her confidence came back. But she never tackled the stage. She was petrified of the crowds who'd assemble each day on location just to see her.

BAWDEN: Your TV credits go way back.

GREENE: I was on Canadian TV from the get-go in 1952. In the US, I did a *Philip Morris Playhouse* in 1953 that was live. I was on *Danger* in 1955. My favorite early series was *You Are There*, re-creations of favorite moments [from history] where Walter Cronkite suddenly appears to question the subject. I was Beethoven on one of those, William Pitt and Charles Stewart Parnell in others. Live! And lots of fun.

BAWDEN: But your first series lead was in—

GREENE: *Sailor of Fortune.* It was made in Britain and Canada and sold in syndication to US markets in 1957 and I was Captain Grant "Mitch" Mitchell. Christopher Lee was in one, I recall, and lots of lesser Brits who just needed a paycheck. Lasted twenty-six episodes before Elstree Films pulled the plug.

BAWDEN: You guest-starred on a lot of TV westerns before starring in the biggest one of all.

GREENE: I visited *Wagon Train, Bronco, Cheyenne, Maverick,* and also did all the other hits of the day from *Shirley Temple* to *Mike Hammer.* I even went back to Toronto for *Norman Corwin Presents.*

BAWDEN: How did you get the lead of Ben Cartwright in *Bonanza* in 1959?

GREENE: Did I know it would run fourteen seasons and 430 episodes? No! I just needed a well-paying steady job, and brother, did I get it. The creator was David Dortort and he doesn't get the credit he deserves. He had written and produced *The Restless Gun* in 1957, so he was riding high. Westerns were everywhere. NBC wanted a family saga western, and boy, did David deliver a beaut.

At the beginning, we were a most nasty bunch and NBC stepped in and asked David to show our common humanity. We evolved. At first the three sons were antagonistic to each other. I asked NBC to stress the team aspect, brother helping brother. In those days we had a full season's guarantee—thirty-nine episodes—so we worked on these problems, strengthened out the story lines, and

Lorne Greene (*right*) with *Bonanza* costars Dan Blocker (*left*) and Michael Landon (*center*). Courtesy of NBC and The Family Channel.

gradually built a relationship with the audience. *Gunsmoke* was our only rival in length of time on air and it, too, concentrated on human relationships.

We debuted Saturday nights at 7:30. It didn't work. Families were out grocery shopping on that night. NBC hunkered down and we spent a second season there. In 1961, we moved to Sundays at 9, which remained our true home, and we bumped off *G.E. Theatre*, which had been on CBS for years. Host Ronald Reagan saw me at a party and was steamed his show got ditched. CBS tried everything against us: Judy Garland, *Perry Mason*, Garry Moore—we blew them all away.

BAWDEN: Tell me about the casting.

GREENE: David thought originally I was too young for the role! I was! So I played older. After all, Pa Cartwright had three sons by three different marriages. David thought the fact I had Shakespeare training wonderful. Pernell Roberts was second casting choice—as Adam, a very thoughtful, serious guy. He finally came to me in some anguish saying he was quitting the series because he was afraid of losing his theatrical training if he stayed away any longer. I told him to sign for three more years and then he could own his own theater, but he left and when I later saw him onstage with Ingrid Bergman I knew he'd made the right choice.

Dan Blocker was always the heart and soul of the series—all was lost [when he died]. He couldn't be replaced. Michael Landon came from *I Was a Teenage Werewolf* [1957] and matured into a dazzling talent who would later produce and direct. He got buckets of fan mail from the girlies.

There never was any rivalry on set. We liked each other. We still keep in touch. But may I salute the directors: Chris Nyby, Joseph Sargent, Bill Claxton, Lewis Allen. They worked very slowly, meticulously, and no producer ever told them to hurry it up. We weren't that big into guest stars, but I do remember fondly Mercedes McCambridge, Joan Hackett, Bill Demarest. I even remember Ted Knight in there. The weirdest casting had to be Marlo Thomas as the little Chinese mail-order bride Tai Lee.

Technical details were remarkable for a weekly hour: Dario Piazza did over a hundred shows as wardrobe head, Bob Miles headed stunts, Haskell Boggs on camera was a master of light and shadows. I thought we were the best-produced show on series TV at that time. Still do.

BAWDEN: Remember the day at Paramount when I visited and you were out on the Alan Ladd western street and I said I felt something amiss?

GREENE: It was designed three-quarter size because Ladd was so small! I looked like King Kong going down that street! And we had a big ranch where we shot the action stuff. We'd shoot action for two or three episodes, day after day. People always ask me why Pa wore the same clothes every day. And I tell them he was a working cowboy. Who needed to dress up? But also we'd shoot the action out of sequence so the last thing we should worry about was wardrobe.

I remember at the Emmy Awards one year I was presenter with the great Barbara Stanwyck. And she bent over laughing—live on TV—when I wondered if we shouldn't amalgamate our two spreads into one gigantic ranch. [Stanwyck played the female owner of a similar big ranch on her own show, *The Big Valley*.] Afterwards, backstage, she snapped, "Don't you ever ad-lib again in my presence" and stormed off. You see, I had broken her poise.

BAWDEN: When do you think the series started to wind down?

GREENE: The day Dan Blocker died, suddenly, tragically. I remember the date: May 13, 1972. He told me he was going to have routine gall bladder surgery and died of a pulmonary embolism. We even mentioned Hoss's passing in a beautifully textured script the next year. But we couldn't last without our moral compass and our fourteenth season ended early on January 16, 1973. Did you know they named a beach in his memory out at Malibu? People still ask me about him all the time.

BAWDEN: American critics recently gave you a rough time at a press conference. What was that about?

GREENE: It all came down to questions about my citizenship. Why aren't I an American citizen? I kept explaining my dual citizenship, but some didn't want to listen. I can take it. I pay my fair share of US income taxes.

I guess the strangest time came when *Bonanza* started and one publicist asked me not to mention I was Jewish. She said having two Jews riding the range—her words—might test American tolerance. The other was Michael Landon. But nobody ever brought it up!

BAWDEN: Why go into another series [*Griff*] so quickly?

GREENE: Because I like to work. But is it too soon? *Bonanza* closed down only nine months ago. The scripts are solid enough—producer Gary Cohen promised me well-written mysteries. I'm partnered by Ben Murphy, and Vic Tayback is also around. But there is the opposition: Carol Burnett on CBS. So I'm not sure how long we can hang on until viewers discover us. It's not like the old days with a full season to get it just right. [*Griff* was yanked after only twelve episodes, with ratings in the cellar.]

[Lorne and I talked again in 1978 on the set of his newest series, *Battlestar Galactica.*]

BAWDEN: Here we go again.

GREENE: This one is already being advertised as *Bonanza in Outer Space.* Glen Larson created it, and Richard Hatch, Dirk Benedict are the younger costars. You know, the network assigns a physician to do all the checkups and she was surprised I'm only sixty-one. She thought with *Bonanza* starting almost twenty years back I'd be well over seventy. Yes, the sets are impressive but this one focuses firmly on family values. [That series lasted twenty-one episodes and was replaced by *Galactica 1980,* which ran twelve episodes. The series was revived many years later as a cable series and was finally a rousing success.]

[My next meeting with Greene was in 1981 on the set of yet another series, *Code Red.*]

BAWDEN: We've got to stop meeting like this.

GREENE: This one will be a hit. I guarantee that. I'm Joe Rorchek, thirty years with the L.A. Fire Department, and Andrew Stevens is my son, Julie Adams my lovely wife. The questions at the press conference to date were all about [fellow cast member] Sam Jones and the nude spread he did for *Playgirl.* I agree this one is a sort of fire version of *Emergency.* It's shot mostly on locations. Now, as always, it's the opposition one has to worry about. And we're up against *60 Minutes.* [*Code Red* lasted nineteen weeks before cancellation.]

[My final chat with Greene was back in Toronto in 1982 when he was doing his final series, *Lorne Greene's New Wilderness.*]

GREENE: I'm happy to be home. I'm happy to still be active. I never did get the movie career I craved. I played Ava Gardner's father in *Earthquake* [1974] and when I told her I was a mere six years older than her, she roared with laughter. One of the great broads of the business and I sired her when I was aged six? But I was in some pretty big TV miniseries: *Roots* [1977] and *The Moneychangers* [1976]. I've even been on *The Love Boat* several times. I really have no shame. If you ask me my favorite piece of acting I'll say a 1971 TV movie, *The Harness* by John Steinbeck, costarring Julie Sommars. Check it out. Academics write me letters about that one. Now I'm working on ecological matters in my new nature show produced by my talented son. So we'll just see where that takes me.

Afterword

Lorne Greene was married twice—first to Canadian Rita Hands from 1938 to 1960. They had two children—twins Charles and Belinda. After they divorced, Greene married Nancy Deale in 1961. They had a daughter, Gillian.

Greene built a home in Mesa, Arizona, that was an exact replica of the Ponderosa ranch manor house he occupied in *Bonanza.*

Greene died in Santa Monica, California, on September 21, 1987, from pneumonia after heart surgery. He was seventy-two.

Julie Harris

Interview by James Bawden

Julie Harris was already on her way to becoming one of the great ladies of the American theater when she began to work in live television drama in the late 1940s. It was a natural place for young Broadway stars: television drama was much like live theater then, peopled with many Broadway players because the great TV drama showcases originated from New York City.

Perhaps for that reason, Harris rose rapidly in the theater world while she also was gaining greater renown in television drama. Her reputation in theater is still a towering one. She was nominated ten times for a Tony Award and won five times, starting with her 1952 win as the first Sally Bowles in *I Am a Camera*, the play that was turned into the musical *Cabaret* and provided a career-making role as Sally for Liza Minnelli.

During the same years, Harris was conquering other media as well as television, where she ultimately earned eleven Emmy nominations and two wins—for *Little Moon of Alban* (1958) and *Victoria Regina* (1961). She made her movie debut in the film version of her Broadway hit *Member of the Wedding* (1952), earning an Oscar nomination for Best Actress. In 1955, she reprised her Tony-winning role in the movie version of *I Am a Camera* and played James Dean's love interest in the 1955 movie *East of Eden*. The recording industry even gave her a Grammy for her audio version of her 1977 Tony Award–winning performance in *The Belle of Amherst*.

And yet a generation of Americans probably remember her best for her supporting role as country singer Lilimae Clements in CBS's popular prime-time soap opera *Knots Landing* (1979–1993).

Setting the Scene

My interview with Julie Harris took place in 1987 at a cocktail party for TV critics with the cast and crew of CBS's *Knots Landing* in Los Angeles.

193

Julie Harris in *Knots Landing,* circa 1981. Courtesy of Lorimar Telepictures.

I had arranged to be seated next to her at the event, and fortunately, nobody else wanted to talk with her one-on-one that night, no doubt because they were more eager to talk with the hot young stars of the prime-time serial drama. As it turned out, that was their loss because Julie Harris certainly had a lot to say.

The Interview

BAWDEN: I sat in on the mass press conference you gave this morning to announce you were joining the cast of *Knots Landing*. But one particular question really irked you.

HARRIS: I was asked if I minded wasting my prime doing TV when I could be starring on Broadway.

BAWDEN: Your answer was priceless.

HARRIS: I pointed out I'd been doing TV since 1948. And *Knots Landing* has great TV actors in the cast. More people will see me in just one episode than in all the plays I've ever done. That's the power of TV.

BAWDEN: I first saw you onstage at Canada's Stratford Festival in 1960. We were studying *Romeo and Juliet* in the tenth grade and there was a trainload of high schoolers from Toronto who arrived at the Stratford rail station just before the Wednesday matinee. I was so impressed—but also shocked to discover you really were not aged twelve.

HARRIS: I was a thirty-five-year old Juliet. You could do that onstage. No close-ups! And I was one of the few Americans ever invited to Canada's Stratford. My costar was a marvelous young Italian Canadian actor, Bruno Gerussi. He later had a hit on CBC-TV in the series *The Beachcombers* that ran, or so I'm told, nineteen seasons. But I'm rather peeved I was never asked back. I think I would have made a dandy Lady Macbeth.

BAWDEN: After the performance you did a Q and A session with the student audience. I remember you told us your son wanted to be a champion swimmer. And when one student told you the way his English teacher had thought of Juliet, you ran off the stage and up to the astonished teacher and said, "You're wrong!"

HARRIS: I don't remember that. I was one of the few Americans invited to play at Stratford. Ray Massey, who was a Canadian, never even got an invite. I thought I'd be a grand Lady Macbeth but eventually that great Canadian actress Kate Reid aced that part.

BAWDEN: Did you always want to be an actress?

HARRIS: I was born in Grosse Pointe, Michigan, in 1925 and I guess I got the urge by listening to a lot of radio dramas, particularly Helen Hayes's CBS Radio broadcasts. My parents were horrified. My mother tried to gently tell me that with my red hair and freckles it was out of the question. I have two brothers and they turned out normal. I finally went to Yale School of

Drama, but only for the first year. As soon as I got my first acting job, I quit. One cannot teach the art of acting. Either you've got it or you should seek employment elsewhere. These days I tell prospective actors to stop waiting tables in Manhattan and go to a regional theater to get some experience.

BAWDEN: Your first TV credit came in 1948?

HARRIS: It was for a CBS anthology series titled *Actor's Studio*. Other unknowns in it were Maureen Stapleton and Johnny Straub. The title of the episode was "The Giant's Stair." I remember nothing of the plot at all. I did three more of these in 1949 and then I made the special *Bernice Bobs Her Hair* in 1951 for *Starlight Theater* and then I was in several *Goodyear Playhouse* shows. All live. Very few people had TV sets then. I certainly never saw any of them. It was opening and closing in a play all at once.

BAWDEN: Tell me about making your first movie, *Member of the Wedding*, in 1952.

HARRIS: Directed by Fred Zinnemann. I'd made my Broadway debut in *Henry IV, Part II* in a part so tiny I'm listed as "performer." I did a lot of these little parts, but in 1950 I finally had the lead as Frankie in *Member of the Wedding*. The great Harold Clurman directed and we had this great success. Playing a twelve-year old was possible because I was distanced from the audience. But in the movies this was difficult. Also my costar, Brandon De Wilde, was two years older by the time of the movie and not quite as precocious. But Ethel Waters was supreme. And to this day Fred says it's his favorite film. I doubt it made back its costs. Today it would be an art house movie and play in tiny cinemas. Stanley Kramer produced it and it was one of the reasons he left Columbia. I think basically it was a filmed play and that's that. I did get an Oscar nomination.

BAWDEN: Then came *East of Eden*.

HARRIS: It was filmed in 1954 before Jimmy Dean went on to make *Rebel without a Cause*. If you ask me, I was a bit too old to play Sabra, but Gadge [Elia] Kazan said he needed a stabilizing veteran to work with Jimmy, who had no experience fronting such a big picture. Ray Massey as the father just hated Jimmy. Said he was immature. Which is true. But Jimmy had such heart. Gadge first tested Paul Newman as the older brother Aron, but he was too dominating. So Richard Davalos was used and Gadge ordered them to room together so they'd know each other as brothers do. Dick came to loathe Jimmy. Ray hated all the tricks Gadge had to use to get that great performance out of Jimmy. To this day Ray does not believe Jimmy could have sustained a long career. I like to think he could have under the right circumstances.

The press misinterpreted what I said when I admitted I was in love with Jimmy during filming. But I meant I really was in love with his character, Cal. It would be too painful to rewatch it today. Jimmy's gone. So is Brandon from *Member of the Wedding*, so I try to avoid it, too, when it runs on TV.

BAWDEN: Didn't *East of Eden* make you hot in the movie world?

HARRIS: In a word, no. I then did *I Am a Camera*, which was shot in England because it was cheaper. Nobody mentions this one these days because it has been surpassed by the musical version, *Cabaret*. I liked being Sally, but I hated acting opposite Laurence Harvey—and Shelley Winters was just plainly out of her comfort zone. I think it made money because it was considered very racy for 1955.

BAWDEN: The same year you went back to live TV.

HARRIS: The first was an hour version of *A Wind from the South* for *The United States Steel Hour*, directed by Canadian Daniel Petrie. And I conquered my fear of live TV right then and there. And I went on to star in live versions of *The Good Fairy* [1956], *The Lark* [1957], and *Johnny Belinda* [1958].

BAWDEN: Didn't you do two separate versions of *The Lark*?

HARRIS: No. You are thinking of *Little Moon of Alban*, which I first did, live, for George Schaefer in 1958. Others in it included Chris Plummer. I never saw it. Then George phoned me up in 1964 and we did it all again with Dirk Bogarde, only this time it was taped. I think it was better because we'd do one scene at a time with multiple cameras. And then catch our breath, and that took about a week to tape.

BAWDEN: How did you get to costar in the movie version of *Requiem for a Heavyweight* [1962]?

HARRIS: I was available and I was cheap. I hadn't done a movie in awhile. I was billed fourth behind Tony Quinn, Jackie Gleason, and Mickey Rooney. Tony was bigger than life, often hard to work against. Jackie never wanted to rehearse and Mickey was all over the place. I'm told the TV version, which ran live, is better, but I never saw it. My character was so prim I thought she might emerge as a stereotype. It was made quickly and efficiently and made its money back but not much else.

BAWDEN: I would love to see the TV version of *The Power and the Glory*, done in 1961.

HARRIS: Me, too. It was filmed, not taped, in a Brooklyn studio using multiple cameras and starred Larry Olivier, as he insisted on being called. The cast included George C. Scott, little Patty Duke, Roddy McDowall, and we did it all within a few weeks. Larry was sailing back to England on a certain date. That meant we went well into the night. Marc Daniels directed it; David Susskind was the producer and he sold it everywhere. I think the reviews were kind but nobody has mentioned this one to me in decades.

BAWDEN: Explain why *The Haunting* [1963] remains your favorite movie.

HARRIS: Because it just worked. The budget was $1 million, so our great director, Bob Wise, shot it in a real house in England. There was no budget for special effects, so this made everything very interior. I read one article where Claire Bloom says I was standoffish. And that's true. I couldn't slip out of my character and be all palsy back at the hotel. I was Eleanor the spinster, repressed and belittled by her own family, at the hotel every night. I thought Claire, with her great beauty, just aced it, and Russ Tamblyn and Richard Johnson were also great. It enjoyed a modest success at the time, but has grown in stature. More people ask me about it than *East of Eden* these days. Lately I have taken not to see it when it runs on *The Late Show*. It truly creeps me out these days!

BAWDEN: You had a reunion with Shelley Winters on *Harper* [1966].

HARRIS: Also with Paul Newman. I tested with him when he was trying to get the part of Aron in *East of Eden*. I liked my part, which was small. I liked my paycheck, which was bigger. I read the book, *The Moving Target*, by Ross Macdonald. I was a junkie who liked jazz. You do know it was originally written for Frank Sinatra [in the leading role]? It was nice to be in such a big hit.

BAWDEN: Talk about *Reflections in a Golden Eye* [1967].

HARRIS: It could have been great. But it was a box office disaster. Liz Taylor accepted it so she could costar with her old pal Monty Clift. And she put up her salary as collateral because Monty was so sick. Then Monty died of a heart attack and Liz had cast approval. She vetoed her husband, Richard Burton, meaning that marriage was on the rocks. Marlon Brando [who took over the lead role] told me he was doing it for the money and he was guaranteed 10 percent of the gross. I bluntly told Marlon he was ruining his reputation with so many bad movies [and should] return to the stage and he got teary eyed and said he'd lost it. I think I really tried. Brian Keith was my husband [in the movie]. What an underrated actor! I don't think [the director] John Huston was up to this one. He didn't have the energy and it never came together. Perhaps the story was unfilmable all along.

BAWDEN: You started doing a lot of TV.

HARRIS: Oh, I was promiscuous, I really was! The same year as *Reflections* I did a slew of guest appearances on the TV hit *Tarzan*. I was in *Daniel Boone* [1968], *Bonanza* [1968], *The Big Valley* [1968], *The Name of the Game* [1969]. And I discovered I loved series TV, I was always treated beautifully.

Barbara Stanwyck was shocked at my quarters and ordered a full trailer for me during my week's stint on her TV western.

BAWDEN: And you jumped into TV movies.

HARRIS: *The People Next Door* [1970]. I loved acting with Eli Wallach. I liked *The Last of Mrs. Lincoln* [1976]; I was Emily Dickinson in the TV version of *The Belle of Amherst* [1976]. Just before I did *Knots Landing* I was on *The Love Boat* [1987] and I had a ball. And I loved Arlene Dahl and Peter Graves! Such a hoot!

BAWDEN: I saw you on Broadway in 1979 in your big hit *Forty Carats*, but you did not get the movie version.

HARRIS: We were playing to packed houses and producer Mike Frankovich comes backstage to tell me he's bought the movie rights and Audrey Hepburn is going to do it. Well, she hadn't made a movie in a decade. And she demanded Mike shoot everything in Rome, where she lived, and he finally backed off and used Liv Ullman and the movie just tanked. And that was a sort of sweet revenge!

BAWDEN: Talk about *Knots Landing*.

HARRIS: They pay me $20,000 an episode. Some weeks I get just one scene. It's a wonderful life. They put me up in a grand hotel. Meaning clean sheets every day and I don't have to do any cooking. Joan Van Ark, who plays my daughter, first interviewed me as a fifteen-year old. And I later got her into Yale School of Drama. Alec Baldwin is my crazy son. He'll be a full-blown star one day. I love this repertory feeling. You know, we're the one country in the world without a national theatrical company. Well, serials like *Knots Landing* fill that void. Everywhere I go people call me Lilimae and I love that.

BAWDEN: What's next?

HARRIS: More theater, more high-priced cameos. I'm into my anecdotage and I like playing slightly dotty old ladies. I really do.

Afterword

Julie Harris was married and divorced three times—Jay Johnson (1946–1954), Manning Gurian (1954–1967), and Walter Carroll (1977–1982). She had a son, Peter Gurian, by her second husband. In 2002, she was given the Lifetime Achievement Tony Award and in 2005 was a Kennedy Center Honors recipient.

Harris died of congestive heart failure on August 24, 2013, at her home in West Chatham, Massachusetts. She was eighty-seven.

Art Linkletter

Interview by Ron Miller

You could argue endlessly over who was the all-time king or queen of prime time in television's golden age, but there shouldn't be much debate over who ruled in the daytime. In my opinion, that would be Art Linkletter. After all, his *House Party with Art Linkletter* ran for twenty-four years, first on radio and then on television.

Like his only real rival, Arthur Godfrey, Linkletter came from a long, solid background in radio—and also had phenomenal success in carrying over his daytime popularity with female viewers to prime-time television, where a large audience of both men and women flocked to his *People Are Funny* program. That series began in 1942 on radio and finally ended its nineteen-year run as a television show in 1961.

As if that were not enough, Linkletter also was a successful author whose *Kids Say the Darndest Things* was a best-selling book, inspired by the segment of his daytime show in which he interviewed little kids, often with hilarious results. What's more, that segment became a show of its own in the 1990s, produced by Linkletter and hosted by comedian Bill Cosby.

Along the way, Linkletter also parlayed his radio and TV fame into a number of roles in movies, sometimes playing himself, as he did in the movie version of *People Are Funny* (1946), but occasionally playing characters sort of like himself in films like *Champagne for Caesar* (1950) with Ronald Colman.

What makes the Linkletter success story even more amazing is the fact that he was abandoned by his parents as an infant, and then adopted by a Canadian minister and his wife, whose own children had died. Linkletter did not know he was adopted and that his real name was Gordon Arthur Kelly until he was twelve. As the adopted son of a traveling preacher who seldom stayed in the same community very long, Linkletter learned quite early to take care of himself and to develop an open and earnest persona that people found attractive.

Art Linkletter. Courtesy of PBS publicity.

Linkletter first distinguished himself as a host and announcer at various fairs and public events. That led to doing the same thing on radio, and soon he was in great demand as a host or master of ceremonies on American radio.

His ingratiating, wholesome manner made him especially popular with female listeners and viewers. Over time, his clever investments and amazing durability as a performer helped make him a very rich man whose best friends were giants of show business like Walt Disney and even political leaders like his old pal Ronald Reagan.

Setting the Scene

Art Linkletter was like family to me, as he was to many youngsters who grew up in the 1940s. I mean, he was in my house just about every day, either on the radio or on television. My mother thought he was like a friend because he was so nice to all those strangers he got to know on his programs and because he seemed to personify all the good qualities one hopes to find in a man.

My only interview with Art Linkletter came in 1998 when he agreed to take part in the publicity effort CBS was making on behalf of *Kids Say the Darndest Things* when Linkletter and CBS turned the old *House Party* segment into a weekly prime-time series with Bill Cosby. Linkletter also made appearances on the program to show film clips of some of his classic talks with children on his old daytime show. I asked to meet privately with Linkletter for an interview and I suspect he agreed because he knew I was from the San Francisco Bay Area, which had played a major part in the start of his show business career. He turned out to be a good-natured, extremely likeable man, just as I had hoped he'd be from all those years I'd been watching him on TV.

The Interview

MILLER: You always seemed at ease with an audience, whether it was a studio audience in radio or an audience on camera in your TV days. Was that natural for you from the start?

LINKLETTER: Being a preacher's son makes you accustomed to being in front of audiences. I worked with my father on a very important part of his Sunday service: the collection.

MILLER: I've heard some people say that you need your audience in order to be at your best.

LINKLETTER: Well, that may be true. I did four feature films and six TV movies. I didn't like the lack of an audience, the repetition of rehearsals, and having to pretend I was someone else.

MILLER: Looking at your long run in radio and then television, you could almost say you've been doing the same sort of thing all those years. How did you happen to find such a comfortable groove for your career?

LINKLETTER: When I started in radio, there had never been a talk show. Ralph Edwards and I originated the "stunt" shows [like Edwards's *Truth or Consequences* and Linkletter's *People Are Funny*]. Before I came on the network [CBS] I did all kinds of quiz and game shows. [He explained that his ability to work with a live studio audience evolved out of all that experience, so he stuck with it.]

MILLER: You have a reputation as a shrewd businessman. Did that also come naturally to you?

LINKLETTER: I like to make my own deals. I've never had an agent. That caused a little problem with my old friend Walt Disney. The opening of his Disneyland was a seminal moment. He asked me to be the master of ceremonies for the official opening show. He asked me to pick two of my friends to be on the air with me, so I picked Ronnie Reagan and Bob Cummings. He had taken me to the site picked for the development before it was built. We spent an hour on dirt roads getting there and I didn't think much of it at the time. Finally, when the park was built we had to talk about the deal for me as his emcee. Walt said, "Art, I'm embarrassed to have to negotiate with you because we're such good friends. Why don't you have an agent like everyone else in Hollywood?" Walt said he'd had lots of cost overruns and probably couldn't afford me. So I said, "Why not just pay me union scale"—which was $220 at the time—"and give me the photo concession at the park—the right to sell all film and cameras at Disneyland for ten years?" He readily agreed—and it probably turned out to be highest price ever paid for a two-hour job!

MILLER: I've been watching you on TV for most of my life and I have to say I'm astounded that you still look like the same man I first saw in my youth. What's your secret?

LINKLETTER: I probably had good genes, although I don't really know about that for sure. [He never knew his birth parents.] I always took good care of myself. Originally, I wanted to be an athlete. I was Pacific Coast backstroke champion at one time and tried out for the Olympic swimming team in 1932. I'm in the Hall of Fame for basketball at San Diego State University. I never smoked and I never drank. In fact, I worked out for twenty minutes before I came down here [for the interview]. I have a good lifestyle and don't let stress bother me. I started on CBS in 1933 and I'm still here. That's longer than Bob Hope was on NBC.

MILLER: The show that really put you on the map was *House Party*, but your most famous part of the show was the segment where you interviewed children—and as I recall, it was just a small part of the program.

LINKLETTER: *House Party* was one of the first magazine shows on television. We had thirty-five different departments. We had lots of experts like Hedda Hopper and Edith Head, but the last five minutes was always the kids. These days I travel about two hundred thousand miles a year and lecture about seventy-five times. People always come up to me and tell me they watched my "kid show." I ask them, "What about the other stuff on the show?" and they don't remember it at all. That devastates me. But it was the only thing that had never been done before and hasn't been done much since.

MILLER: How did you first get the idea to do it?

LINKLETTER: I was trained in college as a schoolteacher and I always enjoyed talking to kids. I first started doing it in my own house in San Francisco, recording interviews with my son Jack, who was then about five. I used these big wax disks back then and was just doing it to keep for the family. At the time, I had a radio show called *Who's Dancing Tonight?* at the St. Francis Hotel in San Francisco. This was a time in the late 1930s and early 1940s when every big hotel in San Francisco had a big-name band. Everybody went out dancing. I'd stop people in the lobby and do interviews with them. One night I put a record on by mistake and out came the interview with Jack. Well, we got a lot of mail about that. So I went home and told my wife, "You know, we ought to do a show with kids." It was really the response to that local radio show that started the whole thing.

MILLER: When you had your network show and decided to add that segment, how did you figure out how to make it consistently entertaining?

LINKLETTER: It was so fresh to hear a kid saying unexpected things. I went for the aggressive kids. I told the teachers in the Los Angeles school system to pick the kids you'd like to have out of the classroom for two blessed hours. I didn't want the good kids who'd never said or done anything bad or made a fuss. I knew that even the aggressive kids who were show-offs would be intimidated a little bit by the lights and cameras, especially the inner-city kids who'd never even seen the inside of a place like CBS. Anyway, the board of education said, "You can't just take the kids from Beverly Hills schools."

MILLER: Did you quickly learn some no-nos about what to ask?

LINKLETTER: The first thing you should never do is ask them something they could answer with a "yes" or a "no." That question's dead, so you have to think of another one. You have to ask them for opinions. What animal would you like to be? What would you do if you were in an airplane and the pilot said you'd just run out of gas? What did your mother tell you not to say today?

MILLER: Did you get to talk to them first before the cameras were on them?

LINKLETTER: Oh, no, I never had a chance to pre-interview them. But I had a little help from the teacher we hired to go around and pick the children up in a limousine every day. On the way in, she'd listen to them as they talked to each other and if they said anything interesting, she'd write me a note about it. The note might say, "This boy's uncle has just been castrated" or whatever. If the uncle had just run off with the church organist, I'd ask him if any of his relatives had moved away recently. I couldn't just ask them, "What about your uncle?"

MILLER: I seem to remember some pretty risqué answers from the kids.

LINKLETTER: We did very little censoring in those days. In those days, the network almost cut you off if you said "pregnant," but kids could get away with saying a lot of things. I asked one kid what he did that summer and he said he had to go to the hospital. So I asked him why and he said, "They circumcised me."

MILLER: Did they ever really shock you with an answer?

LINKLETTER: Once I asked a kid what animal he'd like to be and he said, "An octopus." Well, that surprised me, so I asked him why and he said, "There are a lot of bad boys in my class, so if I was an octopus I could reach out and grab them with my testicles." Well, when the laughter died down, I told him I was going to give him a little biology lesson today—that an octopus has eight *tentacles*. But he grabbed my arm and said, "No, Mr. Linkletter—testicles!"

MILLER: Were there times when the answers were just too honest?

LINKLETTER: Sometimes I'd ask why their teacher had picked them to be on the show and I'd get the real answers, like "My mother's the president of the PTA" or "My dad's the principal of the school."

MILLER: I seem to remember you rarely had a kid return to the show for a second time.

LINKLETTER: When kids came back, they were never as good because once they went home, everybody would tell them how funny they were, so next time they set out to be funny—and they weren't.

MILLER: Did any of the kids ever turn out to be somebody?

LINKLETTER: This one kid had a real deep voice that was amazing for a kid. He became a child actor named George "Foghorn" Winslow and was in several movies. Tom Hanks's wife, actress Rita Wilson, was on the show.

MILLER: Did you ever meet up with any of the kids after they'd grown up?

LINKLETTER: We wanted to find some of the kids as grownups to see what they looked like, but we had no idea where they were. We never kept track of them. We wanted to put them on the new show with Bill Cosby, but not one scrap of paper about them had been kept. So I went on KTLA [a local Los Angeles TV station] and asked for anybody who had been on the old show and wanted to be on the new show to call this number—and the switchboard lit up like a Christmas tree.

MILLER: How did that work out?

LINKLETTER: The reunion show was probably one of the highlights of my life. I kept asking to see the last pages of the script and those rascals kept telling me there were none yet. They just told me to walk out on the stage and Bill Cosby will talk and I should just ad-lib with him. Finally I came out and Bill asked me what I thought of the audience and I said it looked pretty good. That's when Bill said, "Everybody in the audience was a child on your show!" They all stood up. There were tears in my eyes. I'd been off the air for twenty-five years. Then they surged up onto the stage. Bill backed off and let me be surrounded. I was still on that stage with them a full hour after the show ended.

MILLER: I have to ask you why you didn't just host the new show yourself.

LINKLETTER: I did it for twenty-six years and interviewed twenty-seven thousand children. I'm not dying to do another show.

MILLER: Do you think the kids of today are different from the ones you used to interview?

LINKLETTER: The kids from age six on are so much more well informed. I'm talking about the eight-year-old whose grandparents ask them over to fix their video recorders. They're hip kids. But the little kids are the same as they've always been. Their whole world is about discovering things.

MILLER: After all these years and all that you've accomplished, do you have any unfulfilled ambitions?

LINKLETTER: My one unfulfilled ambition in life—and I used to tell Bill Paley [the founder of CBS] this over lunch—was I wanted to be one of the guys on *60 Minutes*. But Bill told me they could never allow a guy who sells products to be a newscaster.

MILLER: I'd say the whole daytime television world has changed quite a bit since you left. What do you think?

LINKLETTER: I think the best of television today is far better than anything we ever dreamed of—and the worst of television is far worse than anything we ever dreamed of. I mention one name: Jerry Springer. He wins it. He's the champion of the dysfunctional society. The only thing I can say in his defense is that you have to have an audience, so you have to criticize who's watching a show. When I hear that he's beating Oprah Winfrey in some cities, my opinion of the average viewer has gone down considerably.

MILLER: But I'm guessing you have no regrets about the way your TV career has gone.

LINKLETTER: It's been a wonderful life. If you spend your whole life doing what you want to do and can do well, you have no complaints.

Afterword

The revival of *Kids Say the Darndest Things* as a regular program was not a big success, but its failure did nothing to dim the already lustrous career of Linkletter, who was given a Lifetime Achievement Award by the Academy of Television Arts & Sciences in 2003 for his daytime television legacy. He has a star on the Hollywood Walk of Fame for his TV work.

Linkletter was a very generous philanthropist and also a major supporter of Republican political candidates. He campaigned loudly against drug use by young people after the suicide death of his youngest child, Diane. He claimed her leap from a tall building to her death was caused by her use of LSD, although no drugs of any kind were found in her body.

Linkletter was a devoted family man whose marriage to wife Lois in 1935 lasted nearly seventy-five years. They had five children. After he suffered a mild stroke in 2008, Linkletter's health declined and he died at his home in the Bel Air district of Los Angeles County on May 26, 2010. He was ninety-seven.

Mary Martin

Interview by James Bawden

If this book were about famous Broadway stars, there's little doubt whose picture would be on the cover: the immortal Mary Martin, who headlined two of the most celebrated Broadway musicals of all time, both from Rodgers and Hammerstein: *South Pacific* and *The Sound of Music*.

Though Martin had a decent enough fling at movie stardom—she shared billing with the likes of Bing Crosby, Jack Benny, and Cary Grant—she never duplicated her Broadway fame at the movie box office.

But Mary Martin is also a legendary TV star for one reason, if none other: her Emmy-winning performance in the title role of *Peter Pan*, the Broadway musical brought to television in a spectacular live telecast on March 7, 1955. As she soared through the air on invisible wires, Martin's performance as Peter Pan was so amazing that she returned the following year to reprise her live performance on another edition of NBC's *Producers' Showcase*.

Martin returned to television on a number of other occasions, including her role as cohost of the PBS talk show *Over Easy* in the 1980s. What's more, she was the mother of an actor destined to become one of TV's all-time most popular stars, Larry Hagman of CBS's *Dallas*.

Setting the Scene

As big a star as Mary Martin was on Broadway, in person she was warm and down-to-earth, with a great sense of humor. It was my impression that she absolutely had nothing left to prove.

I first interviewed Mary Martin in 1979 in her dressing room as she completed her only TV movie, *Valentine*. The location was CBS's Studio City lot in the San Fernando Valley. Martin chatted on and on between takes on what proved to be one of her last shooting days.

Mary Martin as Peter Pan, 1956. Courtesy of NBC publicity and the James Bawden collection.

I met her again with a few other critics in 1981 in the Garden Room restaurant of the Century Plaza Hotel in the Century City part of Los Angeles. She had insisted on a very early breakfast interview to promote *Over Easy*, the new PBS series for seniors that she cohosted with former *Today Show* star Hugh Downs.

In 1982, I met her yet again at the Malibu home of her son, Larry Hagman, and we chatted on a deck overlooking the ocean for what seemed half the night. Many of the other TV critics who attended the party, over one hundred of them, had no idea who she was.

Finally, in early 1990, we chatted over the phone. She was in London promoting the release on video of TV's *Peter Pan*.

The Interview

BAWDEN: Does it bother you that some people now think of you mainly as the mom of Larry Hagman of *Dallas*?

MARTIN: It's his turn. I tell everyone I'm the icon and Larry is the man of the moment. Maybe he'll become an icon with time. He deserves it.

BAWDEN: I always wanted to ask you: how many times did you play Nellie in *South Pacific*?

MARTIN: Honeybee, who was counting? But I'm told it was 1,925 times. Not that I was counting! Of that, 800 times was in London's West End. And I was as nervous at the end of the run as at the beginning.

BAWDEN: Why?

MARTIN: On Broadway you have to pace yourself. I mean, you can't give it your all on a Wednesday matinee because there's a Wednesday night coming up in a few hours. Ezio Pinza forgot that. He'd do two or three Met operas in a busy week. Here he started losing his voice and had to book off sick. He was also fifty-eight. Told me he'd never worked so hard in his life.

BAWDEN: But why nerves? You were on top of the world.

MARTIN: Say a couple from Topeka had saved all year for their week in New York. I couldn't disappoint them. I sang over colds, I ran around in scanties while I had the flu. Ezio booked off sick. I never would. I owed it to the public who had this one chance to see us. As I told my understudy, "Get a library card. You'll be reading a lot of books."

BAWDEN: What's the most important thing about being in a truly long run?

MARTIN: The vitamin bottle. Without it you'll get all run-down. That and a clear conscience. I'd hit the pillow at night and get right to sleep. Worst thing is I missed important events in the lives of my two children. My daughter, Heller, still chides me about that.

BAWDEN: How did you get the part?

MARTIN: [Composer] Richard Rodgers saw me on tour in *Annie Get Your Gun*. That would have been in '48. He phoned me up and made the offer while I was in L.A. The only song he had to entice me was "Some Enchanted Evening," which my character does not sing. And working with a huge Metropolitan tenor scared me to death. But I took it.

BAWDEN: You also contributed to the song titles.

MARTIN: In the shower one morning I had this idea for "I'm Gonna Wash That Man Right out of My Hair." When I started doing it eight times a week my hair started falling out. I had to use baby shampoo! Gee, I wish we'd had blow dryers in those days.

BAWDEN: You expected to star in the movie?

MARTIN: Well, we opened April 1949 and that was always the plan. Then the years started going by and when they decided to finally make it in 1958 I was forty-five. Too old for Nellie? Nobody ever told me. I thought they might go for Doris [Day], but they picked Mitzi Gaynor. So I stopped talking to the boys for a bit because I had to read it in the paper.

BAWDEN: How did you feel when the movie came out?

MARTIN: It made a lot of money, but it was a stinker. Mitzi was the only one who actually sang, the rest of them were dubbed, badly. And all those color filters! What was Josh Logan [the director] thinking?

BAWDEN: Who made the first move to reconcile?

MARTIN: Well, Oscar [Hammerstein] was always a darling to me. Dick Rodgers was very closed up about everything. And Oscar phoned and said they needed me for *Sound of Music*. And I said, "But Oscar, I'm too old!" Which I definitely was this time. There was an audible groan and he apologized and so did Dick. And we were back together and I never assumed I'd get the movie because this time I was really, really old!

BAWDEN: Julie Andrews did it. What did you think of her in it?

MARTIN: Wonderful. But, you know, Julie always goes on about how Audrey Hepburn took *My Fair Lady* from her. [Andrews had starred in the Broadway production.] Do I go on about how Julie took Maria von Trapp from me? [Martin's character in Broadway's *Sound of Music*.] No! Never!

BAWDEN: Your biggest gripe about today's Broadway musicals?

MARTIN: The miking. I was never miked. Can you imagine them daring to mike Ethel Merman? It produces a feeling of artificiality. But now it's expected. I have a very dear friend and when she was out of town in a drama the miking system failed and she refused to go on that night. Mikes take all the intimacy out of Broadway shows, I just hate it.

BAWDEN: You mentioned Ethel Merman. One book on Broadway refers to your feud with Merman. Can you tell me about that?

MARTIN: Not a feud. A rivalry. I don't know her awfully well. But that talent! I guess it started when I did the road tour of her Broadway hit *Annie Get Your Gun* and Ethel was not pleased. But she did come backstage when *South Pacific* was on and told me, "I could never have done that!" And I couldn't have matched Ethel in *Gypsy*. We both had our tries at *Hello, Dolly*. And clips from our live sing-song in 1954 are everywhere. I'm always trying to top her and she says it's the same for her.

BAWDEN: Along the way, you also appeared in a few non-hits on Broadway.

MARTIN: *Kind Sir* [1953] was a romantic comedy with Charles Boyer. It ran 166 performances, but people kept expecting me to sing. Cary Grant loved the story, bought the movie rights, and made it into the movie with Ingrid Bergman [*Indiscreet*] that was a big hit. The big flop was *Jennie* [1963], which Dietz and Schwartz wrote for me. It had one hit [song]: "Kiss the World Goodbye." It was the life of Laurette Taylor and had already flopped as a straight play with Judy Holliday. Incredibly, the Broadway cast album has just been reissued.

BAWDEN: How many times did you do *Peter Pan* on TV?

MARTIN: The first time was 1955. Live. Then we did it again live in 1956. Both times in color. The kinescopes exist but only in black and white. Then we did a carefully taped version in 1960. That's the one that's out on video. It's the worst one because when you're doing it live you have to be in top condition. With tape we would do a scene over and over until all the energy was drained out of it.

BAWDEN: On Broadway it was a limited run in 1954.

MARTIN: Of 125 performances—bankrolled by NBC. Both Cyril Ritchard and I had won Tonys so the TV audience was something fierce, over 65 million. I was doing Broadway's *Sound of Music* when I agreed to the 1960 taping, which was done in Brooklyn. NBC ran it several times but they cut my final thank-you speech and other bits to make way for more commercials. I hate it, I really hate it. It has a "So what?" feeling to it.

There was also a "Black" *Peter Pan*. We went into an unused theater in Houston and after they'd hoisted me up into the heavens I came down covered in soot. Nobody had ever bothered to dust up there. If Orson Welles had his Black Macbeth, I had my Black Peter Pan.

BAWDEN: I've seen a kinescope transferred to video of your TV special with Noël Coward.

MARTIN: *Together with Music* [1955]—ninety minutes with Noël Coward and an audience. I went down to the Bahamas to rehearse with Noël-lie. He'd never done anything like this before. And he kept going up on his lines. We had huge lunches, lavish dinners, wine flowed, and I finally said, "We must go to a bare rehearsal hall and keep plugging away. Because there are no retakes on TV." It was done at CBS studios in Los Angeles. An audience made me even more nervous. I was a wreck but Noëllie sailed right through it letter perfect. I never saw it, of course. I was doing it. Then recently a lady comes up and says, "I love you and Coward." And it turns out there's a bootleg tape out there. I haven't seen it. Apparently everybody else has.

BAWDEN: You loved live TV.

MARTIN: As a challenge. I did a live version of *Born Yesterday* [1956] with Paul Douglas, who was in the original. I think I made a funny Billie Dawn. I did a live color version of *Annie Get Your Gun* [1957] with John Raitt. We did it in front of an audience and that helped, but [composer Irving] Berlin demanded the kinescopes be destroyed after one usage. Said it would damage future rights. But there's one out there, I'm told, and stories about a bootleg video, and this delights me.

BAWDEN: I heard you singing in an old movie I just watched, but you weren't in the cast.

MARTIN: Ah! I know what you're talking about. It was *The Shopworn Angel* [1938] and there's a scene where Maggie Sullivan sings "Pack Up Your Troubles." And she did it on the soundstage and later in the cutting room it was decided she couldn't really sing. So they got me in and I had to sing it based on her lip movements. Which was hard. It took a day. Now, MGM would never hire me to go before the camera because the brass had problems with my irregular face. So that's my sole MGM credit. I can sadly say I worked one day at MGM.

BAWDEN: I've heard you disparage your Paramount period [1939–1943]. But some of those musicals are just fine by me.

MARTIN: Such as?

BAWDEN: *The Great Victor Herbert* [1939], for one.

MARTIN: Okay, so it was very lavish. And it got some Oscar nominations and won one for cinematography. But there's very little Victor Herbert in it. I was paired with Alan Jones and he sang very loud, so I had to sing very loud and that's not the way I usually sing. I mean I sing higher than I've ever sung before or since. You remember Susanna Foster in it, a cute teenager? She sang an F above C in one song. Not my style at all, but it was constantly being

Bing Crosby with Mary Martin in *Birth of the Blues* (1941). Courtesy of Paramount Pictures and the James Bawden collection.

reissued. It's why I've always hated operettas. Incidentally, Herbert was played by the marvelous Walter Connolly, who died tragically within the year. He got his divorce papers from his wife the day before he died: Nedda Harrigan, who turned around and married Josh Logan, so I knew her later. She and Walter had a daughter—Ann Connolly—who played Wendy as a grownup in the *Peter Pan* I was in during the 1954 season.

BAWDEN: Then at Paramount you got to sing twice with Bing Crosby.

MARTIN: He was made for movies, had that intimate style. I was awkward in front of the camera. The first, *Rhythm on the River* [1940], I just watched him and how he'd dial down for a close-up and the movie was a hit. Then he asked me to do *Birth of the Blues* [1941] and that was huge and we later reprised all the numbers on a TV special. He said it was one of his favorites. I wish I could have done all my pictures with Bing.

BAWDEN: Didn't Bing Crosby come backstage after he'd seen you in *South Pacific?*

MARTIN: Oh, yes, and you know he disagreed with me leaving Paramount. He sat very still in my dressing room and said, "Mary, I was wrong. I now see why you left movies." And I told him he should try it and he said "No retakes! I don't think I could."

BAWDEN: Then came two with Dick Powell.

MARTIN: No, three. I sang a wonderful song with Dick. The big all-star one was *Star Spangled Rhythm* in 1942. Dick and I sang "Meet Me Tonight in Dreamland." He had a wonderful voice but he hated doing that kind of stuff by then. He claimed he wanted to change his style and become a tough guy. *Happy Go Lucky* [1943] was set in a fake Trinidad and Paramount played up Betty Hutton, who really wanted to be a movie star. Then we turned around and made *True to Life* [1943], only this time I was top-billed and Dick got third billing because the studio guessed he was leaving. He was a radio writer renting a room from a wacky family. I left to do *Lute Song* in late '43 and I never went back to Paramount. In fact, they never asked me.

BAWDEN: You once said you weren't pretty enough for pictures.

MARTIN: Here's a funny story: at a dinner party at Jack Benny's, I sat next to Claudette Colbert's husband, Dr. Joel Pressman. She was late because she was still working. He thought I was Claudette because he never wore his glasses except at work. He was a research doctor. Paramount had made me up to look like her—bangs, tight curls. At the end of the evening I told him, "I'm not your wife. I don't even like the way Claudette looks!" And I just walked out!

You know, we all had to do glamour shots. When [photographer] George Hurrell got to me in his studio, he'd howl, "The nose! The nose!" Said I was horse-faced "just like Jean Arthur." Well, I happen to think Jean is a real beauty, but that kind of treatment, it got to me.

BAWDEN: But you came back once in the 1946 musical about Cole Porter, *Night and Day.*

MARTIN: Playing myself as I was discovered and sang "My Heart Belongs to Daddy." Jack Warner offered me $20,000 to work just a few days.

I knew what that was really all about. He needed a blond singer and was preparing a film called *Romance on the High Seas*. He wanted to see how I photographed. By the time the film started in 1948 I had committed to *South Pacific*. And Jack went with an unknown called Doris Day. So both Doris and I benefited. But Cary Grant as Cole Porter? I asked Cole why he'd permitted such a travesty. And he said, "It was either Cary or Reginald Gardiner. Who wouldn't like to look like Cary Grant?"

BAWDEN: You once told me about one of the saddest days of your life. Can you recall that for me now?

MARTIN: Late March 1987. I don't know why I answered the phone that day but it was a reporter from Associated Press asking for a comment on the death of Robert Preston. He'd just died and nobody had told me. My darling costar from Paramount and later on Broadway in *I Do, I Do*. Sweet, kind, ultra-talented. And I just crumpled on the floor and wept.

BAWDEN: Why are you doing the TV movie *Valentine* [1979]?

MARTIN: It started with the PBS series *Over Easy*. People said to me, "Mary, why admit you're old?" Well, why not admit it? I loved doing that show. One time I had Lillian Gish and Helen Hayes and our collective age was nearer to three hundred than I care to remember. In *Valentine* I've got a great trouper in Jack Albertson and a fine director from the stage, Lee Phillips. It's about being old and trying to carry on. We did a scene at a seniors' home and an actual resident said, "Mary Martin! I'm younger than you!" So why was she plopped in a home? Because her family had no use for her, I guess. I'm not like that. I'll go on until I drop.

Afterword

Mary Martin was married and divorced twice. Her first husband, Benjamin Jack Hagman, was the father of her son Larry Hagman. Hagman and Martin were married in 1930 and divorced in 1936. She married Richard Halliday, a drama and movie critic, in 1946. They divorced in 1973. He was the father of her daughter Heller Halliday.

Martin was both a Tony and Emmy winner and was a Kennedy Center Honoree in 1989.

In 1982, Martin was seriously injured in an auto accident in San Francisco when the car she was riding in was struck by a vehicle that ran a red light. In the crash, her press agent was killed and her best friend, Oscar-winning actress Janet Gaynor, was badly hurt, later dying from complications. Gaynor's husband, producer Paul Gregory, was not seriously hurt in the crash.

Martin died at age seventy-six at her home in Rancho Mirage, California, on November 3, 1990, from pancreatic cancer. She'd toured US cities in the stage play *Legends* opposite Carol Channing, but refused to take it to New York. In my final talk with her on the phone, she admitted she was very sick but was traveling to London, hoping to see the queen before she went home.

Ricardo Montalban

Interview by James Bawden and Ron Miller

Ricardo Montalban was one of the last Latin American movie stars to be imported to Hollywood by a major studio in the final days of the "Latin lover" period that stretched from the 1920s through the 1940s. Unlike Argentina's Fernando Lamas, who arrived in 1950 and sputtered out of fashion fairly early, Montalban put down deep roots in America, proved his versatility many times over, and finally became a major star after finding a permanent lodging in television.

Though he had appeared in musical "soundies"—the forerunner to music videos—as early as 1941, Montalban had worked mainly in films of his native Mexico until 1947, when MGM gave him a showcase role in the musical drama *Fiesta* and a buildup as the latest romantic Latin lover type.

Tall, dark, and awesomely handsome, Montalban was incredibly promising star material in Hollywood. Able to speak perfect English, with only that essential hint of an accent, he was a sleek romantic partner for young MGM talents like Cyd Charisse and Esther Williams, but he had the skills of a dramatic actor as well.

Because he could play romantic leads and all kinds of ethnic character roles, Montalban became an incredibly busy actor in television from the 1950s on. He was a guest star on virtually all the major shows, from westerns like *Gunsmoke* and *Bonanza* to crime shows like *Columbo* and *The Untouchables* to medical shows like *Ben Casey* and *Dr. Kildare*—even comedy shows like *Here's Lucy*. In 1967 he played the villainous outer space menace Khan in an episode of *Star Trek*, then reprised the role fifteen years later in the feature film *Star Trek II: The Wrath of Khan*.

But the career-changing role for Montalban came in 1977 when he first played a mysterious character named Mr. Roarke in a TV movie called *Fantasy Island*, which racked up big numbers for ABC, spurring a sequel in

Ricardo Montalban. Courtesy of the Spelling Premier Network and Worldvision.

1978, *Return to Fantasy Island,* and then a weekly series that ran from 1978 to 1984.

From then on, Montalban was an iconic figure on TV, even attracting rave reviews for his sexy TV commercials as a spokesman for luxury cars that boasted "fine Cordovan leather," spoken in a tone that made you long for the feel of that leather in real life.

Throughout his long career, Montalban worked unselfishly to make things better for people of Latino background, devoting great amounts of his personal time and money to promoting a better screen image for Latinos, mostly through his efforts as a leader in the Nosotros organization in Hollywood.

Setting the Scene

Each of us separately interviewed Ricardo Montalban on multiple occasions. We have combined our interviews for this presentation.

BAWDEN: I first interviewed Ricardo Montalban in 1973 over lunch in the dining room of Toronto's Royal York Hotel. Montalban walked in and selected a table in the corner "so people won't bother" and ordered breakfast, although it was 1 p.m., "because I slept in this morning to ward off a cold."

He was deeply tanned and extremely courteous. He said he was halfway through a lengthy bus and truck tour with George Bernard Shaw's *Don Juan in Hell*—a staged reading that costarred Paul Henreid, Edward Mulhare, and Agnes Moorehead, who "tried to tell our director—John Houseman—what's what because she's done this one before." Montalban told me, "It's wonderful being in front of a live audience, which is so appreciative of good drama. We read it, of course, from large binders, but we've all memorized everything by now. In college towns we really pack them in."

We chatted for a few hours. I noticed Montalban had barely touched his meal. He said he was going back to his room to rest. He had two more Toronto performances and then would hit Hamilton for one showing only. He waved good-bye as he entered the elevator, but few people seemed to notice him.

We had a reunion in 1981 on the ABC portion of a TV critics convention. His hit series *Fantasy Island* had been running for several years. I sat between him and his gorgeous wife Georgiana. Montalban professed to remember me, but was irked people kept coming by to get the autograph of his costar, diminutive Hervé Villechaize, who was seated at the table with a glamazon date, who told me she was six feet six.

MILLER: My interest in the career of Ricardo Montalban probably began in the late 1950s when I realized I had an intense interest in the culture of people from different ethnic backgrounds from mine. At San José State University, I had two Mexican American roommates who became dear friends. My exposure to Latino food, music, and culture was intoxicating, and when I ultimately became a journalist I was deeply attracted to stories about the way Latino people were treated in American society and depicted on the screen.

That's one reason I followed the activities of the Nosotros organization once I became a television columnist. In 1977, my first year as a full-time syndicated columnist, I learned that Ricardo Montalban was coming to San Francisco to talk about Latino issues as well as his acting career at a Spanish-language radio station. I made arrangements to do an interview during his visit. Then, just a few minutes before I left for San Francisco, I received a phone call from a publicist friend at ABC who told me Montalban's *Fantasy Island* had just received a series commitment from the network after the ratings success of two TV movies that served as pilots. In those days before everyone carried a cell phone, my ABC friend told me they'd been unable to reach Montalban that morning, so would I give him the good news when we met for our interview that morning?

That turned out to be a magic moment for me when I first met Montalban for our interview in the presidential suite of the Mark Hopkins Hotel in San Francisco. Always a warm and gracious man, Montalban was especially happy to see me once I confirmed the good news he'd been expecting about *Fantasy Island.*

Over the years that followed, Montalban was happy to remember me and fill me in on his latest issues and activities. We had two more opportunities to talk privately after that. We sat side by side at a small dinner party at MGM in the early 1980s. His wife—Georgiana, the half-sister of actresses Loretta Young, Polly Ann Young, and Sally Blane—was at our table, along with my wife, Darla, and Sam Elliott and his wife, Katharine Ross.

Our final interview was on the set of *Fantasy Island* in 1983 where he was filming a dance scene with Cyd Charisse, his former dance partner from his first MGM film, *Fiesta.* That final meeting demonstrated again how thoughtful Montalban could be. He had remembered my interest in his early career and asked the network to invite me to the set so I could meet Cyd Charisse and watch them on the dance floor one last time. (Ironically, Montalban was no longer able to move about freely due to a severe leg injury, so he and Charisse had to be photographed from the waist up as they were rotated atop a turntable-type platform on the dance floor.) That day on the set in Burbank remains another magic memory for me—both Montalban and Charisse were in most charming moods.

The Interview

MILLER: I suppose one of the abiding myths about you is that you first came to America in 1947 to star in MGM's *Fiesta.*

MONTALBAN: That's true. I came here in the 1930s to get an education. I went to Fairfax High School in Los Angeles and that's where I first appeared anywhere as an actor—in a school play.

MILLER: In those days, it was common for studio talent scouts to show up at school plays, looking for "stars of tomorrow." Did anybody discover you in that school play?

MONTALBAN: You're right. A talent scout did see me and tried to sign me. That was in 1939.

MILLER: So what happened?

MONTALBAN: My older brother told me to forget that nonsense and go to college. I was supposed to be an engineer. When I graduated from high school, my brother took me to New York to go to college. I gave it a year to see if I could make it, but I also began to get small roles in stage plays.

MILLER: I guess your future as an engineer fell apart when you were given a chance to test for a major role in a big Hollywood movie.

MONTALBAN: The role was the male lead in MGM's *Tortilla Flat* from the John Steinbeck best seller. I tested for the role opposite a young singer from Xavier Cugat's orchestra, but they wound up giving the male part to John Garfield and cast Hedy Lamarr as the Mexican girl.

MILLER: Hey, that sounds like a familiar tune for Hollywood—casting an Anglo as a Mexican boy and an Austrian girl as his Mexican sweetheart. How did that make you feel?

MONTALBAN: Hollywood has a way of stomping on your dreams. But I'm forever optimistic.

MILLER: Did that missed opportunity sour you on an acting career? That's about when you went back to Mexico, wasn't it?

MONTALBAN: No, I was forced to return to Torreón [his hometown in Mexico] because of the sudden illness of my mother. I needed to stay there until she recovered. But I finally decided to try for parts in Mexico City's film industry.

MILLER: How did that work out?

MONTALBAN: I quickly became a star in Mexican motion pictures and made thirteen of them.

BAWDEN: Now we come to your return to the States on an MGM contract. Can you describe your first days at MGM?

MONTALBAN: It's a blur. There was a walkabout to all the sets. That took the better part of a day. I met Clark Gable on the set of *The Hucksters,* never thinking I'd be working with him someday. I saw Barbara Stanwyck striding to the dubbing room. We'd work together on *The Colbys* forty years later. Every one of the twenty-nine soundstages was in operation. I had to submit to numerous screen tests. Were my teeth okay? Was my hairline too low? Did I need a more Anglo name? "Ricky Martin" was suggested and I shouted, "No!" That I remember.

BAWDEN: Just out of curiosity, what was it like to work with Stanwyck when you finally did so in *The Colbys*?

MONTALBAN: She was seventy-nine years young and never missed a line. After the lunch break, she stood at the main door with her stopwatch, clocking us in. She'd shout, "Where the hell is Moses? [costar Charlton Heston] Roarke? You're two minutes late!" She was a sheer delight. She said her house was broken into and she needed money from [producer] Aaron Spelling to refurbish it. That's an excuse. Like all of us, she craves approval and one more round of applause.

MILLER: You had forged a reputation as a romantic leading man in Mexico's cinema, so now you got the plush treatment from MGM. Were you prepared to find out they wanted you to become the dance partner of their latest dance discovery, Cyd Charisse?

MONTALBAN: I felt totally inadequate in her presence as a dancer. But I had a wife and four children by then. If the studio said that's what you've got to do, then that's what I did. I didn't consider myself a klutz, but I was totally inexperienced as a dancer. In those days, I was there just to dress up the scenery.

MILLER: Cyd Charisse claims you had a natural talent for dancing and were eager to learn. How did the two of you start off?

MONTALBAN: She took me by the hand and led me through the dance number we had to do. For some reason, I could create the illusion that I was a dancer.

MILLER: But this was a woman who eventually was the partner of the two greatest dancers in movie history—Fred Astaire and Gene Kelly.

MONTALBAN: Instead of being disappointed that she had to dance with someone who had never danced before, she made me feel very comfortable.

MILLER: If you see *Fiesta* today, you certainly look like you belong together on the movie screen.

MONTALBAN: I call that number a half-assed flamenco! But the studio liked it so much that they kept putting us together again—in *The Kissing Bandit* [1948], in *On an Island with You* [1948], in *Sombrero* [1953]. They even loaned us out to Universal in 1951 for *Mark of the Renegade*. [In that one, Montalban was a dashing bandit named Marcos and Charisse was the sultry Manuella.]

BAWDEN: She was just one of the many glamorous leading ladies you played opposite. Who were your favorites?

MONTALBAN: That's being un-chivalrous, but June Allyson was sweet and kind to this newcomer. I got into shape swimming with Esther Williams. She said I could really dog paddle. I had to replace Fernando Lamas in *Latin Lovers* [1953]. He and Lana Turner [his costar in the movie] were real-life sweethearts and that romance went sour. What did I get for this? MGM dropped my contract after five years as they were dropping everyone by then.

MILLER: Do you regret the passing of that golden age of musicals that you were a part of in your early career?

MONTALBAN: We don't dream like we used to dream. We don't glamorize or make things so much bigger than life. The audience may still want to see dancing, but I think something has been drilled into us lately that the screen should be used for something relevant. I think the tenor of the times around the world—the conflicts and threats of war and so on—have made people a little more aware of what's going on. Perhaps they feel that something like that [lighthearted musicals] is nonsense.

BAWDEN: Before you left MGM, you managed to get some good dramatic roles. Do you have a favorite?

MONTALBAN: *Mystery Street* [1950], directed by a very young John Sturges. A lot of it—the exteriors anyway—were shot in Boston, even Harvard. The cast was terrific and included Jan Sterling and Elsa Lanchester. It went out as a programmer, top of a double bill. As a Latino cop, I avoided all of the usual stereotypes. The script was by Richard Brooks and Leonard Spigelglass. John Alton shot it beautifully. I watched it on TV recently and it really holds up.

MILLER: Once you were dropped by the studio, was that a wake-up call for you?

MONTALBAN: Parts were not assigned to me anymore. Overnight I was faced with the problem any Latino actor faced in Hollywood. In those days, the only parts Hollywood offered were the extremes—forever the bandit, the uneducated peon, the gigolo, or Latin lover. Many times I had to turn down a part I really needed because of the way a Mexican was portrayed.

BAWDEN: Do you feel your advocacy of Latino causes made you box office poison with some producers?

MONTALBAN: Undoubtedly. Some producers got it, but others simply chose to hire somebody else.

MILLER: That's when you started taking lots of smaller non-leading roles in television. Some would say that helped you develop into a very good character actor.

MONTALBAN: I took the jobs that others wouldn't take because they were afraid to work in live television. As a result, television opened doors for me that motion pictures never could have opened.

MILLER: I'm guessing that also made movie producers see you as more than the stereotypical Latino. You played a Japanese man in *Sayonara*, for example. But haven't you always argued that the role of a Mexican should always be played by a Mexican?

MONTALBAN: Well, I say that because there are so many good Mexican actors and so few roles available for them. But the actor in me says the only yardstick by which an actor should be measured is his talent and ability. If Eli Wallach can portray a Mexican bandit better than me, he should get the part. All we ask for is that we be allowed to compete.

BAWDEN: At one point, though, you played several American Indians.

MONTALBAN: I wasn't politically aware at the time. I tried to stress the dignity of the American Indians in *Across the Wide Missouri* [1951] and *Cheyenne Autumn* [1964]. I had a talk with Jack Ford on *Cheyenne Autumn* [Ford was the director] and he said he'd done a disservice to them in the past, but there weren't any Indian actors at the time. So I tried my best to suggest the dignity of my character, Little Wolf.

MILLER: Because of your long success at expanding the horizons for Latino actors, you were in great demand as a spokesman for others who wanted to follow your path. What motivated you to get so deeply involved with Nosotros and other groups?

MONTALBAN: I couldn't just stay home and play tennis. I like to think that, in the orchestra, I was a piccolo that added maybe two notes to a symphony of three thousand notes.

MILLER: In today's entertainment world, you're an iconic figure, but do you ever look back with nostalgia at the golden era of Hollywood that you once tasted?

MONTALBAN: In those days, we were in the hands of people who loved the business. I worked with Mr. Louis B. Mayer [head of MGM production when Montalban was there]. There was a man who loved the business. Now we're in the hands of Gulf & Western and Coca-Cola. Let's be realistic about it: it's a business. I don't think we have the dreamers, the visionaries we used to have—because of economics.

BAWDEN: Before *Fantasy Island*, you seemed to be surviving by doing a host of guest appearances on television series.

MONTALBAN: One could get about $2,500 for a week's work on *Playhouse 90*, *Riverboat*, *Adventures in Paradise*, *Schlitz Playhouse*, *Climax!* But usually I could only work once a year on those shows. My income shrank dramatically. We had to sell our big house and buy a small one in a less desirable neighborhood.

BAWDEN: Meanwhile, MGM was sinking fast. How did that make you feel?

MONTALBAN: Sad, but grateful I'd been there during the last glorious years. If a *How the West Was Won* suddenly popped up and the studio seemed ready to roll again, I was very enthusiastic. Then another slide began.

BAWDEN: What was the last time you worked on the MGM back lot?

MONTALBAN: *The Singing Nun* in 1968. Nothing else was in production picture-wise, but there were a lot of TV shows on the lot. In 1966, I'd done a gaggle of *Dr. Kildare*s as the same character back at MGM, but when I wandered around, all I could see was dry rot. The *Meet Me in St. Louis* house was barely standing and nobody had mowed the lawn for years.

BAWDEN: To keep busy, you even started doing commercials.

MONTALBAN: I was the spokesman for Chevy for years and, boy, did we need that money.

BAWDEN: Looking back at those years, there was one famous TV gig.

MONTALBAN: Khan on *Star Trek* in 1967. Why didn't I save that script? Can't remember. Got great notices, but the series only lasted a few years. Then fifteen years later comes *Star Trek II: The Wrath of Khan*. What happened to my costume? I'd not known *Star Trek* would surge because of those TV reruns.

BAWDEN: You did have a recurring role on the series *Executive Suite* [1976–1977]. I remember meeting you on the set while interviewing the Canadian actress Sharon Acker.

MONTALBAN: I did that for eight episodes. The CBS president said he found it all a bit too oversexed for CBS, so he canceled it after one season, replacing it with *Dallas*, which was super sexy!

MILLER: When it comes to fulfillment of dreams, though, you must have really felt satisfied when you were offered the role of the mysterious Mr. Roarke on *Fantasy Island*. Though he has the romantic appeal of the Latin lover characters you used to play in MGM musicals, he also has great depth of character and an almost holy demeanor.

MONTALBAN: He's the man who makes people's fantasies come true. I look forward to having my own fantasy come true—that we'll live in a world where there are no passports and men live together in harmony, racial and ethnic differences overlooked for the good of mankind.

MILLER: Do you see any signs of that fantasy coming true?

MONTALBAN: As I grow older, I have fewer dreams, fewer fantasies, but as I said before, I'm forever the optimist.

BAWDEN: How do you get along with your costar Hervé Villechaize?

MONTALBAN: No temperament at all. He says we never see eye to eye on things, which is true. [Villechaize was under five feet in height.] He has the most statuesque girlfriends.

BAWDEN: There's a lot of speculation about Mr. Roarke. Does he have a secret?

MONTALBAN: I know exactly who Mr. Roarke is, but I'm not telling you that!

Afterword

Ricardo Montalban won an Emmy Award as supporting actor in a dramatic series for a recurring role in four episodes of *How the West Was Won* (1978).

Montalban's last roles in both motion pictures and television were as a voice actor in animated films—the 2006 movie *The Ant-Bully* and in a 2009 episode of the TV cartoon series *American Dad*. In the latter, he played a Latino general.

He was also a co-founder and the first president of Nosotros, the organization that works tirelessly to improve the image and impact of Latinos in films and television.

Montalban's only wife, Georgiana, died in 2007, and he died on January 14, 2009, at his home in Los Angeles of congestive heart failure. He was eighty-eight.

Harry Morgan

Interview by James Bawden

There's a well-known axiom in show business, especially in the old world of burlesque: "If you want to be the top banana, you have to start at the bottom of the bunch." In truth, some actors eventually learn that being the top banana isn't all it's cracked up to be, and you can have a very satisfying career with a perch a little lower in the bunch.

Such an actor was Harry Morgan, one of America's great character players, who spent years as a sidekick or second banana in feature films, then moved to television series, where supporting players can be just as beloved as the star whose name is on top.

Though Morgan occasionally moved up to the leading actor ranks—most notably in the spin-off shows *Pete and Gladys* and *After M*A*S*H*, which promoted his supporting characters in the original shows to star status—he was never that successful as the star of the show and happily returned to second banana status afterward.

In a career that spanned more than half a century, Morgan had a long list of major accomplishments. He was a member of the original Group Theater and was in the original cast of Clifford Odets's *Golden Boy* on Broadway. He won acclaim for his work as a key supporting player in some of the greatest of all westerns, including *The Ox-Bow Incident* (1943), *Yellow Sky* (1948), and *High Noon* (1952). But mostly he's remembered for his greatest supporting roles in three long-running TV series—*December Bride*, *Dragnet*, and *M*A*S*H*.

During much of the 1940s, Morgan was known as Henry Morgan, but he switched to Harry Morgan to avoid confusion with popular humorist Henry Morgan, who frequently appeared in films and on radio and television.

Harry Morgan, circa 1954. Courtesy of Universal-International publicity.

Setting the Scene

I treasured my yearly encounters on the set of *M*A*S*H* with Harry Morgan, the great character actor from years of golden age movies and television. I'd been covering the series even before it went on the air, starting with a luncheon interview on the Sunset Strip with cast member Loretta Swit, who was still an unknown. I remember she flounced in wearing her tennis whites, and the CBS press representative, who'd worked with Doris Day for years, almost fainted at what she deemed an egregious breach of etiquette.

When TV critics used to preview the new season at the Century Plaza Hotel in Los Angeles, I'd frequently tiptoe out of some boring press conference to walk out the hotel back door and through the back gates of the Twentieth Century Fox studio next door. If Loretta Swit grew tired of talking to me, she'd happily pass me on to Harry Morgan, who always greeted me as a long-lost friend and always asked me back the following summer.

"You actually watched *Pete and Gladys*?" I remember him asking me with some wonderment after I'd mentioned seeing his long-forgotten early TV sitcom from the 1950s.

And in 1988, when he came to Toronto to film an episode of *The Twilight Zone*, he invited me on set for a grueling last day of shooting that didn't wind up until well past midnight.

The Interview

BAWDEN: What do you remember about your first big film, *The Ox-Bow Incident*, the classic film about a frontier lynching? Some critics regard it as the best-ever western.

MORGAN: Well, those critics are correct. Wild Bill Wellman [the director] wanted to make it so badly he bought the rights from producer Al Hurley at Paramount and virtually gave the property to [Fox production chief] Darryl Zanuck. Now, this whole thing was made in 1941, and when Zanuck watches the final cut in a screening room, he yells at Bill, "You bastard! This is a great movie. But it won't make a penny, damn you. How the hell am I gonna market this to women and children?" And he stormed out and kept the film on the shelf for two years. And only after he joined the army himself did the film sort of sneak out on double bills. And it lost a bundle.

The production costs were so low because most of the scenes were done inside soundstages. The mountain location was a set made up of bits and pieces of other sets. The western street was the one used in grade-B Cisco Kid movies. You can also see it in *The Gunfighter* [1949].

[In the film, Morgan plays the partner of drifting cowboy Henry Fonda. Both find themselves caught up in the action of a lynch mob.] We had a great cast. [Oscar winner] Jane Darwell came in on one day's notice and replaced Florence Bates, who fell from a horse. I can't believe all the good actors in it: Tony Quinn, Harry Davenport, Dana Andrews at the beginning of his Fox career. By the time it came out, Dana [who played one of the lynching victims] was a far bigger star from *Laura* and critics wondered why he'd accepted such a small role here.

Bill Wellman rode Hank Fonda mercilessly. He'd wanted Gary Cooper, who just refused to do something that inflammatory. It took me a bit to get used to Hank's moodiness, but when you acted with him he made you better. He's very taciturn, stoic, soft-spoken. People strain to hear what he's saying. When he reads the letter from the hanged man you could hear a pin drop in the movie theater. I should know. I was there, and the audience came out at the end and nobody was talking. Their heads were down. Hank was shocked the studio just dumped it. The censors put up a huge fight, saying whole scenes were un-American, but Wellman shouted them down, I was told. Wellman had to do two bad pictures for Fox without any input just so he could make it. For a flop movie, it has resonance. People keep mentioning it to me. I just loved playing Art Croft. It was a great way to jump-start my movie career. But I never again worked with Henry Fonda, although we were both in *How the West Was Won* [1962].

Wellman remembered me and used me again in *Yellow Sky* and the location was Death Valley. And I'd tease him, "Bill, why can't we make this one inside a safe, cool soundstage?" Because the temperature would soar to 120 degrees and our original leading lady, Paulette Goddard, got so frazzled she quit and Anne Baxter flew in on a special plane to replace her.

BAWDEN: What do you remember about *State Fair* [1945], the original screen musical by Rodgers and Hammerstein?

MORGAN: That I had one scene as a carny barker. I didn't even have a name. I'd watch for weeks because they didn't know when they'd be using me. Easiest salary I ever pulled in. All the songs had been prerecorded and those setups took hours to get right. I don't remember seeing Rodgers and Hammerstein around. They were missing on my days. The fair was too clean for my liking and too modern. And Fay Bainter and Charlie Winninger looked more like grandparents than parents. But I can truly say I was in a hit musical—even if I didn't get to sing.

BAWDEN: You also were in the classic film noir *Somewhere in the Night* [1946].

MORGAN: It was Joe Mankiewicz's second turn at directing. I'd also been in his first, *Dragonwyck* [1946], which wasn't box office. You could tell because Zanuck handed him a medium-budgeted thriller. A dilettante named Anderson Lawler supposedly produced it, but we never saw him on set and he never worked at Fox again.

Joe borrowed John Hodiak from MGM and he was a good actor. He never had star presence. I would have thought this was Ty Power's territory, but Joe said Ty was committed to *The Razor's Edge*. But once Lloyd Nolan ambled into camera range halfway through, it was game up. Lloyd is my candidate for best-ever movie actor. A lot of good people were in it: Sheldon Leonard, Richard Conte, and in one scene there's Josephine Hutchinson doing a great job. It came and went without much attention. Watch it and a few days later you'll be thinking of all the holes in the plot.

BAWDEN: What do you remember from *The Big Clock* [1948]?

MORGAN: That Ray Milland [who had won the Oscar in 1945] was so big at the time he had veto power over the director and major cast players. He chose John Farrow to direct, who was a real pepper pot. Look, the whole thing was patterned after *Time*'s Henry Luce. Charles Laughton took days to find his character and then he stayed in character. I was a muscle guy named Womack, his masseur and hired gun. Charles said I gave the loveliest massages. His wife Elsa Lanchester was also in it and she watched our scenes together. She'd shout, "Charles, do not underact here!" As if Charles ever under acted. He'd play with words and it was hard to keep a scene going.

BAWDEN: How did the TV series *December Bride* come your way?

MORGAN: Because I told my agent I wasn't proud. I'd do TV. Needed a steady job. I was married with kids by then, freelancing after my Fox years. Waiting for weeks for the telephone to ring was deadly. I got the argument up and down it would ruin me in pictures. Made me hotter than ever. Started it in 1954 and I'd just made *The Glenn Miller Story*, which was my highest-grossing hit. In 1955 I still managed three pictures on the side, including *Strategic Air Command*.

BAWDEN: How was *December Bride* done?

MORGAN: Very carefully. After all, our two girls, Spring Byington and Verna Felton, were on the sunny side of sixty. We started off with an audience—we shot at Desilu—but those two couldn't always remember lines. So we finally did it without bleachers and all the tension was gone and they never forgot a line after that, with only the crew to play off. Freddie De Cordova was the director and he used the same technique he'd used on *Burns and Allen*. We took about three to four days per episode. We worked Saturdays the first year. Parke Levy created it and he was always there for script consultations. But he never had another hit. He later created *Many Happy Returns*, which ran one season, 1964 to 1965.

Dean Miller and Frances Rafferty were the newlyweds. It was very amiable. I was the next-door neighbor, Pete, and I told jokes about my wife, Gladys, who was never ever seen. It just goes to show you. It ran 155 episodes, but CBS was always happy because it was family friendly. Levy told me Lily was created after his own mother-in-law. I remember a teen named Joel Grey played her nephew a few times. A happy cast. For a family show, we were on late—Mondays at 9:30 p.m. But our lead-in was heavenly: *I Love Lucy*. Anything would have been a hit after *Lucy*. CBS made big money in syndication after cancellation in 1959. Today it's disappeared.

BAWDEN: You then went right back at it with *Pete and Gladys*.

MORGAN: I had a bad feeling about it from the start. Gladys was funny as long as people didn't see her. And Cara Williams as Gladys was an accomplished actress. She was married at the time to John Barrymore Jr. The show never jelled. Levy really worked on the scripts. Nothing happened. We did seventy-two episodes in two years. We got quite desperate, but nobody was watching. In fact, we lost viewers over that two-year period against *Riverboat* on NBC.

BAWDEN: After all that TV, you got a great movie part in *Inherit the Wind* [1960].

MORGAN: As Judge Coffey. It was the Scopes monkey trial, but they had to change the names of everyone. Spence Tracy was really Clarence Darrow, Freddie March was William Jennings Bryan. The two greats both were double Oscar winners and both were vastly competitive. Every time Spence spoke very quietly, Freddie would start fanning himself to provide some distraction. I was in every courtroom scene, of course, but I had little to do except listen and occasionally interject something. It worked wonderfully onstage, less so here because there were attempts to open it out a bit. When Spence took an Oscar nomination and Freddie didn't, there was much press comment. I think March has the harder part, although his side wins. He just got to the bombastic essence of Bryan. It didn't make a lot of profit because our leads were both over sixty. It's an old man's picture. I looked like a kid next to these two titans.

BAWDEN: I'm intrigued by *The Richard Boone Show* [1963–1964] because it was very different.

MORGAN: After *Medic*, Dick Boone could write his own ticket at NBC. And he asked for a TV repertory hour—different story every week, but with the same cast of actors. Sometimes I'd have the lead, on other occasions I'd get one line. NBC loathed it. It didn't fit in any of their boxes at all. The cast included Lloyd Bridges, Bobby Blake, Laura Devon, Jeanette Nolan, Warren Stevens; I can't think offhand of the others. We started in September 1963, got walloped every week by *Petticoat Junction* on CBS. NBC lost patience and canceled us in March after just fifteen episodes.

BAWDEN: Your next series was the flop *Kentucky Jones* [1964–1965].

MORGAN: Only seven episodes were made. We got several time slots and flopped everywhere. Dennis Weaver was determined to show he could be more than *Gunsmoke*'s limping Chester. It was too twee, too much removed from reality. Nobody is that clean-cut. I played a character named Seldom Jackson. I was seldom, if ever, funny in that one.

BAWDEN: You've said one of the most important movies you made was *Dark City* [1950]. Why?

MORGAN: Because it's where I met Jack Webb and he was a journeyman character actor at the time. I think he had just made *Sunset Blvd.* at that point. We had scenes together, clicked, and I figured he had forgotten me. Although, as a joke, I'm unbilled in [Webb's] *Pete Kelly's Blues* [1955]. Fast-forward sixteen years and Jack phones me up and says he's remounting *Dragnet* and needs a new partner. The original guy, Ben Alexander, was busy doing another police show [*Felony Squad*] with Howard Duff. So we meet and I agree to do *Dragnet '66* as a TV movie and it gets grand ratings and Jack has a three-year contract because he's considered so powerful at NBC. I played Gannon and in four seasons—we started at the halfway mark in '67—we made ninety-eight episodes, enough to sell big-time in syndication. Look, I was over the age limit to play a cop, but so was Jack. He can be a funny guy on set. But he insists on that staccato rhythm to scenes and some actors just can't do it. When David Janssen later did a series for Jack, David was in tears because he couldn't talk like that. We'd do a half-hour episode in three days and there were rarely retakes.

BAWDEN: You just couldn't stay away, could you? Next up was *Hec Ramsay* [1972–1974].

MORGAN: I blame it all on Dick Boone. He got me into it and he played a turn-of-the-century private detective and sheriff. I played Doc Amos. We did eight of those starting in 1972 and we usually were on once a month as part of that mystery wheel. NBC considered it very expensive because of the period accoutrements and Dick has such a hot temper he'd always be shouting at the NBC executives who'd wander by. All we had to do was match the ratings for *Columbo* [another show in the "mystery wheel"], which we certainly didn't. So I was unsurprised we got canceled.

BAWDEN: How did you land *M*A*S*H*, your most famous gig?

MORGAN: Well, I was on there first in 1974 as General Bartford and I rather liked the atmosphere. And when McLean Stevenson left to do his own series, they hired me as Colonel Sherman Potter the very next year and I stuck with it until the bitter end in 1983. You were on set for the farewell episode, I recall, but it wasn't the last one filmed. We just did it with the TV critics in town so you pests would leave us alone. Everybody cried during that show. I certainly did. It was the best thing I've ever done and my obit will read: "'*M*A*S*H*'s Colonel Potter Dead,'" I betcha.

The rest of us had weekends off. Not [the show's star] Alan [Alda]. He was always working on scripts in his office all Saturday with producer Burt Metcalfe, if in town. Sometimes he'd fly back to New York to say hi to the wife. It was very collegial. We shot one episode a week. Script readings around a table started off the week. Alan never became careless just because the show was such a hit. The show was shot leisurely with a lot of takes. I can't say enough about that guy. Of course, it was all a metaphor for the Vietnam War then raging [though the show was set during the Korean War]. But CBS suits kept their distance.

Alan liked to tell the story that he got the worst decrepit, dusty sound-stage because Fox was not expecting it to be a hit. And Fox executives argued he could do it only in three or four days because that's the time that was allotted to *Nanny and the Professor*. But we showed 'em.

This one continues to reap millions in syndication. It's the gold standard. I was closest to Loretta Swit. I admire her beauty and her acting ability. And I really miss just going there every day, I really do.

BAWDEN: You really couldn't stay away from series, could you? Next came the sequel series *After M*A*S*H* [1983–1984], and I remember you were very glum when you took me to lunch on the set.

MORGAN: Glum isn't the word. It was *Pete and Gladys* all over again. *M*A*S*H* had ended and a few of us did this ill-advised sequel. Trouble was people at home kept waiting for Alan Alda to come through the door and he never did. There was no reason to do it. [Writer] Larry Gelbart was always on the set, typing new dialogue like mad. Jamie Farr [who played Klinger] would look at the pages and say to me, "Is this funny?" and I'd whisper, "No!" Bill Christopher [Father Mulcahy] wasn't a happy man, I can tell you. It's never been seen since. Thank you, God!

BAWDEN: You had another flop with *Blacke's Magic* [1986].

MORGAN: CBS owed something to Peter Fisher, who created *Murder, She Wrote*. The concept was fine but it only ran three episodes before getting

Henry Morgan (*left*) with Loretta Swit and Alan Alda in *M*A*S*H,* 1974. Courtesy of CBS publicity.

pulled. Hal Linden was a great magician, I was the dad. I think we clicked as a team. In the old days CBS would have given it a year to find itself. Competition was so cutthroat that was no longer possible. After all, it took a full season for *M*A*S*H* to take off.

BAWDEN: Then came *You Can't Take It with You* [1987–1988].

MORGAN: I was Martin Vanderhof. People expected the hit play, but this was contemporary, which was a wrong decision. After three episodes, we got the phone calls saying not to come to the set that day because we were canceled.

BAWDEN: And now here we are. It's 1988 and it's after midnight as you wait for the last scene of "The Curious Case of Edgar Witherspoon" on the Canadian remake of *Twilight Zone.*

MORGAN: It was a good part. I grabbed it. The rest of the cast is Canadian—Cedric Smith, Barbara Chilcott, Eve Crawford. I can tell the director, René Bonnière, is French Canadian because he always shouts, "*Acsheeeonnn!*" But look, I'm seventy-three; I should be weeding my roses.

[Two years later, CBS arranged a phone interview for me with Morgan, who popped up as costar with Walter Matthau in the 1990 TV movie *The Incident*, which was followed by the 1994 TV movie sequel *Incident in a Small Town*.]

BAWDEN: So, you're at it again.

MORGAN: I just couldn't turn down working with Matthau, who says he wanted somebody older to make him look young. And he's an actor's actor, very determined to make everyone look good. Walter plays an over-the-hill lawyer determined to defend a Nazi soldier of murder charges in a Colorado town in 1944. I'm the no-nonsense judge who gives him the case, hoping he'll lose it. Walter is a one-take wonder. He knows everything about camera angles and he has that quiet confidence to even incorporate a blooper or two into his character's essence. But this is it, I swear.

Afterword

As it turned out, that wasn't it. Morgan kept acting through the 1990s with guest spots on *The Jeff Foxworthy Show*, *Grace under Fire*, and *3rd Rock from the Sun* (he had three stints as Professor Suter). He last acted in the 1999 short subject *Crosswalk*.

Harry Morgan was married twice and had four children. He died peacefully at home from complications of pneumonia. He was ninety-six.

Noel Neill

Interview by Ron Miller

Long-lasting stardom is a rare commodity in Hollywood, and it's even rarer indeed for an actor who almost never was top-billed in a feature film or a TV series. But actress Noel Neill was and always will be a star because of the chance she got to be a major part of a cultural phenomenon. If her name isn't that familiar, then maybe it will help to know the name of the most famous character she ever played—a role she owned from the minute she played it and, in my opinion, still owns today: Lois Lane. That's right: Superman's main squeeze, the fearless reporter on the *Daily Planet* who worked side by side with reporter Clark Kent and never suspected he was really the Man of Steel. Well, at least not for a long, long time.

Neill was an untrained young starlet in the 1940s, appreciated by young men who saw the pinup photos she posed for, but not much adored by the studios, who gave her small roles in mostly forgettable movies. She was, in fact, going nowhere until she was cast as the comic book "girl reporter" in the 1948 serial *Superman,* which became a runaway hit in its day. Bear in mind that playing the female lead in a Saturday-morning cliffhanger serial was then considered a substantial step below the big time for an actress. Only kids would see you and they wouldn't appreciate your acting—if you even had the chance to actually do any acting in a serial.

But Superman was already on his way to being a cultural phenomenon— the most famous comic book superhero of all time. And Noel Neill was the physical embodiment of Lois Lane. Millions of little boys grew up loving her just like Superman did, and wanted someone just like her for a girlfriend or wife.

Neill was so convincing as Lois that she was brought back to make the 1950 sequel, *Atom Man vs. Superman,* then went on to reclaim the role from TV's first Lois Lane, Phyllis Coates, and played her from 1955 to 1957

Noel Neill, the screen's first Lois Lane, with George Reeves as TV's *Superman*. Ron Miller collection.

opposite George Reeves in *The Adventures of Superman*, the popular television series.

Though some actors would balk at being so closely identified with a single role, afraid that it would forever typecast them, Neill realized there was a huge positive side to it: she was the screen's first Lois Lane, which not only made her a star for the rest of her career but also made her a Hollywood icon. She dined out on that glory for the rest of her years.

To underscore the fact that she wasn't forgotten, director Richard Donner gave her a cameo role in *Superman,* his 1978 big-screen reboot of the Superman legend, along with Kirk Alyn, the actor who played the Man of Steel opposite Neill in those two early serials. Neill and Alyn play passengers on a train who see the teen Clark Kent racing past them, "more powerful than a speeding locomotive." A subsequent telecast of the movie added outtakes that showed Neill and Alyn as the parents of Lois Lane, played in the movie by Margot Kidder.

Modern filmmakers continued to use her, often in nostalgic cameos. She was featured (not as Lois) in a 1991 episode of the *Superboy* TV series. She played Aunt Lois in the 2004 film *Surge of Power: The Stuff of Heroes* and had a small role as Gertrude Vanderworth, the dying elderly wife of villain Lex Luthor, in the 2006 big-screen movie *Superman Returns.*

For years, Neill turned up at comic book conventions and movie nostalgia events to sign autographs as the screen's first Lois Lane. Two books have been written about her by Larry Thomas Ward—*Truth, Justice & the American Way: The Life and Times of Noel Neill, the Original Lois Lane* (2005) and *Beyond Lois Lane* (2007), which documents Neill's other movie and TV work and her modeling career.

In 2010, Neill was honored with the unveiling of a statue of Lois Lane, modeled on her, in Metropolis, Illinois, the city that's known as the official home of Superman.

Setting the Scene

I was one of those kids who grew up seriously infatuated with Noel Neill, so it was a major head trip for me to have a chance to meet her in person in 1986. The interview was arranged because Neill was involved with the promotion of a "Superman Marathon" by a local TV station in San José, California, where my newspaper was headquartered. Sixty episodes of the *Adventures of Superman* TV show were telecast. Neill had videotaped some commentary for the marathon, along with Jack Larson, who had played Jimmy Olsen in the show.

In those days, I was living in the L.A. area, covering TV and the movies for the paper and its feature syndicate. I drove to Neill's home, perched on a hillside in Santa Monica, and spent the afternoon chatting with her about her unusual career in films and TV.

Neill was then sixty-five and still slim, deeply tanned, and very attractive. She was warm and gracious and even shed a few tears when I told her how much I adored her as a kid and how jealous my friends and I were of that stupid Superman, who never seemed to even give her a little kiss—when we were all dying for the chance to do so.

The Interview

MILLER: It has always struck me as curious that your most famous role was playing a newspaper reporter and, in real life, you were the daughter of a newspaperman.

NEILL: That's true. My father, David Neill, worked for years with Fairchild Publications and later became news editor of the *Minneapolis Star-Tribune*. Naturally, I was going to study journalism in college.

MILLER: So what happened to the plan?

NEILL: I graduated from high school in January, half a year ahead of my friends, and I was going to college, but not until the fall. So my mom and I decided to take a little trip to get away from the cold weather. We left Minnesota for California, where we had friends and relatives. One of our friends was head of the music department at NBC. Our friend knew I had sung with a band in high school and suggested I audition for a singing job that was open at the Del Mar Turf Club. I thought it would be a kick—and I got the job!

MILLER: How did a job at a racetrack club lead to a movie career?

NEILL: In the early 1940s, the Turf Club was a hangout for Hollywood stars. One of the club's owners was Bing Crosby. He took a liking to me and asked his brother Larry, who was an agent, to see if he could get me work at Bing's studio, Paramount.

MILLER: I guess that worked or else you'd be a reporter today.

NEILL: It sure did. I became a contract player there, so I decided to skip school that year. From then on, things just started to happen.

MILLER: Between 1940 and 1944, you made a lot of brief appearances in films, but received few screen credits. For instance, I've noticed you in three films of the Henry Aldrich series from Paramount, but you weren't a regular in the series and never played the same role.

NEILL: Don't forget I had no real acting experience, so I was given a lot of small roles while I tried to learn my craft. They put me in a lot of teen comedies and westerns, but nothing much came of it.

MILLER: So after Paramount finally dropped you, you got the break of your life at Columbia from producer Sam Katzman, the so-called Keeper of the Bs because he made so many B pictures there. How did that come about?

NEILL: I had long, dark hair at the time and Sam Katzman thought I looked like Lois Lane. My agent had looked Sam up and asked him if he had any work for me. I'd worked for Sam before and he knew I could say two lines in a row without blowing it, so I got the job.

MILLER: Did you have any idea how that role was going to stick to you in future years?

NEILL: No. I wasn't into comic books, so I'd never heard of Lois Lane. It was just a job to me. At the time, it just seemed like this silly little show. I had no idea of the impact it would have.

MILLER: Lois is supposed to be smitten with Superman. How did that work out when you met Kirk Alyn, who was going to be playing Superman?

NEILL: We really didn't get along. He had a great ego. He was married to Virginia O'Brien at the time and she was really the breadwinner. Kirk was always kind of a smart aleck and would make a play for all the ladies on the set, which I thought was pretty low for a married man.

MILLER: That must have been fun. You did fifteen twenty-minute chapters of *Superman* with him, then fifteen more in the sequel. Did you feel better about him when you were reunited for your cameos together in the 1978 *Superman* movie?

NEILL: Let's just say I'd prefer to never see him again.

MILLER: Some modern feminists look back at Lois Lane as a breakthrough character, a plucky woman who was competing with men in a high-profile job. Did you feel that way about her back in 1948 when you were bringing her to life on the screen?

NEILL: Nobody had time to even think about characterization in the serials. They didn't have the time or money to mess around with that. In the serials, Lois had little to do but be caught by the heavies and saved by Superman.

MILLER: So we know how you felt about your first Superman, but what about your second one—George Reeves in the *Superman* TV series?

NEILL: We weren't close friends, but I always liked and admired him. He was a good actor and had really studied, but he was permanently typed as Superman.

MILLER: Reeves's death by gunshot is one of the enduring Hollywood mysteries. One theory is that he committed suicide because he was so depressed by his stagnant career. What do you think?

NEILL: I don't think he killed himself. He was unhappy about being typecast, but he was smart enough to realize he couldn't do much about it. I know he was looking forward to doing the next twenty-six episodes because they were giving him a nice raise. We all felt he was mentally all right, but I guess it's always going to be a mystery.

MILLER: Did they decide right away to cancel the popular *Superman* TV show when Reeves died in 1959?

NEILL: Every muscle man in the world came looking for the job, but they finally decided it wouldn't work because people were so used to seeing George as Superman. When they decided not to go on, I felt it was time for me to get out of the business.

MILLER: What do you think of the current Superman and Lois Lane? [Christopher Reeve and Margot Kidder were then making their fourth and final film in the series, *Superman IV: The Quest for Peace*.]

NEILL: I like both of them as actors, but I don't like some of what they do on the screen. They say you shouldn't mess around with a legend. Now Lois knows who Clark Kent really is, they're in love and in the sack. I think people are offended by that.

MILLER: Of course, you're speaking as the Lois who never even got a kiss from the Man of Steel.

NEILL: The closest I ever came to that was in a TV episode where Lois dreams she's about to marry Superman. It was the only time I ever got out of that crummy suit. But even then there wasn't a kiss—not even a handshake!

MILLER: Are you comfortable with the publicity that usually comes to you every time there's a new Superman project heating up?

NEILL: I'm not trying to get back into movies, so publicity is meaningless to me. But I do enjoy the feeling of love so many people have for me whenever I go on the road and meet fans of the serials and the TV show.

MILLER: What about Lois? If she were a real woman, would she feel as loved as you have been all these years?

NEILL: I doubt it. I'm afraid she'd be an old maid somewhere, still pining away for Superman.

Afterword

In the years after our interview, Noel Neill moved, first to Metropolis, Illinois, then to Tucson, Arizona, where she suffered a fall in her home and was disabled with a badly fractured hip. She died on July 3, 2016, in Tucson from natural causes. She was ninety-five.

Neill was married three times. Her first marriage was annulled and the other two ended in divorce. She had no children and had no living relatives at the time of her death.

Donna Reed

Interview by James Bawden

Donna Reed was one of those precious few genuine movie stars who came to television in the 1950s and somehow managed to settle her screen image into a comfortable groove that really fit her real-life personality as a wholesome, family-oriented modern woman.

Though she won the Best Supporting Actress Academy Award for her performance as the Honolulu prostitute in the 1953 *From Here to Eternity*, perhaps her most beloved screen role was in Frank Capra's Christmas classic *It's a Wonderful Life* (1946), in which she played the loyal wife of James Stewart.

Reed was born January 27, 1921, in Denison, Iowa, as Donna Belle Mullenger. She was a bright student in high school and a campus beauty whose wholesome, glowing looks helped lead her to Hollywood in the 1940s, where she became a busy starlet at MGM and soon moved up to leading lady status.

Though never a top box office drawing card, Reed was a reliable leading lady who found her métier in television with her own comedy series, *The Donna Reed Show* (1958–1966), which returned her to the warm kind of homemaker she had played in *It's a Wonderful Life*.

Setting the Scene

It was in June 1980 that I first met Donna Reed at the posh Baltimore Hotel in Phoenix, Arizona, where CBS was conducting its fall TV previews for visiting TV critics. Despite the temperature, which was hovering over one hundred degrees, Reed remained calm and collected through a day's worth of interviews. I'd arranged to lunch with her in the hotel restaurant, and she was civil and charming and amazed I admired so many of her best movies.

245

Donna Reed as Donna Stone in *The Donna Reed Show,* circa 1958. James Bawden collection.

Three days later, the CBS press group flew to Los Angeles and that night we were all taken to Larry Hagman's beachfront estate in Malibu for a barbecue. Waiting on the doorstep was Reed, who had joined the cast of Hagman's TV series *Dallas.* We wound up spending another hour on the back patio "catching up," as Reed put it.

The Interview

BAWDEN: How did you get into the movie business?

REED: Well, it was certainly a long way from Denison, Iowa, where I was born in 1921. I've never lost my small-town roots. Milking cows is hardly the way to become an actress. My [high school] chemistry teacher loaned me the book *How to Win Friends and Influence People* and it changed my outlook on life. I started getting great grades and the lead in the school play. But there was a scene in *It's a Wonderful Life* where I had to throw a rock through a windowpane and director Frank Capra called for a stunt double. I said I could do it and it was all accomplished on the first take. So there's always a little bit of Denison in me.

I'd always thought about acting but my aunt had me enrolled at Los Angeles City College because the tuition was cheap and she insisted I finish my associate degree in teaching as a fallback. Only then did I get an agent who took me to MGM, where I screen-tested. I made my debut [as Donna Adams] in a tiny part in *The Get-Away* [1941] opposite Bob Sterling. But MGM head Louis Mayer hit the roof and said it sounded Germanic and changed it to Donna Reed.

BAWDEN: You quickly went up the ladder as an MGM starlet?

REED: My second film was *Shadow of the Thin Man* [1941], where that great star Myrna Loy told me, "Stop acting and start being. Make it as simple as possible." Best advice I ever had. I was competing with other starlets such as Virginia Grey, Laraine Day, and Ann Rutherford. MGM played us off against each other, but we remained fast friends. I did a requisite outing in *The Courtship of Andy Hardy* [1942] and, yes, Mickey Rooney made a pass, which I rebuffed. I was in *Eyes in the Night* [1942] with Edward Arnold as a blind detective. I had a better part in *The Human Comedy* [1943]. I remember director Clarence Brown told me he thought I had a bright future. That made my day!

BAWDEN: You were criticized as the pallid ingénue in *The Picture of Dorian Gray* [1945]?

REED: I was rushed in as a last-minute replacement and our director, Albert Lewin, told me not to even try a British accent. The picture was all Hurd Hatfield and Angela Lansbury, but neither managed to make a career out of it. When Mr. Mayer finally figured out what it was all about, he exploded. [The leading character's decadence and corruption cause his picture to age.] But the picture was finished by then. Critical response was mild but it made a fortune at the box office.

BAWDEN: What did you think of the war picture about PT boats, *They Were Expendable* [1945]?

REED: [Director] John Ford said I was not his kind of leading lady. Too educated, too strong! This was the first postwar picture for Robert Montgomery and the studio was petrified of losing him. Jimmy Stewart had refused to return to the studio and said he preferred freelancing. Ford used to torture John Wayne something awful by praising Bob's war record and saying, "But Duke, you shot your Japs on the Hollywood soundstages!" And Wayne would burn with fury. I think it's a fine picture, but postwar audiences were not as yet interested in reliving the war.

BAWDEN: In what way were you involved in the movie about the making of the first atomic bomb, *The Beginning or the End* [1947]?

REED: The Manhattan Project involved my chemistry teacher from Denison and I got MGM interested in making a movie of it. But when the time came for casting, MGM picked my pal Audrey Totter over me for that one! That's gratitude for you!

BAWDEN: Instead you made one of your all-time best movies, *It's a Wonderful Life*?

REED: It was a case of availability. Frank Capra needed a quick replacement for Jean Arthur, who walked out saying she was too old for the part. Gary Cooper did likewise, replaced by Jimmy Stewart. People think [that] on a Capra picture we all stood around playing practical jokes. Frank had a definite idea on everything. One day I opened the door and said, "Hello" ten times until he was satisfied. And it was made for Jimmy and all those character stars he brought from picture to picture. But Frank took so long to make it that costs could never be recouped, no matter how popular it was. He was devastated when it lost money and he never again made such a challenging movie. The picture went into public domain, meaning it could be shown on TV stations every Christmas. And now NBC has acquired rights and struck a new print and it's a classic.

BAWDEN: Your last MGM film was *Green Dolphin Street* [1947].

REED: It was bought for Katharine Hepburn, but after [Hepburn had] a string of box office stinkers, it was given by Mayer to Lana Turner! Lana was a living doll, but never an actress. It was set in New Zealand and so phony I thought I better get away to another studio. So I declined MGM's renewal of my contract and signed a joint deal with Columbia and Paramount, figuring I could do one picture a year for both.

BAWDEN: How did that go?

REED: I was in *Beyond Glory* [1948] and *Chicago Deadline* [1948] with Alan Ladd, who was smaller by an inch than me, but a dedicated family man and box office tops at the time. Both were for Paramount. Then I did *Saturday's Hero* [1951] and *Scandal Sheet* [1952] at Columbia, both with John Derek, who was prettier than I was. *Hangman's Knot* [1952] was with Randy Scott, *Trouble along the Way* [1953] with Duke Wayne.

BAWDEN: Then you got *From Here to Eternity*?

REED: Again, it was a case of being available. Director Fred Zinnemann spent half the budget on the huge salaries for Burt Lancaster, Montgomery Clift, and Deborah Kerr. Did you know she replaced Joan Crawford, who left in a snit after Freddie refused to grant her wardrobe approval? Columbia studio head Harry Cohn said he had to cast [the role of the prostitute] from the studio roster, meaning either Audrey Totter or me. And Fred tested us and thought Audrey too blatant. She'd played a lot of dames. He told me [this] was a refined whore and she only craved to open a women's fashion shop back home. Scenes with Monty were difficult. He always had to be in the mood. But he trusted me and worked with me beautifully and I think I acted better than ever.

BAWDEN: And you won the Supporting Oscar. Was it a surprise?

REED: Well, Frankie Sinatra and I won for support. Deborah didn't win [for Best Actress]. I felt she should have. And Monty and Burt cancelled each other out [in the Best Actor category]. But it won as Best Picture and Best Script and Director. And it made a fortune. But my career was slipping anyway. I was a leading lady, [but] not a big star. And my kind of small picture faded over the next few years.

BAWDEN: In other words, you weren't getting the big roles being an Oscar winner should have brought you?

REED: I did the [Dean] Martin–[Jerry] Lewis picture *The Caddy* [1953] the same year. I did westerns: *They Rode West* [1954] and *The Far Horizons* [1955], where I was Sacajawea, to my everlasting shame. I went back to MGM for *The Last Time I Saw Paris* [1954], shot on the back lot but not in Paree, and a Glenn Ford thing, *Ransom* [1955]. I made my last leading woman movie *The Whole Truth* in 1957, but it wasn't released until the next year and failed miserably.

BAWDEN: *The Donna Reed Show* turned everything around for you in 1958. How did that come about?

REED: My husband Tony Owen [the producer] set it all up. We cast a theater actor, Carl Betz, as my husband and our kids were Paul Petersen and

Donna Reed with Montgomery Clift in *From Here to Eternity* (1953). Courtesy of Columbia Pictures publicity.

Shelley Fabares. Campbell's Soup bought it and ABC picked it up. It definitely was not *Mother Knows Best*. Gene Reynolds directed many of them. He later set up *M*A*S*H*. All kinds of great character actors guested: Jack Albertson, Mary Treen, Virginia Christine. The wonderful writer Bill Roberts created it, but with kid costars they needed schooling as well.

When I watch today, I'm annoyed by the laugh track, but the network insisted. I notice the all-white cast, which was America in 1958 in the suburbs. My character, Donna Stone, was not a Lucy scatterbrain. But she also had a funny streak of her own. She didn't work because she didn't have to work—and that was 1958. I remember at an affiliates meeting arriving with my real children, which deeply disturbed some of the wives of the station owners.

It was a huge success, but after four years I was terribly tired. So ABC signed us for three more years—that had never been done before—and guaranteed us huge wealth in reruns. It meant a total of 274 episodes. They have been running forever after. ABC used them in the afternoon for the next decade. People today are fascinated by the portrait they paint of America pre-Vietnam. And we are accused of being too cozy and socially conservative. But we did hire a blacklisted couple who wrote more than thirty episodes because I felt the blacklist so very wrong and immoral.

I remember on the last day of shooting, I took Paul [Petersen] aside and told him he'd have a hard time getting grown-up parts and now he helps other ex–child stars find their way in adulthood. But afterwards I didn't need to work and I didn't. I remarried and settled in Seattle.

BAWDEN: You became involved in protesting the Vietnam War.

REED: Had to. I couldn't understand who we were fighting and why. And I said so, infuriating such old pals as Duke Wayne. I'm conservative, but not right wing.

BAWDEN: Why was there never a TV movie reunion for *The Donna Reed Show*? Everybody else seemed to be doing it.

REED: But there was. It was all set up and ABC was on board and then I phoned Carl Betz, who I hadn't talked to in a few years. The moment he came on the line my heart started pounding. He couldn't speak above a whisper. Carl had gone onto another hit show, *Judd for the Defense*, and we'd grown apart. I started crying. He sounded so desperately sick and he told me, "I'll soon be dead from lung cancer." He died in January 1978, and I refused to go it alone. ABC said, "Why not turn Donna Stone into a widow?" And I said simply, "Enough!"

BAWDEN: But you did return to acting in 1979 with the TV movie *The Best Place to Be*.

REED: I was always doing things, but I wasn't acting. My [third] husband, Grover Asmus, and I settled in Seattle. I had enough money. I adored my new lifestyle and then Ross Hunter phoned me one day. He'd commissioned this movie *The Best Place to Be* as a comeback vehicle for Audrey Hepburn, who finally did not want to do it. So he had a poll taken of mature actresses and who starched well with TV audiences. My name was number one because the show had never left TV. It was still in reruns. So he phoned up and sent a script and I did it. Efrem Zimbalist was in it plus his daughter Stefanie and Tim Hutton. It was a two-parter and ratings hit the roof.

BAWDEN: Then came *Deadly Lessons* [1983] and two episodes of *Love Boat* [1984]?

REED: My slasher credit! They juiced it up after I left. What else can I say? I was schoolmarm Miss Ward, Bill Paxton was in it, Larry Wilcox from *CHiPs*. It was TV so the slashing had to be minimal. On *Love Boat* I was with Efrem Zimbalist Jr. again and others included Gene Kelly and Yvette Mimieux.

BAWDEN: Then the phone rang again!

REED: And it was Lorimar [production company]. I was told Barbara Bel Geddes is out of *Dallas* because she had open heart surgery and can't recuperate in time. We need a new Miss Ellie like yesterday. And a few days later I was on the set getting wardrobe fittings. And I was married on the show to Clayton, played by Howard Keel, but we had never met. He came to MGM in 1949, two years after I left. I was told right off: no imitations of Barbara. I don't look like her or sound like her. That's TV soap opera for you. It's a level of opulence I have never seen on any other TV show I was associated with and I love everything about it. I'm just starting up, I have a multiyear contract, and who knows what great things will happen?

Afterword

But only bad things ensued for Donna Reed. After completing her first season on *Dallas*, Reed was in Paris when she read newspaper accounts stating she'd been dumped for Barbara Bel Geddes, who had recovered and was back on the show. Nobody had bothered to phone Reed. She sued successfully for breach of contract.

Donna Reed died in Beverly Hills on January 14, 1986, of pancreatic cancer, less than two weeks before her sixty-fifth birthday. Of the *Dallas* cast, only old pal Howard Keel had phoned to talk to her during her final illness.

After her death, her husband, family members, and several friends, including her TV daughter Shelley Fabares, established the Donna Reed Foundation for the Performing Arts in her hometown in Iowa, which provides scholarships for talented students. She has been honored with a star on the Hollywood Walk of Fame. She was a Golden Globe Award winner for her TV show and earned four Emmy nominations for her work on the show.

Ann Sothern

Interview by James Bawden

In the early 1950s, when the television medium was still in its infancy, the networks were quite desperate for star power. Though many people were willing to watch virtually anything on TV because of the novelty of it, the networks needed well-known stars whose presence on TV would induce more people to buy television sets and get in the habit of watching it night after night.

But the decision makers who ran the movie studios still saw TV as a competitor that would give the public a reason not to buy movie tickets, so they forbade their stars from doing any television. That helped create a steady demand for the services of the growing number of famous movie stars who were no longer tied to studio contracts.

One of them was Ann Sothern, whose run at MGM was over. She seemed to be tailor-made for the new medium. In the 1930s and 1940s, Sothern starred in a popular series of movie comedies built around a brassy showgirl named Maisie. There were ten films in all and the B-level production values made them almost like what would become the standard format for a TV situation comedy series in the 1950s.

Though Sothern also was a fine dramatic actress and a talented singer— she had sung the Oscar-winning song "The Last Time I Saw Paris" in the 1941 musical *Lady Be Good*—her experience in the *Maisie* films made her the perfect choice to star in the 1953 television comedy series *Private Secretary*, which became a hit show and brought her back to nationwide fame overnight.

Sothern went on to star in two more weekly series after *Private Secretary*, revitalizing her career and giving a whole new generation a reason to think of her as a genuine TV star.

Ann Sothern in *Private Secretary*, circa 1953. James Bawden collection.

Setting the Scene

When Ann Sothern arrived for our first interview in 1974, I almost didn't recognize her. The lady that emerged from her Rolls-Royce at L.A.'s Century Plaza Hotel wasn't the sassy blonde from the *Maisie* movies or TV's *Private Secretary*, but rather someone who could pass for a grown-up Baby Jane, complete with baggy trousers and her hair done up in long ringlets. She must have

254

noticed the look of surprise on my face because she quickly explained she was currently playing someone who looked like that in a TV show and wanted to "stay in character."

Although I talked to her on the phone a half dozen times in later years, we never met again face-to-face. Still, I have many memories of my chats with this colorful actress, who was a star at both Columbia and MGM in the 1930s and 1940s, then became a star all over again in the television era.

The Interview

BAWDEN: Describe your first day at Columbia in 1934, and meeting with studio boss Harry Cohn.

SOTHERN: I just sat there with my mouth open. He's striding around his office and talking very loudly: "I've got a problem with yer name: don't like it." [Her name then was her real one—Harriet Lake.] I asked him, "What's wrong with it?" And he said, "Too common. There's Arthur Lake. There's Florence Lake. No more Lakes! We'll have to change it. I'm picking Sothern for your last name out of respect for E. H. Sothern, an actor I adored. Now you pick the first name, honey, and be quick about it!" So I chose Ann because it was my mother's middle name and mainly because I just wanted to get out of that situation. And days later when I'm at the pay wicket there's nothing for me—but there is [a check] for Ann Sothern. The change went right through in days.

And speaking of "Lakes," that moniker never hurt Veronica Lake, did it? Years later, I run into Jack Lemmon at a party and he says how he's new at Columbia and Harry is trying to change his name and tells him the "Ann Sothern" story and Jack says, "I still like Harriet Lake better," and the old man erupts in rage. Well, Jack got to keep his own name, but I must confess I did grow to like Ann Sothern.

BAWDEN: Tell me about your first Columbia picture, *Let's Fall in Love* [1934], a dandy little satire on Hollywood.

SOTHERN: My first day on the set and I'm told my dark red hair photographs badly and aestheticians rushed in and dyed it platinum blond. Jean Harlow was all the rage that day. We shot it in eighteen days, which was positively leisurely at Columbia. Edmund Lowe was the star—very sedate and full of himself, but he helped me through some rough patches. Gregory Ratoff was the daffy producer; he was playing himself. Betty Furness was in it, Tala Birell, and an oldie named Marjorie Gateson. Thirty years later I'm watching the CBS afternoon soaper *The Secret Storm* and there's Marjorie still stealing every scene she's in.

BAWDEN: When Cohn didn't have something for you, it seems he loaned you out.

SOTHERN: I finished *Let's Fall in Love* in the morning and in the afternoon started *Melody in Spring* [1934] across town at Paramount. Norman McLeod directed it and it was one of a number of vehicles made for the team of Charlie Ruggles and Mary Boland. Lanny Ross was my love interest. He was Paramount's backup crooner to Bing Crosby, a nice guy who never went very far.

BAWDEN: And back at Columbia you made *The Hell Cat* [1934], *Blind Date* [1934], *The Party's Over* [1934].

SOTHERN: Ten-day wonders. Bob Armstrong in *The Hell Cat* had just finished *King Kong* [1933] and then this! I have never seen this one on TV. Never! Neil Hamilton was my leading man in *Blind Date* and I remember Mickey Rooney played a little brat. Other than that I'm drawing a blank. *The Party's Over* sums up what life was like at Columbia. The films were bad, I was bad. When a critic gave me the title Queen of the Bs, why, I just felt awful.

BAWDEN: But then came two A musicals, *Kid Millions* [1934] and *Folies Bergère de Paris* [1935].

SOTHERN: *Kid Millions* was an Eddie Cantor vehicle. He made one a year and Sam Goldwyn lavished sets, chorus girls, even Technicolor at the end. We shot and shot. Ethel Merman was in it. We've been friends ever since. George Murphy was my beau in it and we later worked together at MGM. I was photographed lovingly. It was like taking a pep pill, going on that set every day.

Then I was loaned out to Twentieth Century for *Folies Bergère,* Maurice Chevalier's last US picture [for several decades]. His box office was sliding. His ego remained intact. Hated the other leading lady, Merle Oberon, who primped and primped, kept us all waiting. But he was quite a showman. They later remade it twice—with Don Ameche and then Danny Kaye. Maurice's next American picture was *Love in the Afternoon* twenty-two years later. He could have stayed on, but he demanded top dollar and the best in sets, direction, and his box office was waning. He hated the score and decided to interpolate his standard "Valentina," which he'd first done in the 1920s.

BAWDEN: Your last year at Columbia you made six pictures. When did you sleep?

SOTHERN: Oh, we'd make these in two to three weeks at most. The product kept getting worse, not better. Harry did not know how to make stars.

256

He just ran out your contract with as much work as possible. In 1936 I made six terrible B pictures. I had become the stock bland ingénue and it hurt. I knew I'd have a short career if this kind of thing kept up. I started to get loan-outs for Bs: *Smartest Girl in Town* [1936] was actually made at RKO with Gene Raymond, while *My American Wife* [1936] was a B I made in ten days over at Paramount with Francis Lederer. He was supposed to partner me in *The Whales of August* [many years later, in 1987] but withdrew because of illness. Gene [Raymond] and me were sold as B versions of Astaire and Rogers. *Dangerous Number* [1937] was for MGM and *Fifty Roads to Town* [1937] was a Fox B with a new guy, Don Ameche. I got so despondent I remember I crashed Frank Capra's bungalow on the Columbia lot and begged for the role of the little tart in *Lost Horizon* [1937), but Frank was very rude, told me I was a B picture floozy.

BAWDEN: Then you just faded away.

SOTHERN: My husband Roger Pryor was a dance band leader and I joined his band and sang for my supper. I was living off the bracelets I'd bought in palmier days. I was on the road in some town in Ohio and Bing Crosby phones and offers me the girl part in *East Side of Heaven* [1939], but I had a contract with my husband. [Joan Blondell got the part.]

When the tour ended, Ralph Bellamy, who I met on the set of a stinker called *Eight Bells* [1935], told [director] Tay Garnett I was available and he used me as the second femme lead in *Trade Winds* [1938]. Freddie March and Joan Bennett were the stars, Ralph and I supplied the comedy. Tay told me to go study old Joan Blondell flicks because he wanted the part to be played broadly. I told him I was as funny as the next girl but the story got back to Joan and she accused me of stealing her act, if you can believe that. *Trade Winds* came about because Tay and his wife, Patsy Ruth Miller, took a world cruise and shot footage everywhere, which got back-projected at United Artists and they built sets around that! Today those transparencies look so phony but fans thought we actually were in all those places.

BAWDEN: Is that how your career got back on track?

SOTHERN: Yes—and then MGM offered me a script called *Maisie* based on the story "Dark Dame" by Wilson Colliman, which had originally been bought for the late, great Jean Harlow. Fox offered me *Hotel for Women* [1939] with Linda Darnell. I made both and at the end of the year had two firm contract offers and I picked MGM. I had personal meetings with [MGM studio head] L. B. Mayer, who envisaged a whole set of *Maisie* movies. The Andy Hardy films were making buckets for the studio. I said okay but only if I could do a big-scale musical or comedy every year as well.

257

Fox offered more dough [than MGM], but [studio boss] Darryl Zanuck had fallen for Linda Darnell, the nominal star, and ruthlessly cut my part. So I said no thanks and Zanuck went berserk and said I'd never work again at his studio. And I didn't—at least for a decade.

BAWDEN: How did the MGM deal work out?

SOTHERN: Well, in 1940 I made two successful *Maisie* movies. *Congo Maisie* was made on the Tarzan set and was a remake of *Red Dust* [1932]. *Gold Rush Maisie* was a sort of poor man's *Grapes of Wrath*. I also redid *Dulcy*, which Lynn Fontanne had created on Broadway and on loan-out I did *Brother Orchid* at Warners. I replaced Joan Blondell, who had just left the studio, so I got another blast from her. I loved Eddie Robinson's competitiveness. In one scene we're in the back of a convertible and Ralph Bellamy is driving. His character was a whiz with bird calls and Ralph got a bit carried away with his whistles. Director Lloyd Bacon bawls, "Cut!" and Eddie runs over and shouts, "Ralph is interpolating more bird whistles in this damned script than are actually called for! Tell him at Warners we do not improvise!" And he stormed off the set.

BAWDEN: So why did the Maisie character take off and become so popular?

SOTHERN: In 1941 we made two more, *Ringside Maisie* and *Maisie Was a Lady*. Can't understand her popularity. Must have been the times. The war was looming, people liked take-charge dames. Every *Maisie* flick cost $350,000 to make and returned profits always twice that number. Once I was in Mr. Mayer's office complaining about the series and he took me to a window and showed me construction of a new soundstage which profits from *Maisie* made possible. He said *Congo Maisie* made more profit than *Ninotchka*, if you can believe that! We made them in under a month, using standing sets. I got a lot of leading men who were on their way up—from John Carroll to John Hodiak. MGM had lots of character stars to plop in, and as time went on the lengths ballooned and the films became top-of-the-bill attractions. On *Gold Rush Maisie* I had little Virginia Weidler to work with, a darling, but MGM soon cast her out to make way for Judy Garland. Maisie was always stranded somewhere and some guy was always trying to save her.

BAWDEN: You seemed to get all the other parts you'd wanted.

SOTHERN: Oh, no. Every actor has disappointments. I was all set for *Waterloo Bridge* [1940] with Vivien Leigh, but was felled by an attack of appendicitis. Then later on when I was pregnant with my daughter I had to give up working with Spencer Tracy and Kate Hepburn in *Without Love* [1945]. Lucy Ball replaced me and she also replaced me in *Du Barry Was a*

Lady [1943] when I couldn't finish *Swing Shift Maisie* [1943] in time. And I also ceded the second lead in *The Harvey Girls* [1946] opposite Judy Garland. Angela Lansbury replaced me.

BAWDEN: But you finally got a big musical in *Lady Be Good.*

SOTHERN: A hard one to make. Take a look at the credits where Ellie Powell gets first billing. In the movie she doesn't dance at all until the halfway point. And her character was basically in support of me and Bob Young. As filming progressed, our parts were built up on orders of Mayer and hers cut to the bone. She was furious and stopped talking to me for almost thirty years. But I could do nothing. She did have that great number "Fascinating Rhythm," directed by Busby Berkeley, but she felt ruined and her last two movies at Metro were costarring Red Skelton. I introduced [the song] "The Last Time I Saw Paris," written by Jerome Kern, and it got the Oscar as Best Song, although it hadn't been written expressly for the picture. But where was it in *That's Entertainment* [1974]? I wasn't there because I'm told the producer hates blond sopranos.

BAWDEN: What happened with *Panama Hattie* [1942]?

SOTHERN: Oh, you've seen it? Trouble was the producer started it going with [director] Norman McLeod again and we had the same continuity problems. So he tells me to go up to San Francisco for a weekend and catch Ethel Merman in the road tour [production of *Panama Hattie.*] He said not to tell Ethel I was doing the movie, as if she never read *Variety*! But I went backstage and she was very gracious, never assumed she'd do it as a movie. All this time they're building up Red Skelton's part to the point he was finally getting first billing. But the movie wasn't about him. We started and stopped it, I went off and did a *Maisie* picture. Finally they let Norman go and brought in Roy Del Ruth, who demanded they film more of the Cole Porter score than they were going to do, and we shot more weeks of bridging material. A mess, yes, and it cost over $2.5 million. But it grossed over $4 million. It was MGM's big musical of the year and all in blazing black and white.

BAWDEN: In 1943 you also made *Cry Havoc* with a virtually all-female cast.

SOTHERN: About the nurses at Corregidor. I was on downtime when director Richard Thorpe said Joan Crawford had walked out of the studio rather than do it. I read the script, my part was okay, and we went at it. The ladies included Margaret Sullavan in her last MGM movie, Joan Blondell, Marsha Hunt, Ella Raines, Fay Bainter, and Diana Lewis, who had just married Bill Powell. The gossip columnists, including Hedda [Hopper] and

Louella [Parsons], all asked to come on set because they expected fireworks from this bunch of bitches. But nothing happened. Maggie kept calling me "Maisie" to get me going but I merely smiled, and Joan Blondell kept ribbing me about stealing her act. We finished on time every day except when it was raining. Maggie had a strange clause that said she couldn't act in the rain, something about bad luck.

BAWDEN: It was about your last good movie under contract to MGM.

SOTHERN: I did one terrible comedy, *Three Hearts for Julia* [1943], with Melvyn Douglas that year and the requisite *Maisie* [*Swing Shift Maisie*]. In 1944, I only did *Maisie Goes to Reno* and then booked off pregnant. Mayer was livid. He took everything personally and my last two pictures in 1946 were *Up Goes Maisie* and *Undercover Maisie,* released in 1947.

I was promised if they needed me I could come back. I had one song—"Where's That Rainbow?"—in *Words and Music* [1948]. In 1947 I went over to RKO and did *Indian Summer* with Alexander Knox. The studio hated it so much they put it on the shelf for two years. [It was released as *The Judge Steps Out.*] And over at Warners I did *April Showers* with Jack Carson. That one I only recently saw on TV and I told a columnist we got away with a lot in those days. I mean it was a Jack Carson vehicle where we did old songs and hammed it up. But it was a success at the time.

BAWDEN: How did you get your best movie ever—*Letter from an Unknown Woman* [1948]?

SOTHERN: [Writer-director] Joe Mankiewicz phoned and sent over a script. He said I had the best part, but I'd have to take third billing behind Jeanne Crain and Linda Darnell, two Fox contractees. This script was a beaut, not a word was changed. What doesn't Joe know about women? My husband in it was Kirk Douglas and he made the requisite pass and I sort of caved in for a bit. But actors have massive egos and nobody is more egotistical than Ole Cleft Chin. After we finished, he dropped me just like that. It was akin to a divorce. We shot so much of it in New York State I actually was feeling that I should move there. Joe asked me to come back for *All about Eve* [1950] as the playwright's wife, [the role] Celeste Holm would eventually take. But MGM had hired me back for two pictures and I couldn't fit Joe in.

BAWDEN: How did it feel being back at MGM?

SOTHERN: I was Jane Powell's mom in *Nancy Goes to Rio* [1950]. It was based on an old Deanna Durbin picture. Joe Pasternak produced both and he was obsessed about breasts. He kept telling me to put on a bigger bra but would never have suggested that to Jane Powell. She was playing a teenager, although in real life she was twenty-two, married, and had a kid. But she had a huge fan base. It made buckets of dough.

Then I did *Shadow on the Wall* [1950]—real noir territory, where a child sees me commit murder. Nancy Davis [Reagan] was cast as a counselor. She walked around as if she owned the studio. She did. She was dating MGM vice president Benny Thau! There were tiffs about her attitude and she's hated me ever since and the film just didn't amount to much. Then I lost momentum again by going to Broadway in a very shaky comedy called *Faithfully Yours* opposite Bob Cummings. He was continually tinkering with it but it never quite jelled, although we lasted for sixty-eight performances.

BAWDEN: How did you get to TV?

SOTHERN: I was off for almost two years with hepatitis. I needed work badly so MGM resuscitated *Maisie* as a syndicated radio show. We'd already done it [from] 1945 to 1947 on CBS. They recorded the shows right in my living room because I was so weak I couldn't travel. When I recovered I got third billing in a mystery called *The Blue Gardenia* [1953] starring Anne Baxter, but I hated director Fritz Lang. He was so nasty. I could see my time in movies was passing. So I joined with an MGM producer, Jack Chertok, and we approached [new MGM boss] Dore Schary about turning *Maisie* into a TV series to be made at the studio. He blew his top. MGM go into TV? Why, the very idea! He couldn't think out of the box. None of that old guard could. So we approached CBS with an idea for *Private Secretary*. It really was "Maisie Goes into Business," that's what it was. Don Porter was my boss, Mr. Sands, who ran a talent agency. And we started in February of 1953 and ran for four seasons. Lucy Ball started *I Love Lucy* in October 1951, and Eve Arden started *Our Miss Brooks* in October of 1952, so those two beat me to it. But Loretta Young started her show in October 1953, so I beat her.

We did twenty-six episodes a year, alternating with *Jack Benny* on Sunday nights at 7:30. We were sandwiched between *Lassie* and *Ed Sullivan*, a great time slot. I definitely did not dress like Maisie. The clothes had to be just a bit outlandish, but look affordable. After all, I was getting a secretary's wages. She was what every secretary secretly wanted to look like. We shot an episode a week to maintain the quality but eventually there were quarrels with Jack [Chertok] about the outside work I could take, so in 1957 I sold the reruns—all 108 half hours—to syndication. I got 42 percent of the profits, which was over $1 million. They retitled the reruns *Susie* and it ran in daytime slots for years and years. Reruns were just being born!

BAWDEN: You then formed Anso Productions and returned with *The Ann Sothern Show* [1958–1961]?

SOTHERN: The last time I played Susie was on an episode of *The Lucy-Desi Comedy Hour*—the opener, to be precise—and Desi said, through Desilu, he wanted to bring me back to TV. CBS signed and this time I was an upscale Maisie named Katy O'Connor. We debuted in the fall of 1958 with that wonderful old character actor Ernest Truex as my boss in a hotel situation. But the fans deluged me with letters: "Where was Don Porter?" Finally CBS ordered me to fire Ernest and bring back Don Porter as the manager of the hotel. In this one I got to boss the men around a bit. Jesse White was also back and Ann Tyrell as my secretary. I was at "that age" by then so I designed my own clothes and I got a lot of old pals as guests: Lucy, Eva Gabor, Van Johnson, Joe E. Brown. We ran ninety-eight episodes on that one. In the third year we were opposite another Desilu show, *The Untouchables,* on ABC, and it killed us. Desi said he could no nothing, but I wondered. And this series never went into reruns as it should have.

Then CBS offered yet another comedy called *Atta Boy, Mama,* casting me as a small-town mayor. We filmed the pilot but it reeked and I just walked away from it, although CBS wanted to go ahead. Then Desi came up with *The Mothers-in-Law* [with Sothern and Eve Arden] and peddled it to CBS, which said Eve Arden and I had similar comedy styles. I was busy elsewhere when Desi finally sold it to NBC with Kaye Ballard and Eve in the leads.

BAWDEN: What happened?

SOTHERN: I'd been Maisie. I'd been Susie, I'd been Katy. Time to be just plain Ann for a bit. Moved to New York with my daughter and I enrolled at the Actors Studio. Stella Adler spots me in class and her jaw drops open. But I wanted to dispel all that sitcom shtick that had been getting me by. And I did succeed. I played a shabby prostitute in *Lady in a Cage* [1964] and the reviews were fantastic. My first day on set, I was all dolled up as an aged hooker and [the film's star] Olivia de Havilland just walked right by me. Didn't recognize me at all. Took [union] scale and a deferred salary to do it and wound up making big bucks because it was such a hit. But no Oscar nomination in support as I'd hoped because the movie sparked a big debate on violence.

BAWDEN: You had a whole new career.

SOTHERN: I then did *Sylvia* [1965] as Carroll Baker's blowsy sidekick. The picture went nowhere fast, but I had a beautiful scene in a restaurant, breaking down and admitting I was nothing more than a big fat slob. Now that scene was difficult to do! *Chubasco* [1968]: that was just plain hard slog-ging. Christopher Jones is of the mugging school of acting and I felt I was pulling teeth. He was a Method actor, all mixed up. You should never bring your problems to the set.

Then I drifted into TV movie work. Trisha Sterling [her daughter] was going to New York to make one called *Death of Innocence* and I went along as her dramatic coach. Kim Stanley left after the first day and I was asked to step in. The very next day I had this heavy confrontational scene with Shelley Winters and I sort of mauled her. Another good one from that period was *Weekend Nun* [1972] with Joanna Pettet. I was the aged mother superior, try-ing to convince this disillusioned woman to stay in the convent.

BAWDEN: But you also retained a TV connection.

SOTHERN: In 1965, Viv Vance decided to leave *The Lucy Show* and "Lu-squeal" phoned and offered me a running part as Countess *Framboise*— that's cheese, you know. [Sothern was wrong. That's the French word for rasp-berry, not cheese.] And I did seven or eight of these over the season and had a ball. But Lucy was in bossy mode. She'd show me how to do every line, every reaction shot. And frankly I did not want to be tied down as her second-in-command. So I departed. I did the voice for *My Mother the Car* [1965]. I'd record episodes in the studio and decamp. Easiest money I ever made.

BAWDEN: You have a reputation as one of Hollywood's craftiest businesswomen.

SOTHERN: Guilty as charged! There'll never be a benefit for this gal. For years I had a sewing circle back in Idaho and a dress shop nearby. There was a ranch to raise black Angus and I finally sold most of these. People still write for copies of my album *Sothern Exposure*. One thing I don't do are the talk shows. Not at those prices!

BAWDEN: What are your comments on *That's Entertainment!*, the pop-ular film made up of scenes from MGM hits of the past?

SOTHERN: Try adding a "Not" in between the other two words. I just wasn't there. Jane Powell wasn't there. Jeanette MacDonald and Nelson Eddy were mocked. Believe me, they knew exactly what they were doing. They never got serious about those songs. They happily sang them with a lot of irony at times. The producers tried to stuff too much in, cutting down scenes to the bare bones. I did go to a special sneak preview at Metro on invitation. Just before the lights were doused, in tottered a very old gal. It was Norma Shearer, once the queen of the lot. That night nobody in the big crowd recognized her.

BAWDEN: Tell me about your next picture.

SOTHERN: Curtis Harrington directed. It's called *The Killing Kind* [1973]. A brilliant new actor, John Savage, is amazing. Ruthie Roman is around. It's my favorite performance. We shot everything in a Victorian mansion and the look is as far away from Metro as possible. I never cared how I look. Here I look awful, a real nasty mother, and I was quite done in emotionally when it was over. Next week I'm off to Hong Kong to make *Golden Needles* [1974]. I'm a mah-jongg parlor hostess. Back with Burgess Meredith after how many years? I'm continuing to seek out work, which is great therapy.

Afterword

During the 1980s, Ann Sothern moved to a ranch in Idaho with daughter Trisha and curtailed her acting, although she managed a cameo in the bad TV movie remake of *A Letter to Three Wives* (1985). Still later, she costarred with Bette Davis and Lillian Gish in the 1987 feature film *The Whales of August*. I phoned her the day after she received a Supporting Actress Oscar nomination for that film and asked her how it felt to finally get an Oscar nomination for her acting.

"It's only taken me sixty years!" she told me. "I feel awful for Bette and Miss Lillian for being overlooked. It was some shoot, let me tell you. Very rough conditions. We lived out of trailers. Bette is cantankerous, you know, and loves to pick fights. I had to grin and bear it. One day our wonderful director, Lindsay Anderson, was explaining to Miss Lillian the kind of close-up he wanted of her and Bette shouts, 'God damn it! Don't you know, Mr. Director, that old bag invented the close-up?' So I'm glad I did it, even if it half near killed me."

As it turned out, Ann Sothern didn't win the Oscar—it went to Olympia Dukakis for *Moonstruck*. And *The Whales of August* was her last credit. Sothern died of heart complications on March 15, 2001, at her Idaho home. She was ninety-two.

Robert Stack

Interview by James Bawden

Robert Stack was destined to be a leading man on-screen from the start because he was a handsome, trimly built young man who looked good in either gentlemanly dress or the rugged style of an outdoorsman. He was the son of a wealthy advertising executive who divorced Stack's mother when the boy was just a year old. Stack was raised by his mother in Europe and learned English as a third language. (He spoke fluent French and Italian as a child.)

Signed by Universal Pictures in 1939, Stack was treated at first like a male starlet, drawing romantic roles opposite the studio's younger leading ladies, but he soon graduated to more serious roles before he was called to service in World War II.

After the war, Stack appeared in several A pictures, including MGM's *A Date with Judy* (1948), in which he chose sweet Jane Powell over blossoming beauty Elizabeth Taylor, and was the second male lead to John Wayne in the hit *The High and the Mighty* (1954). He also helped make film history by playing the lead role in Arch Oboler's *Bwana Devil* (1952), the movie that launched the 3-D boom of the 1950s. He finally was taken seriously as an actor playing a drunk in the acclaimed *Written on the Wind* (1956), for which he earned a Best Supporting Actor Oscar nomination.

But it was television that provided Stack the venue for genuine major stardom. As sober-sided lawman Elliot Ness in *The Untouchables,* he won the 1960 Emmy as Best Actor in a Drama series. He went on to other television series roles and many feature films afterward.

Trim and fit into his later years, Stack was an outdoor sportsman and a respected rifle marksman in competitions.

Robert Stack as Eliot Ness, circa 1959. Courtesy of NBC publicity.

Setting the Scene

I first met Robert Stack at an NBC press party at the Pasadena Ritz Carlton Hotel in 1987, and we met again at his Beverly Hills home the very next summer. Though the day was blazing hot, Stack's wife Rosemarie nevertheless served high tea because she felt that's what a Canadian would appreciate. I found Stack friendly and eager to talk about past accomplishments on both occasions.

The Interview

BAWDEN: You just know my first question must involve your giving Deanna Durbin her first screen kiss in *First Love* [1939].

STACK: At one point I was deeply disturbed by *that* question. But it's hardly asked these days because fame recedes and the younger interviewers don't even know who Deanna Durbin was. But to answer your question: boy, was I nervous! And the director, Henry Koster, tried out all sorts of kisses, from a peck on the cheek to a full-blown smooch. What wasn't known at the time was Deanna and I were both the same age—nineteen. The publicity department had shaved a few years off her age to make her seem even more extraordinary.

When she appeared on the scene, that was it for Shirley Temple. Deanna's films saved Universal from bankruptcy, but already she was complaining about being typecast. And it [the kiss] was a big event at that time. It made newspaper front pages. We were reunited for a second film: *Nice Girl* [1940]. But it didn't get the same reception. And no, we haven't kept in touch. She's lived in France for decades. [Durbin died in 2013.]

BAWDEN: You are a fifth-generation Los Angelino?

STACK: Sixth. My family was old money and we'd spend part of every year in Europe. In fact, English became my third language. My grandfather was the opera sensation Charles Wood, but I can barely carry a tune. I was into sports and with my brother won the Outboard Motor Championships in Venice. At sixteen, I was a champion skeet shooter.

BAWDEN: How did you get into the movies?

STACK: I never considered acting. But I was visiting a friend at Universal Studios in 1939 and producer Joe Pasternak saw me and arranged a screen test with contract player Helen Parrish. And I got a part in *First Love*. First I had to have my hair darkened because Joe said blond leading men shouldn't exist. It was done by Jack Pierce, who did makeup on those Wolf Man pictures. The day we finished shooting, Joe loaned me to MGM to play a Nazi character in *The Mortal Storm*. It had Jimmy Stewart and Margaret Sullavan as leads, and another young Nazi thug was an unknown Dan Dailey.

BAWDEN: You became a Universal male ingénue.

STACK: I was costarred with Gloria Jean in *A Little Bit of Heaven* [1940]. Jean was the second-string Durbin. Universal wanted to show Durbin they had another potential singing star as backup. I just went from picture to picture: *Badlands of Dakota* [1941], *Eagle Squadron* [1942], and right in there again on loan-out for *To Be or Not to Be* [1942] as Carole Lombard's secondary squeeze. I was shaking with fear, but I'd known Carole forever. I used to go skeet shooting with her husband Clark Gable. Just before the film was released, she died in a plane crash and here was this wonderful comedy and audiences weren't laughing but instead were in tears.

BAWDEN: After six years off for war work, what did you expect when returning to L.A. in 1948?

STACK: That I'd be forgotten, which was true. Had to start at the bottom once again. Then Duke Wayne offered me the lead in *The Bullfighter and the Lady* [1951], which he was producing. The great Budd Boetticher directed. I go down to Mexico and want ace bullfighter Gilbert Roland to show me all the tricks of the trade. It was finished and great at 124 minutes and then they cut it down to 87 minutes. Budd had been a bullfighter. He pulls no punches in these gory scenes. I think it is one of the great classics nobody seems to have seen.

Then Duke invited me on board *The High and the Mighty*, which really was an all-star disaster movie, the first of its kind. When I signed for it, the two big female stars were going to be [Barbara] Stanwyck and [Joan] Crawford and both left because they felt their parts were not big enough. I think one critic called it "*Grand Hotel* in the air," which is perfectly correct. Yes, it was filled with clichés, but the point is we started these clichés in this movie.

BAWDEN: Soon you were over at Universal International and making your favorite movie.

STACK: *Written on the Wind* in 1956. Our great director, Douglas Sirk, described it to me as opera without the music: a real weepie. A river of oversized emotion was on display, but we were told to talk in earnest terms. The sets were gorgeous and yes, it is soap opera, but on the highest level. It was Dorothy [Malone] who won the [Supporting] Oscar. I was nominated but lost. Sirk, you know, told me my character, Kyle, was really a latent homosexual, hence his drinking. Which made everything strange because Rock Hudson [who was gay in real life] was in it as well. I mean everything was bigger than life and, boy, did it make a bucket of dough.

Rock, Dorothy, and I got together for another Sirk epic, which I think a better film: *Tarnished Angels* [1957] from the William Faulkner novel *Pylon*. Here was a terrific yarn set in the '30s about former war aces, but Sirk insisted it be shot in black and white and audiences failed to show up. One day we're out on location and Rock tells me, "Look up!" And one of the vintage planes had a banner: "It's a Boy!" Rock set that up because my son had just been born. Rock was that nice a guy.

BAWDEN: So how did you wind up on TV as Elliot Ness, the starring role in the huge hit *The Untouchables* in 1959?

STACK: I was at home on a Friday night and Desi Arnaz phoned me in a huff. Production was supposed to start on Monday on a new TV pilot titled *The Untouchables,* which would run over two weeks on *Desilu Playhouse* on CBS. Desi said he had a firm series commitment and needed me as Elliot Ness. Desi warned me not to waver as he'd next phone Van Heflin.

I have heard that the Mafia actually ordered the assassination of Desi for inflicting such hatred on Italian Americans. But I can attest that Walter Winchell had a weekly pay packet of $25,000 just for his rat-tat-tat introductions. By the way, CBS passed on the show and ABC bought it up the same day. CBS chairman Bill Paley said it was too violent for his family-friendly network. But there was a boycott of L&M Tobacco and the company moved on as sponsor.

But look at the pilot: Jerry Paris, Anthony George, Chuck Hicks, and I were the only actors retained from the pilot for the actual series. The others asked for hefty pay raises and Desi dumped them. Another thing I vividly remember: when Desi came on set one day and said we were cleared for the first time to say "prostitute." Of course, the Italian Defamation League came right after us and Desi [agreed in writing] that all the fictional criminals we later used would have non-Italian last names!

BAWDEN: Why do you think it was such a monster hit?

STACK: Because it was a new form of TV. You know, Desi poured a heck of a lot of dough into the sets, production values, and he got big-name guest stars. You start with the directors: oldsters like Tay Garnett, Abner Biberman, and up-and-comers like Howard Koch, Paul Wendkos. A lot of big names wanted to be on it: Barbara Stanwyck, Joan Blondell, Keenan Wynn, Cloris Leachman, Peter Falk—I mean, I was constantly being surprised. And the first executive producer was Quinn Martin. Need I say more?

BAWDEN: It ran four strong seasons and 119 episodes, but started to falter in the fourth year?

STACK: We ran out of actual characters. And then we had Elliot pursuing Nazis in World War II, which just did not work. ABC wanted a kinder Ness, thinking that would pep us up, but instead viewers tuned out in droves. You do know that in the first year we knocked off *Playhouse 90* on CBS, which rather saddened me. The second season we knocked off CBS's *The Ann Sothern Show*, which shot beside us and was another Desilu show! Our own downfall was very swift. By year four, we'd run out of baddies.

BAWDEN: Why come back to TV with *The Name of the Game* in 1968?

STACK: Loved it. A ninety-minute dramatic series—that was something new. There were three stars, including Tony Franciosa and Gene Barry. Tony was the roving reporter, Gene was the publisher, and I was Dan Farrell, who had jumped from the FBI to crime reporter. It ran on Friday nights and was a big hit at first. My episodes came on every third week. But how to keep up that level of quality? A very young and dewy Steven Spielberg directed one show. Steven Bochco was one of the writers. Within the parameters of network drama, it was big stuff. Then Tony brawled with the network and left and Bob Culp came in. And ratings continued to drip away.

BAWDEN: Why return with *Most Wanted* in 1976?

STACK: It had a full season of twenty-two episodes, had Quinn Martin at the helm, and we shot all over Los Angeles. But it never got that toehold. *Strike Force*? It was on in 1981, Fridays at 10 opposite *Dallas*? Need I say more?

BAWDEN: And now you're the series host of *Unsolved Mysteries*?

STACK: I'm very excited. Obviously it's my background, starting with *Untouchables*. The production values are full force and never seedy as I feared. I like narration. I did radio dramas way back when and the interactive feel this series has is terrific. We get the viewers into the solving process and we crack tough cases. We really do. It's a new way of telling true stories. I'm finally getting praise for my voice. Who knew? I adore doing it. And in hiatus I'll do five episodes of *Falcon Crest* [opposite] the great Jane Wyman. Okay, so I gave Deanna Durbin her first kiss. Maybe I'll give Jane a peck or two as well.

Afterword

In the final years of his career, Stack did a great deal of voice work in animated films and TV programs, a tribute to his strong, masculine manner of speaking.

Stack's autobiography, *Straight Shooting*, written with Mark Evans, was published in 1980. His greatest career achievement probably was his Oscar nomination in the Supporting category for *Written on the Wind*.

Robert Stack died at age eighty-four of a heart attack on May 14, 2003. He had been treated for prostate cancer before his fatal heart attack. He was married only once, in 1956, to actress Rosemarie Bowe, who survived him. They had two children.

Ed Sullivan

Interview by James Bawden

If you set out to pick the ideal person to become a major star in the new television industry, Ed Sullivan surely would have been very, very low on a long list of candidates. For one thing, he was neither an actor nor a performer, but rather had built his reputation as a newspaper columnist. What's more, Sullivan was not overloaded with visual appeal. He wasn't very imposing in his physical framework, had features that few ever described as pleasant-looking and, even worse, his face was often set in a somewhat dour expression.

But theoretically, all Sullivan had to do was introduce acts in what amounted to a televised weekly variety show that originally was called *Toast of the Town* before it finally was dubbed *The Ed Sullivan Show*.

Sullivan the TV performer was so wooden in his presentation that mimics almost immediately began to make fun of him. Most particularly, there was comedian Will Jordan, whose embarrassing imitation of Sullivan was saved for posterity on a double-sided phonograph record titled *Roast of the Town*. Sullivan himself got such a big kick out of Jordan's routine that he booked Jordan as a featured act on *Toast of the Town*, where he became a comedy sensation.

Amazingly, *Toast of the Town/The Ed Sullivan Show* ruled the ratings for CBS on Sunday nights from 1948 to 1971. It became TV's premium launching pad for popular acts, and when it presented such talents as Elvis Presley or the Beatles, it soared to astonishing ratings heights that attracted viewers from all across America.

Sullivan's one-hour show became such an institution in TV's first twenty years that books have been written about its influence on American culture and home video collections of its episodes still command a steady viewership.

Ed Sullivan. Ron Miller collection.

Setting the Scene

I was the summer student intern at Canada's *Globe and Mail* in 1970. On a sweltering August day when our TV critic was on vacation I was told by the entertainment editor to proceed to CBC-TV's Toronto headquarters, dubbed "The Kremlin," to interview the great TV star Ed Sullivan.

First impressions: he was already heavily made up because he was due to tape an introduction to a Christmas special at CTV's cavernous studios in Agincourt. Surrounded by a huge staff, Sullivan served hot tea and digestive cookies, although I noticed he only drank ice water.

"What's this? The B team?" he joked when I walked in, but it only took a few detailed questions to get him in reminiscing mood.

The Interview

BAWDEN: You started your newspaper career covering sports, so I wonder if you could fill me in on what happened to the Hamilton Tigers hockey team, which moved to New York City in 1924. I've always wanted to ask you this.

SULLIVAN: They were sold and moved to New York City as the New York Americans and I covered them all the time. But they never had their own arena. They always operated out of Madison Square Garden with the New York Rangers. And they still managed to pull in big crowds until the Second World War when the team disbanded in 1942. All the players were Canadian and, with Canada at war, there weren't enough able-bodied players to go around and the Americans just folded and disappeared.

BAWDEN: Before you were on TV, you spent decades on radio.

SULLIVAN: Right through the '30s. In 1938, on my radio program, I had a contest: should Norma Shearer take the part of Scarlett O'Hara in *Gone with the Wind?* A majority of those polled said no and Norma subsequently declined the part. I'm not sure she ever forgave me.

BAWDEN: You know the critics say you're stiff and awkward.

SULLIVAN: I'm always stiff and awkward. Right this moment, actually. But again, it's not about me. People don't tune in every Sunday night to see me.

BAWDEN: You were famous for your feuds.

SULLIVAN: I never feuded with anyone. They feuded with me. I had the big show. They always wanted something, you see. When [TV critic] Harriet Van Horne said I was stiff and lifeless I wrote, "Dear Harriet: You bitch.

Sincerely, Ed Sullivan," and I signed it. Is that a feud? When Jackie Mason gave me the finger live on TV, I didn't use him again for years. A feud? Not really.

BAWDEN: What was your biggest on-air blooper?

SULLIVAN: I was so nervous one night I asked the songstress Dolores Gray to stand and I said, "She's currently starving on Broadway," and everybody laughed. They knew what I meant. And Dolores later told me it was the best publicity she'd had in a while.

BAWDEN: The strangest act you ever introduced?

SULLIVAN: When the former movie star Frances Farmer sang on-air in 1957 and we were ready to cut away if anything happened. But she was fine.

BAWDEN: Why do you think you've lasted so long?

SULLIVAN: Because I'm not in show business. I'm the outsider looking in. I still write my column for the *New York Daily News*. I still consider myself a newspaperman first and foremost. People don't tune in to see me. I can't dance or sing or tell a joke, I'm the emcee, and I get out of the way as quickly as possible.

BAWDEN: How did you get your start in newspapers?

SULLIVAN: At the *Port Chester Daily* in high school. In 1918 I got my first full-time job at the *Hartford Post*. I was at the *New York Evening Mail, Philadelphia Bulletin,* and by 1927 I was sportswriter at the *New York Evening Graphic*. I replaced Walter Winchell as columnist on the *Graphic* in 1929 and did it better, which is why Walter hated me. Now I'm with the *New York Daily News* and my column "Little Old New York" is still a going concern. I approach everything from the perspective of a reporter. I'm out most nights still gathering items and verifying each and every item, I can assure you.

BAWDEN: Have you ever reached a level of comfort on TV?

SULLIVAN: No, never. I'm on guard always. What could go wrong does go wrong. And because it is all live, there's an air of excitement. That's why people still watch—the rest of TV these days is all taped. And very boring and predictable.

BAWDEN: Did you ever wonder why you were such a hit?

SULLIVAN: Because in 1948, there were few choices. No clickers, so a viewer had to cross the living room to change channels. Sure, the time period was perfect for the whole family to watch—we started Sundays at 9 p.m. and went an hour earlier within eighteen months. And we always got the best guests, thanks to a superb booking department. It was a show the whole family could watch. You'd be amazed what I couldn't do. If I had a black performer on, CBS censors would warn me not to get too close or even clasp hands. I usually told them to go blow.

BAWDEN: The other networks tried everything to dethrone you in the ratings.

SULLIVAN: In 1949, we got our 8 p.m. slot, which turned us into a family show. I think NBC got serious in 1951 with *Colgate Comedy Hour*. In 1957, NBC tried *Steve Allen,* but we consistently beat him. I think we also had strong lead-ins from *Lassie* and then at 7:30, *Jack Benny* and *Ann Sothern.* In 1956, ABC tried westerns, first with *Cheyenne* and then *Maverick.* And then NBC plopped Steve at 7:30—so I made sure our big names were on right at 8 and then again at the close at 8:30 so NBC wouldn't gain traction with whatever sitcom they ran at 8:30.

BAWDEN: Any trouble ever booking guests?

SULLIVAN: No, because everyone had to be on the show. We'd plop movie stars in the audience. That was a plug for whatever movie they were promoting. I've always had a great booking department that was very important in looking for up-and-coming comics. People like Joan Rivers started with us on TV. Hardest time for me was at the Saturday rehearsal where we timed everything down to the last second. We always overbooked and I'd have to tell a comic or singer we couldn't include them. They got full salary though.

BAWDEN: Canadian Frank Shuster has an interesting anecdote about his first time on your show.

SULLIVAN: Canadians had been telling me for years about Wayne and Shuster on Canadian TV. We first used them in May 1958. And it was their brilliant skit on Julius Caesar called "Rinse the Blood off My Toga." It timed in at twenty-two minutes. That would have made it the longest ever skit on my show. I begged to be allowed to cut a few minutes out. Nope was their answer. In later skits I made sure I could at least plop a commercial break in the middle. But that skit was talked about all over the country for weeks after. They wound up with sixty-seven skits, which is a record for the show.

BAWDEN: You got all of Broadway's stars on.

SULLIVAN: We had Mary Martin and Ezio Pinza touting *South Pacific,* Rex Harrison and Julie Andrews singing from *My Fair Lady.* I'm trying to think of somebody who refused. I'll have to think of that.

BAWDEN: Now that I've got you, I want to ask you about the 1957 movie *The Sweet Smell of Success* with Burt Lancaster as a predatory Manhattan columnist. People must ask you if anyone really could have such power, and also did you recognize yourself as the columnist who always ate dinner at a different nightclub?

SULLIVAN: Well, Walter Winchell was a real out-and-out bastard. I'd never use a lot of the gossip he used to ruin people. When he said Bette Davis had jaw cancer, which was untrue, he ruined her career for years. My wife thought it could be us as the other columnist and spouse because it's true we did eat out. And about power: with nine newspapers in town there was a lot of competition. But I preferred to tout talent and Walter wanted to destroy anyone who refused to bend to his will. That era evaporated after a few strikes, so today there are only three dailies left. In the '30s there could be as many as seven editions of every newspaper.

BAWDEN: Here you are in Toronto about to tape in July your Christmas special, but up at rival network CTV.

SULLIVAN (*laughing*): This is the cheapest place to make a huge Christmas special with skaters and carolers, and it's being done at CTV because they have the largest videotaping studio in the world. Just ask Billy Graham, who uses them extensively. CBC okayed the location because their facilities are antiquated. And by the way, I once did the show live from Toronto at your O'Keefe Center, and you critics roasted me because I only had one Canadian songstress—Juliette—on the roster. I said video is okay for one Christmas special, but it has to be live the rest of the year.

BAWDEN: You understand, I have to ask you about the drooping ratings this past year.

SULLIVAN: If you chose to live by the ratings, you must also die by them. I'm fully aware the bloom is off. We got huge numbers when we had the Beatles on. Same with Presley. It's harder to get those gigantic acts these days. And homes today may have more than one TV set, meaning family viewing is fractured. I'm determined to soldier on. I want to hit twenty-five seasons, I really do. I've got some big names I'm dickering with. I welcome change. I'm taping this special and I might go that route more in the future.

Afterword

Reports suggest that Ed Sullivan was very bitter about the cancellation of his weekly TV series and he refused to do a final telecast officially signing off the show. In the years that followed, Sullivan was portrayed a number of times on the screen, most often by his favorite imitator, comic Will Jordan.

Sullivan was married only once, to Sylvia Weinstein, and the two had a daughter, Betty Sullivan. Betty later married Bob Precht, the producer of *The Ed Sullivan Show*. Ed Sullivan died of esophageal cancer at a New York hospital on October 13, 1974. He was seventy-three.

Danny Thomas

Interview by Ron Miller

Danny Thomas was the ideal performer for the first decade of network television: a talented, ambitious man with experience—as a comedian used to working in front of a live audience in clubs, as a radio actor who was both a member of a comedy ensemble and then the star of his own radio program, as a movie actor who had played a few leading roles in feature films, and even as a singer who had made records.

What's more, Thomas was eager to learn his way around in the new medium of television, even though he wasn't all that crazy about it at first. His earlier training gave him the ability to soak up knowledge as he worked in early TV, which probably accounted for his later success as a producer of television programs and developer of talent both in front of and behind the TV camera.

In the show business world of the early 1950s, Thomas was rather unusual. He was the son of immigrant parents from Lebanon, an ethnic-looking character who often called himself "an Arab" and used dialects in his comedy. Though not conventionally handsome, he had a lively personality that lit up whatever room he happened to be in at the time. From the start, he was the kind of guy millions seemed to want to invite into their living rooms via the television set.

Born Amos Jacobs Kairouz in Deerfield, Michigan, on January 4, 1912, he later borrowed the first names of two of his brothers to become Danny Thomas, a name that looked a lot better on marquees than the one he started out with.

Thomas first attracted national notice as a regular on NBC Radio's *The Bickersons,* starring actor Don Ameche and singer Frances Langford as a constantly bickering husband and wife. Thomas played Ameche's brother Amos. Thomas also played the role of Jerry Dingle on Fanny Brice's *The Baby Snooks*

Show and appeared as himself several times on NBC's *The Big Show,* a variety program starring Tallulah Bankhead.

In his nightclub appearances, Thomas was basically a monologist who told longer, more complex humorous stories, often heavy in ethnic dialect. His work soon attracted the attention of movie studios, and MGM used him first in support of child actress Margaret O'Brien in *Unfinished Dance* (1947) and *Big City* (1948). By 1951, he had moved up to the leading role of composer Gus Kahn opposite singer Doris Day in Warner Bros.' *I'll See You in My Dreams,* and in 1953 he had the leading role in *The Jazz Singer,* the remake of Al Jolson's famous 1927 film, cast opposite yet another pop singing star, Peggy Lee.

But television was to be the most rewarding medium for Thomas, who began working in live shows like *All Star Revue* (1952) as a variety performer. In 1953, he starred in a situation comedy built around his persona—*Make Room for Daddy,* also known as *The Danny Thomas Show.* A huge hit, it ran until 1964. After that, he returned in *The Danny Thomas Hour* (1967–1968), then did a sequel to his original show, playing an older version of his original character, Danny Williams, in *Make Room for Granddaddy* (1970–1973). He starred in three more series: *The Practice* (1976–1977), *I'm a Big Girl Now* (1980–1981), and finally *One Big Family* (1986–1987)

As a producer, Thomas had a fabulous run of success. With various partners, he produced *The Dick Van Dyke Show, The Andy Griffith Show, The Mod Squad, That Girl* (starring his daughter Marlo Thomas), and three shows that starred character actor Walter Brennan: *The Real McCoys, The Tycoon,* and *The Guns of Will Sonnett.*

A devoted Catholic and generous philanthropist, Thomas's greatest achievement in that field was founding and supporting the famous St. Jude's Children's Research Hospital in Memphis, Tennessee.

Setting the Scene ♦

The first time I met Danny Thomas face-to-face was on a tour of NBC's Burbank, California, television studios in the late 1970s. I was part of a group of tourists being led through the facility by an NBC page when a door popped open and Danny Thomas appeared, heavily made up for a gig on a program being taped there. He seemed genuinely happy to see everybody and immediately launched into a plug for his favorite charity, St. Jude's Children's Research Hospital.

The next time was a much more professional meeting—an interview on the set of *One Big Family,* the new show he was then doing for syndication to local TV stations around the country. He was on his lunch break and the first thing he did when we met—before he even shook my hand—was hand me his personal business card. It read: *Danny Thomas, Out of Work Entertainer.* It was his little private joke—and a good one.

The interview that followed was very pleasant and I came away from it knowing what I had suspected over all the years I'd been watching this fellow on the screen, big and small: that he was a genial and truly loveable guy—as well as a legend in his time.

The Interview

MILLER: At this stage of your life, people like me keep referring to you as a legendary icon of show business. I'm sure you're recognized wherever you go. How does that feel?

THOMAS: I've never really been impressed with me. I'm terribly critical of myself. I stand in line at theaters. I stand in line to get a hot dog. People see me standing in line and they say, "What are *you* doing here?" And I say, "What are *you* doing here?" And if they say, "Well, I'm getting a hot dog," then I say, "So am I, lady!"

MILLER: I don't know. The idea of Danny Thomas having to get his own hot dog is a little shocking.

THOMAS: Hey, I go to these fast food places to eat lunch and sometimes to eat my dinner, too.

MILLER: Okay, with all your fame and fortune, what keeps you that humble a guy?

THOMAS: You have to be brought up in the street. I had very little academic education. I had just one year of high school. I'm not proud of it. But as it turned out, by being a street kid, I was being educated in the business I've been in. I was a busboy, a night watchman, a punch press operator, sweeping up the plugs off the floor at a coal yard in Toledo. I learned to set type at the Boys' Club and I learned how to cobble shoes. If I didn't happen to wind up in show business, I might have been a printer's devil or a shoemaker.

MILLER: So you developed a love for hot dogs at an early age?

THOMAS: If I had $2, I always had one of those dollars in my shoe. That meant you could always buy two hot dogs with mustard, a piece of pie, and a cup of coffee. And I still love it! To me, it's a hell of a meal.

MILLER: So you were raised in a home where you had to help out with paying for groceries. I heard you sold newspapers to help out as a kid.

THOMAS: My dad wouldn't accept charity. One time the social worker came by with half a bushel basket filled with a ham, potatoes, five pounds of flour, brown sugar, and some margarine that looked like lard. My father threw it out on the front porch and told the social worker, "I feed my own family!"

MILLER: I know my own dad came up the hard way, too, working on a farm like a grown man when he was just a kid. But I never knew poverty as a kid. How did your own children react to hearing your hard-luck stories from your childhood?

THOMAS: My son Tony one day told me, "Dad, I love to hear those stories, but what am I going to tell my kids? I was born in Beverly Hills and I had a brand-new car when I was sixteen." My daughter, Marlo, got in on a little of this for her first three years when we moved to Chicago and I played on radio as an actor and worked in the old Fifty-One Club, which was my springboard. They [his kids] didn't know anything about hunger or not having any new clothes.

MILLER: Part of the legend about you is that while still in your teens, you sold candy at a burlesque theater and watched those funny comics every day. How important was it to be exposed to those amazing guys who had to seize the attention of crowds of men who only wanted to see girls in skimpy outfits?

THOMAS: The truly funny guys [from that era], when they just walked on the stage, you started laughing. Jesse White had it. Sid Melton had it. Mary Wickes. Bill Dana.

MILLER: When you began to do comedy, you were a monologist, a brand of humor that you don't see much anymore.

THOMAS: There are no more storytellers. My stock in trade, when I play clubs, is that I'm a storyteller. A storyteller comes out and says something like, "Two Jews met on a street" and off he goes. Myron Cohen was the best, but he died. It's a different kind of humor that the kids have today. As a matter of fact, for a while here [while doing his final series, *One Big Family*] we were having trouble getting the kids tuned to my kind of humor, my delivery.

MILLER: By now, I'm thinking, you must have a world of experience working with kids. In the 1940s, before you were a household name, MGM put you into two movies featuring their top kid star of the period—Margaret O'Brien.

THOMAS: I wasn't myself in those movies. I did *The Unfinished Dance* with Margaret and I played a Greek. Then in *Big City* with her, I was a Jewish cantor.

MILLER: As long as we're talking about your movie work, how did you like appearing in the musical *Call Me Mister* [1951] with Betty Grable?

THOMAS: I hated that. If it wasn't for Betty Grable, I'd have run away from that one. She was so dear. There's another person who never was impressed with herself. To me, she was beautiful.

MILLER: How did it feel to step into the role that turned Al Jolson into a movie star when they remade *The Jazz Singer* in 1953?

THOMAS: There was nobody better than Jolson, that's for sure. I remember Mr. Jolson couldn't get a job for fifteen years. I met him one day while I was sitting in the Hillcrest Country Club with my manager. [George] Jessel was there. [George] Burns, [Jack] Benny, Danny Kaye, Eddie Cantor. They were sitting around this big table and Mr. Jolson said to me, "You know, boy, I envy you. They say you've got something on the ball." He never would have said that to one of his peers. He said that to a fledgling that was just getting on. They used to say he was a great egotist, but that wasn't the sound of a great egotist. Then he said, "I'd give a million dollars if someone wanted me."

MILLER: Wow, what do you say to someone who feels that neglected after such a fabulous career?

THOMAS: I asked him why he didn't produce another Broadway play for himself or something like that. And he told me, "That would be *me* wanting me. I need someone else to want me. Good luck to you, kid. And let me tell you something: when they want you, bathe in it, because the time will come when they won't want you anymore."

MILLER: That's a sad story and a sobering one, I guess.

THGMAS: That was just before they came out with *The Jolson Story* [the 1946 film that put Jolson in demand again.]. Thank God he didn't die before they wanted him again.

MILLER: Though you worked your way up to leading roles in movies, a movie star career never seemed to happen for you. Why?

THOMAS: I made a lot of money in nightclubs. I was very highly paid and I never really was interested in the movies. We turned down *Marty* [the 1955 Academy Award winner]. That's when I was doing *Make Room for Daddy* and we just couldn't give them eight or nine weeks. Being a solo nightclub performer to me was a flight to the moon. You had no cues or anything. The orchestra is there and they play you on and they play you off. Talk about egotism! You could get egotistical real fast when you find out you're conducting an audience the way you conduct an orchestra. You're the bullfighter and the audience is the bull.

MILLER: When television really started booming in the early 1950s, you seemed to be a natural for it and made a lot of appearances on *The All Star Revue*. How did you like the new medium? Did it feel like a perfect fit for you?

THOMAS: I hated television because I never had the time to do the parts of my act that they insisted I do. I'm talking about *All Star Revue*. I alternated with Jimmy Durante, Ed Wynn, and Jack Carson, God rest their souls. They wanted me to do "The Ode to the Wailing Syrian." It ran eighteen minutes, but they gave me six and a half minutes. The "Flat Tire with No Jack" story, for which I became quite well known, ran eight to nine minutes. [They said it was too long.] Finally, I quit. I decided television was for idiots. Walter Winchell [the columnist] said I thought the people who watched television were idiots, but I meant those of us who were doing it, throwing away our material built up over a lifetime, material that would have lasted you for years in clubs. I thought it was a dragon that would eat you alive.

MILLER: Well, obviously you grew to like it a little better.

THOMAS: The solo performer never would make it on TV. But the sketch comic did, so you had to become a sketch comic.

MILLER: Once you started doing a situation comedy built around you own persona—a nightclub comic trying to be a good father to his children— you really clicked. But you also started to be a role model for American fathers of the 1950s. What's your formula for being a good dad?

THOMAS: If there's a secret, it's discipline with love. You see, discipline shows that you care. It works once the kid understands the reason you discipline him is that you love him.

MILLER: Did you try to work that philosophy into your TV show?

THOMAS: We did an episode of *Make Room for Daddy* where Jean Hagen [who played his wife] told me, "You're yelling and screaming too much at the kids." So I just let them do anything. That leads to a scene where my daughter Terry [Sherry Jackson] breaks down and tells her brother Rusty [Rusty Hamer] that it means Mom and Dad don't love us anymore. To them, we proved conclusively that discipline means you care.

MILLER: One actor you worked with on *Make Room for Daddy* who, like you, came from radio, was that wonderful comic actor Hans Conried, who played your Uncle Tonoose. What do you remember about him?

Danny Thomas with his second *Make Room for Daddy* family, circa 1957. *From left:* Rusty Hamer, Angela Cartwright, Sherry Jackson, Thomas, Marjorie Lord. Ron Miller collection.

THOMAS: You know, he was quite a Shakespearean actor. I first met him when I was making the movie *I'll See You in My Dreams* [1951]. He'd come up to me [while they were doing the TV show together] and say, "Must I do this garbage again?" Then he'd go out on the road and when he came back, he'd say, "You know, Dan, everywhere I go, it's 'Uncle Tonoose, Uncle Tonoose.' Nobody ever mentions my King Lear." Among my people, he was a patriarch. We kissed his hand.

MILLER: What do you think was the best program of all the programs you did on TV?

THOMAS: *The Practice* [1976–1977] is the best thing I ever did. It was produced by my son Tony and Paul Junger Witt, who's like a son to me. On *Daddy*, I was playing me. Whatever happened at home in that show was me.

But *The Practice* was acting—a performance. I hated them [the NBC network] for canceling it. They never should have done it. There's an audience out there that needs heroes. He [the character he played] was a cantankerous old man, sure, because he had no patience for hypochondriacs. He was a doctor who made house calls and chided his son for being a corporate-type doctor. He had a lot to say.

MILLER: I guess you weren't so unhappy when *I'm a Big Girl Now* [1980–1981) was canceled since it wasn't too well received, even though Tony produced it.

THOMAS: Marlo called me and said, "Daddy, tell Tony that girl [Diana Canova] shouldn't have a steady job. She should be having a tough time. What Tony has there is *Make Room for That Girl.* If the audience doesn't care about you, then that show's going to fail."

MILLER: Now you're embarked on yet another comedy series. Did you ever consider just retiring and concentrating on your charitable work?

THOMAS: A retired person with nothing constructive to do is a dead person. You know, at first I wasn't crazy about doing it. It means five days a week. Your legs go first and my legs are hurting me now, I guess from standing on the concrete floors so long. But I'm still a very active man and I look forward to coming to work.

MILLER: You've worked with several generations of young comedians. What do you think of the new people coming up now?

THOMAS: Today everybody starts on top. You go on the [Johnny] Carson show first or [David] Letterman. You go on with your six to eight minutes and you're a smash. Then you get booked into a club and the most material you have is maybe twelve minutes, but people expect you to be on for forty-five minutes to an hour. But you shot your wad and that's it. You have to have someplace where you can stink. Somewhere to be bad and still be acceptable. You have to go someplace where you can turn your garbage into gold. I mean, boy, we were bad [in the beginning]! I have some old kinescopes from my early days on television and whenever my ego takes over, I just go down to my projection room and run one of those. And I yell at myself: "You stink!"

MILLER: How would you sum up the life of a comedian?

THOMAS: We're a strange breed. This is a ministry for us. It's serving the public and looking out for their mental welfare. You make 'em forget their troubles. My mother said it better than anyone: "If you carry all your yesterdays around with you, you'll be a hunchback before you're twenty-one."

Afterword

Danny Thomas filmed twenty-two episodes of *One Big Family*, but it was not a success in syndication and lasted only one season. However, his legacy in television is almost without peer. He won the Emmy in 1954 for best comic actor in a series for *Make Room for Daddy*, and he is remembered as one of the greatest TV dads of all time.

Thomas was married only once, to his dear wife Rose Marie, who was the mother of his three children, all of whom went into show business. Daughter Terry was a popular singer, daughter Marlo was the star of her own hit comedy series, *That Girl*, and has made many appearances as a dramatic actress. Son Tony is copartner of Witt-Thomas Productions, which has turned out some of TV's greatest hit shows, including *The Golden Girls* and *Soap*.

Over the years, I've talked with both Tony and Marlo Thomas on several occasions and always found them to be as warm and thoughtful as their father was to me during our time together. In July 1996, I asked Marlo for her thoughts on her dad. This is what she told me: "I'll never have a better champion than my dad. In fact, when I was in a play, I always made sure he came on opening night because I knew there'd be one person in the audience who'd think I was perfect. In the beginning, he said, 'I don't know if you're going to make it. It's a very tough business. There isn't anything I can tell you. It's not like being a lawyer where you go to law school like your dad and then you put up your shingle: Thomas & Son. I don't know whether lightning's going to hit this family twice, but if you really, really want it, then it'll be worth it to you.'"

Danny Thomas died on February 6, 1991, in Los Angeles from heart failure. He was seventy-nine. He's interred in a special mausoleum at St. Jude's Children's Research Hospital in Memphis. His wife, Rose Marie, is interred beside him. She followed him in death in July 2000.

Vivian Vance

Interview by James Bawden and Ron Miller

For anyone who grew up watching *I Love Lucy*, it is impossible to imagine Lucy Ricardo without her ever-willing accomplice in comedy, Ethel Mertz, at her side. In real life, the chemistry between the two actresses who played those parts— Lucille Ball and Vivian Vance—was so potent that they worked together as often as they could even after the original *I Love Lucy* was already part of TV history.

Like most expert "second bananas," Vance was a talented performer in her own right and had solid stage experience before coming to television in its early years to help create one of the all-time most popular and beloved comedy shows. Born Vivian Roberta Jones, Vance disappeared into her TV character and became Ethel Mertz just the way Ball became Lucy Ricardo. Her contributions to television comedy are now indelible and unforgettable.

Setting the Scene

Both of us interviewed Vivian Vance on different occasions. Our interviews have been merged for this presentation, but we explain the separate conditions of our interviews in this section.

BAWDEN: I talked with Vivian Vance in the summer of 1970 in the coffee shop of the Westbury Hotel as she awaited her limousine to take her to Toronto's CFTO studios, which had the largest videotaping stage in North America. Vance was in town guest-starring in the taped TV production of *The Front Page*, which had been revived on Broadway with Robert Ryan, Helen Hayes, and George Grizzard. Vance had been added to the supporting cast, along with Estelle Parsons and John McGyver.

MILLER: I met with Vivian Vance in July 1974 when she was starring in a production of the stage play *Everybody Loves Opal* at the Cabrillo College Summer Theater in Aptos, California. She was much more sophisticated than

Vivian Vance. James Bawden collection.

Ethel Mertz ever was on her best day. Vance was loaded down with heavy turquoise bracelets and was delicately toying with finger sandwiches left over from an enormous buffet luncheon the college had put on in her honor. She had an infectious giggle that I thought was like somebody's charming grandmother on her third glass of elderberry wine.

The Interview

BAWDEN: One of those TV encyclopedias hails you as one of the best second bananas in the business.

VANCE: I love that because I think I was pretty good at it. My job was to react to Lucy Ball's antics and sort of be the audience. My job was not necessarily to be the funny one. And it kept me employed for more than a decade.

BAWDEN: How did you get started?

VANCE: I was born in Kansas—the year is none of your business. But by 1930 I was in the very first-ever show at the Albuquerque Little Theatre. I went to Broadway and worked my way upwards. In 1937 I had my big break, replacing Kay Thompson in *Hooray for What*, which was a semi-success. Then in 1941 I got star billing alongside Eve Arden and Danny Kaye in *Let's Face It*. I costarred in the hit *The Voice of the Turtle* [1945] and then moved to L.A., thinking I could get work in movies.

I had supporting roles opposite Claudette Colbert in *The Secret Fury* [1950] and with Jane Wyman and Charles Laughton in *The Blue Veil* [1951]. Desi Arnaz screened both of them. He told me about plans for the comedy series *I Love Lucy* and was looking for a couple to play the building superintendents. Lucy wanted Bea Benaderet, who she'd worked with on radio's *My Favorite Husband*. Bea was already gainfully employed on *The George Burns and Gracie Allen Show*. [Desi had] already hired veteran supporting character Bill Frawley as Fred Mertz. I tested and became Ethel Mertz.

MILLER: What did Desi see in you that made him think you'd be the perfect Ethel Mertz?

VANCE: I've never been able to figure it out. He first saw me onstage in *Voice of the Turtle*, but I was playing "the other woman" and I was supposed to be sleeping with Mel Ferrer. I was using long cigarette holders, wearing Hedda Hopper hats—that sort of thing. I was just the opposite from Ethel Mertz.

BAWDEN: When did Lucy warm to you?

VANCE: Took a while. She insisted on a clause saying I had to be twenty pounds heavier than she was and wear dowdy frocks. But, after some episodes, I showed that I knew how to make her look good and my acting experience onstage was valuable because we worked in front of a live audience.

BAWDEN: Did you ever warm to Bill Frawley?

VANCE (*chuckling*): Never! His contract said he could not drink the day of the performance. There had to be no smell of liquor on his breath. He

Vivian Vance (*left*) with Lucille Ball in *I Love Lucy.* Courtesy of CBS publicity.

was an irascible curmudgeon. He'd often treat me like dirt. Guess he was a Method actor. And Bill was twenty-two years my senior and he looked it. A crusty old bachelor who lived with his sister. Completely uncollegial. Would never run lines with me. And yet the public loved us together. Go figure that out.

MILLER: As silly as some of the stuff you and Lucy did on the show, I always felt you were like somebody I might meet in real life.

VANCE: We always tried to keep our characters human, even though we were a bunch of clowns.

MILLER: Lucille Ball has a reputation for being a very hard taskmaster when she's working. Did that ever put a strain on your friendship?

VANCE: She's a talented, driving lady. I think one of the reasons Lucille and I remain close friends is that one balances the other. Lucille had more ambition than I had and made me work harder than I ever wanted to work. She pulled me along and taught me a lot of things I was too lazy to do.

MILLER: Were the Lucy Ricardo and Ethel Mertz characters fully developed in the scripts when you first started playing them?

VANCE: We developed them over time out of our own experiences. For example, I told the writers that Lucy is so beautiful and lots of beautiful ladies in real life have a lady around them who's not too attractive. I just asked them not to make me too unattractive or it wouldn't be believable.

MILLER: In the years since the show ended, Lucy has given Desi lots of credit for making the show a big hit. How much of a boss was he while you were working with them?

VANCE: There was no boss on that set. He would have been trampled by the crowd. Everybody was allowed to have his say at every story conference. We rehearsed three days, then sat in a room, sometimes to 4 a.m., and fought out every word, every scene. Desi was the arbiter of taste on the show, but we settled disputes by a vote of the principal performers.

BAWDEN: On more recent sitcoms like *The Mary Tyler Moore Show* they do two complete shows a night and pick the best from both.

VANCE: Are you kidding? Do you know the price of film? [*I Love Lucy* was filmed.] They can do that these days with tape, which can be reused. We'd do a scene until we got it right. But once we got going that never happened. We had so many dry runs for every episode, starting with a table read and then a dress rehearsal. Something complicated like Lucy stomping those grapes as the other gal tries to brawl: that was pre-filmed. Same with the chocolate assembly line. We couldn't keep beating those chocolates, so we rehearsed and rehearsed and then filmed it once and then showed that to the audience.

MILLER: For all that, though, it always looked as if you two were making it up as you went along.

VANCE: Lucille and I always wanted our routines to look like we were doing them for the first time. But we might have been doing that routine for seventy-two hours before we got it right.

BAWDEN: One critic said you had achieved TV immortality as Ethel Mertz. How do you feel about that?

VANCE: It's cute, but being Ethel was also a straitjacket. People meeting me today are surprised I do wear contemporary clothes and I'm not at all like her. I was acting. And there are many sides to me.

BAWDEN: People assume, with the endless reruns, that you are very wealthy.

VANCE: We got paid for the first six repeats—same as the people on *Leave It to Beaver.* Next question, please.

BAWDEN: Tell me about the hour-long *Lucy-Desi Comedy Hour* shows that followed *I Love Lucy*.

VANCE: Lucy had to do those to keep the anthology series *Westinghouse Playhouse* on the air. We'd film them over a week and then show them to an audience. When Tallulah Bankhead showed up it was a week of tension and turmoil. But I think the show was funny. The ones with Bob Cummings and Fred MacMurray went nicely, too. With Red Skelton and Lucy, it was a week of one-upmanship on both parts. Lucy is very competitive. When she later guested on Danny Kaye's show, look out! They stopped speaking to each other by the end of the week!

BAWDEN: You came back for *The Lucy Show* in 1962.

VANCE: I did eighty-one episodes and then I left. I'd remarried, my husband lived in Connecticut, and I was flying home weekends. I became a nervous wreck. Besides, the pay wasn't all that great. Lucy said she'd get Ann Sothern [to replace Vance] but Ann refused, even at double the salary I was getting, telling Lucy she was a tightwad. I'd come every season; same thing with *Here's Lucy*, which I was just on. By the way, the original creator of *I Love Lucy*—Jess Oppenheimer—sued Lucy, claiming he was the creator of that fabulous character and she settled because it was true. I got to expand my horizons. I did quite a number of Red Skeltons, which were fun. I had a good part in *The Great Race* in 1965. I work as much as I want.

BAWDEN: Why was there never a spin-off series for the couple Fred and Ethel Mertz?

VANCE: Because I wouldn't do it. I said to Desi: "You mean I'll be stuck with that reprobate for another five years? I think not." And Bill immediately jumped to *My Three Sons* anyway. Then Desi offered me the lead in a new sitcom, *Guestward Ho*, he'd sold to CBS, but I thought the premise too slim and I passed. He was enraged and signed Joanne Dru and I even did a guest appearance to help out, but it lasted twelve weeks. I never let him forget that one.

BAWDEN: You were there the very last night of the Lucy-Desi partnership?

VANCE: I was up in the gondola of the soundstage watching Lucy do her last scene ever as Lucy Ricardo, the very last scene of *The Lucy-Desi Comedy Hour*. And it got to me and I was teary. I'd spent almost a decade with this gang and this was it and I blubbered like a baby. Desi was standing next to me and he was teary-eyed, too, because it wasn't just the end of a show that had become an institution, it was the end of the marriage as well. Running Desilu had taken so much out of him he started philandering, and that was it as far as Lucy was concerned.

Afterword

Vivian Vance was married four times, first to Joseph Danneck Jr. from 1928 to 1931, then to George Koch from 1933 to 1940, then to Philip Ober from 1941 to 1959, and finally to John Dodds from 1961 until her death. She died in Belvedere, California, on August 17, 1979, of bone cancer that was related to breast cancer. She was seventy.

Robert Vaughn

Interview by James Bawden

Robert Vaughn will always be remembered as one of the most intellectual and discerning actors of his era—a well-educated man who had a doctorate degree in political science. He even looked intelligent, no matter if he was playing a scheming Nazi or a grim-eyed hero of international spy capers.

Though he had several significant roles in feature films, Vaughn made his lasting impression as a star of television programs, starting with his role as the commanding officer of Gary Lockwood in *The Lieutenant* (1963–1964), his first starring role in a weekly series. He followed that with his most memorable role as Napoleon Solo in *The Man from U.N.C.L.E.* (1964–1968), by far the most successful of the many knockoffs of the James Bond spy thrillers on the small screen. Altogether, Vaughn starred in eight different weekly TV series, including his role as General Stockwell in the 1986–1987 season of NBC's *The A-Team*. Beyond those shows, Vaughn was extraordinarily busy through his career as a guest star in TV movies, miniseries, and other stars' weekly shows.

Setting the Scene

It was a cold and frosty spring morning in 1982 when I first interviewed Robert Vaughn one-on-one. We were seated in a warm limousine in a parking lot in the Toronto suburb of North York. Vaughn was in town to costar with Karen Black in a new TV mystery movie. Things had been going wrong for ten days on this shoot, and Vaughn, cuddled under a blanket with a tweed winter coat on, didn't seem at all interested in talking at first. But I'd researched my subject and I thought I knew what he wanted to talk about.

Robert Vaughn in *The Man from U.N.C.L.E.*, circa 1964. Courtesy of CBS publicity.

The Interview

BAWDEN: You wrote one of the best books about the blacklist: *Only Victims: A Study of Show Business Blacklisting* [1972]. You may be the only actor I've ever met who got his Ph.D.

VAUGHN: My agent said, "Why stir up all that old stuff? It might lose you a job or two." But it didn't and I'm glad people are still reading it.

BAWDEN: What was your feeling when working with someone who was a victim of the blacklist?

VAUGHN: Well, I didn't know Vincent Sherman was blacklisted at one point when he directed me in *The Young Philadelphians* in 1959. Nobody wanted to admit anything back then.

BAWDEN: You came from a family of actors?

VAUGHN: My father, Gerald Vaughn, was primarily a radio actor. Mother, Marcella Gaudel, preferred stage. They divorced and I grew up with grandparents in Minneapolis because Mother was on the road most of the time. I enrolled at University of Minnesota in journalism, but that only lasted a year. I then moved to L.A. to be near my mother and finally got an M.A. in theater arts from Los Angeles State College.

BAWDEN: When did you first act?

VAUGHN: I got my first paycheck for an episode of *Medic* in 1955 starring Richard Boone. I still remember the title [of the episode]: "Black Friday." My first film was *The Ten Commandments* [1956]. I was an idolater worshipping the golden calf. You can also see me racing in a chariot right behind Yul Brynner. What fun that was!

BAWDEN: I'd heard Burt Lancaster discovered you.

VAUGHN: I promptly went undiscovered. I tested for him. He'd seen me in the L.A. production of *End as a Man* [the 1953 play by Calder Willingham adapted from his novel]. But I got drafted and that was that. The plum role of Steve Dallas, which I was offered, went to Marty Milner. I was a failure before I'd ever been a success.

BAWDEN: I think you know what movie I have to ask about.

VAUGHN (*giggling*): Well, I just love *Teenage Caveman* [1959]. It was the ultimate in schlock! I mean, I had the most beautiful coiffure you'll ever see. And yes, I got to keep my wardrobe. You know, somebody said it was made in two days. We toiled on that masterpiece for almost two whole weeks. I mean, there's a sweetness here, a silliness. We shot in Griffith Park. The lunches were stale sandwiches. And I stepped on glass and had to go to the E.R. I think the ending makes up for a lot, don't you? [The film has a surprise ending.] Didn't they use it again in *Planet of the Apes*?

BAWDEN: You earned a Supporting Actor Oscar nomination for *The Young Philadelphians* [1959].

VAUGHN: After this one, Paul Newman bought out his Warner Bros. contract. [Newman was the main star of the picture and didn't get an Oscar nomination himself.] It was low budgeted, but director Vincent Sherman was determined to turn it into a sprawling saga. He packed it with scene-stealing veterans like Otto Kruger and Billie Burke. I had these scene-stealing moments as the drunken scion of high society and I just ran with it. And thank you for remembering.

BAWDEN: That led to roles in some pretty popular pictures?

VAUGHN: I think everyone in *The Magnificent Seven* [1960] eventually became a star. But for most of 1960 I did the rounds of TV dramatic series: *Checkmate, Laramie, The June Allyson Show*. It was the same the next year: a dozen TV appearances plus the circus epic *The Big Show*. I asked Dick Powell for career advice when I was on his anthology series and he said, "Get a TV hit series and you'll be a movie star. [James] Garner and [Steve] McQueen are the examples to follow. The big studios are no longer in the business of making stars on their own."

BAWDEN: So you took his advice with *The Man from U.N.C.L.E.*, starting in 1964?

VAUGHN: We made 104 episodes in four years. Sam Rolfe created it for MGM TV and he'd created *Have Gun, Will Travel* before that. Rolfe also created or developed for TV *The Delphi Bureau, Matt Helm, Delvecchio, Kaz*. That's a pretty great record anyway you look at it. So NBC basically gave him a blank card to develop a James Bond–type spy caper.

First point: I wasn't the first choice by either Sam or NBC. I know the actor's name, but won't tell you. In the pilot, which never aired, you can also spot Will Kuluva. He was replaced by the wonderful Leo G. Carroll. THRUSH stood for nothing in the show, but in one of the paperbacks written after the show's success, they call it Technological Hierarchy for the Removal of Undesirables. Of course, we rode the James Bond wave and were very successful for two seasons. Glamorous, but deadly. In the third season, NBC told us to camp it up and viewers deserted in droves. The studio made a fortune on the sales of paraphernalia. I got a very tiny cut, I can tell you. Ian Fleming [creator of James Bond] was asked by producer Norman Felton to give our character a name and he suggested Napoleon Solo. I'm told Fleming watched every episode and loved it. I think he would have loved even better a split of the profits.

BAWDEN: This was a very sexy show for network TV in the '60s.

VAUGHN: Suggestion is the sexiest weapon of all. Cool is what we were. The average TV viewer was being introduced to a new world of coolness. Young guys wanted a Solo-like suit. This was a gadget-laden show, although today they look mighty primitive. David McCallum was portraying an intelligent Russian. What fun! And the producers spent a fortune on the stunts. The cinematography was as good as in any big movie feature. And today boxed sets are selling like hotcakes. It's a credit I'm proud of.

The day Joan Crawford came in for a guest part was something. She arrived with her retinue. She was back at her home studio, MGM, for the first time since 1953. She told me she was jetting to Britain to make a film called *Berserk*, "which will put me on top again." But it didn't.

BAWDEN: There were stories of a feud with costar David McCallum.

VAUGHN: Nothing could be further from the truth. That stuff was planted in the gossip columns to stir things up. We liked each other and we still keep in touch. Both of us live on the East Coast these days. I mean, we share a common history.

BAWDEN: You disliked the spin-off, *The Girl from U.N.C.L.E.*?

VAUGHN: Yes! It simply diluted the main product. It started as an episode of our show, but starring Mary Ann Mobley and Norman Fell. They were replaced by Stefanie Powers and Noel Harrison. But because she was a gal, no killings were allowed. Instead, she used karate chops to disable the meanies. I just thought two hours of this a week was overkill. It was cancelled in 1967 and we only lasted until January 1968.

BAWDEN: But such TV success never made you a movie star.

VAUGHN: No, that era had ended. I got good parts in *If It's Tuesday, This Must Be Belgium* [1969], *The Bridge at Remagen* [1969], *The Mind of Mr. Soames* [1970]. And I still did TV. I was Tom Paine in the Canadian TV series *Witness to Yesterday* [1974]. Then on US TV I was Harry S. Truman in the film *The Man from Independence* [1974]. I was sheer evil incarnate in *The Towering Inferno* [1974], an all-star disaster epic. I kept working.

BAWDEN: Why, then, go back to TV for the series *The Protectors* [1972]?

VAUGHN: The premise was great, but not enough dough was pumped into it. It had a very thin look to it. Both in the abbreviated stories and the rushed camera work. I was a crime fighter in London, allied with Nyree Dawn Porter in Paris and Tony Anholt in Rome. For one thing, the stories needed a full hour. Everything was rushed. Our producer Gerry Anderson had done puppet shows and this wasn't his thing. I was relieved when it was over, but people still stop to ask me about it. Friends watched and told me I looked bored. And I really was.

BAWDEN: You like doing TV miniseries?

VAUGHN: So far I've done *Captains and Kings* [1976], *Washington: Behind Closed Doors* [1977], *Centennial* [1978], *The Blue and the Gray* [1983]. The pay is great; I'm still a TV name.

BAWDEN: What about *Emerald Point N.A.S.?*

VAUGHN: Here we go again. I think this one might go. CBS is very high these days on family-oriented soaps. We've got a good cast: Dennis Weaver, Maud Adams, Andrew Stevens, Richard Dean Anderson. On today's TV there's no place [for a show] to falter and then find itself. You have to start with all cylinders roaring. And we're up against *Monday Night Football* and NBC movies, so you never know. [The show lasted only thirteen episodes.]

BAWDEN: I have to ask you about your reunion movie, *The Return of the Man from U.N.C.L.E.* [1983].

VAUGHN: Well, we had Sam Rolfe do the screenplay. It was good to get together again. But Leo G. Carroll was gone. The '60s were gone. We were living in a different age. Patrick Macnee from *The Avengers* was drafted to replace Leo. We had George Lazenby, who really was Bond, but was called J.B. in our movie. [Lazenby had played James Bond in one movie, *On Her Majesty's Secret Service* in 1969.] But I think you can't go home again. I don't think there'll be another. Not with me anyway. [In 2015, a lavish feature film version of *The Man from U.N.C.L.E.* was released, starring Henry Cavill as Napoleon Solo. Cavill is best known as the current movie Superman. Neither Vaughn nor any other members of the original TV cast appeared in the film. However, it was a rousing financial success, grossing more than $100 million worldwide.]

Afterword

Vaughn persevered. He costarred in the 1998 TV series *The Magnificent Seven*. In 2004 he costarred in forty-eight episodes of *Hustle* and in 2012 was in thirteen episodes of *Coronation Street*. He won an Emmy as Best Supporting Actor in the 1977 miniseries *Washington: Behind Closed Doors*.

Vaughn was married once—to Linda Staab in 1974. They adopted two children. He died in a hospice in Ridgefield, Connecticut, of acute leukemia on November 11, 2016, just a few days short of his eighty-fourth birthday.

Jack Webb

Interview by James Bawden

Jack Webb was one of the most successful of all stars from the early days of television, a talented writer, director, and producer as well as a stylistic actor whose technique was imitated—and at times parodied—throughout his phenomenally successful career.

Webb made his first series of breakthroughs as an actor and writer for radio in the postwar days of the 1940s before television dominated the home entertainment scene. Based in San Francisco, which was one of several regional production centers for network radio, he began as the host of his own comedy series, then gradually segued to drama, producing a number of popular radio shows, including *Pat Novak, for Hire, Johnny Madero, Pier 23,* and finally *Dragnet,* which became a sensation on radio and paved a new path for him to television.

Before *Dragnet* became a television hit, Webb had appeared in supporting roles in several major films. He was in *The Men* (1950), Marlon Brando's first film, playing a hospitalized ex-G.I. pal of Brando, and *Sunset Blvd.* (1950), portraying a drinking buddy of screenwriter Bill Holden. But most important was his role as a crime technician in *He Walked by Night* (1948), a fact-based documentary-style police procedural that inspired his interest in adapting true crime stories from the files of the Los Angeles Police Department when he created *Dragnet.*

Webb's approach to the crime show was unique, involving no-nonsense dialogue ("Just the facts, ma'am") and a storytelling style that sounded more like the reading aloud of an actual police report than a fictionalized crime story. Once it moved to television, *Dragnet* became a national rage. The theme song was a top hit on the record charts with Ray Anthony's instrumental version. Comic parody artist Stan Freberg did a recording called "St. George and the Dragonet" that became a chart-topper. The TV show was turned into a hit

Harry Morgan with Jack Webb (*right*) in *Dragnet,* circa 1967. Courtesy of Nick at Nite publicity.

movie in 1954, starring Webb. And reruns of the program, syndicated under the title *Badge 714,* racked up huge profits.

Before the show left the air for the first time, Webb busied himself writing, producing, and starring in feature films like *Pete Kelly's Blues* (1955), also based on a Webb-created radio series. A lifelong jazz fan and cornet enthusiast, Webb starred as a cornet player and band leader. His grim military drama *The D.I.* (1957) earned him critical raves, though it wasn't a box office hit. [Webb's third wife, Jackie Loughery, was featured in the film.]

In his later years, Webb had a spotty record as a producer. He took over production of the hit series *77 Sunset Strip* and made a number of radical changes that spelled disaster to the series. But his efforts on producing the series *Adam-12* and *Emergency!* were both notable successes.

Time and again, though, *Dragnet* was rekindled for television and even the movie screen, if not by Webb, then by others. It remained his signature program—a milestone in TV history.

Setting the Scene

My first chat with Jack Webb began weirdly—with a ride in the back of a Los Angeles Police Department paddy wagon, along with a gaggle of TV critics.

It was some publicist's idea of a novel way to whisk us from the Century Plaza Hotel to Universal Studios to go on the set of Jack Webb's latest TV series, *Mobile One.* It was June 1975, and the others ran onto the sets to confab with the show's star, Jackie Cooper, other cast members, and John Carradine, who was the guest star that week. Instead, I headed for Jack Webb's office—he was the executive producer—and we sat for several hours, talking about the past while the show's publicist complained we should be concentrating on the new show, not the good old days.

The Interview

BAWDEN: How did you get into show business?

WEBB: I was born in Santa Monica in 1920, but grew up in Bunker Hill, which is part of Los Angeles. I went to St. John's University in Minnesota, where I majored in art. During the war I enlisted in the Army Air Corps and after discharge got a job announcing on San Francisco's ABC station: KGO Radio. It was there I created my first series for radio, titled *Pat Novak, for Hire,* [about] a private detective. My costar was another unknown—a burly Canadian named Raymond Burr. It was all tough-guy talk, and I also created such shows as *Pete Kelly's Blues* and another titled *Johnny Madero.*

BAWDEN: I have to ask you what you remember about acting in the movie masterpiece *Sunset Blvd.*

WEBB: Not much, as I had a very tiny part as Bill Holden's bud. There's a party scene in my crowded apartment that I liked a lot. I wasn't on the set much and nobody noticed me in the reviews.

BAWDEN: How, then, did you attain stardom as Joe Friday in *Dragnet* so soon after?

WEBB: I'd done other bits in films. I'm a technician in the 1948 thriller *He Walked by Night.* It was done in a documentary style and had me thinking of using L.A.P.D. files to re-create real cases. L.A.P.D. chief Bill Parker was a real asset and I wrote and starred in *Dragnet* for NBC Radio. We premiered in 1949. Audience reaction was instantaneous.

NBC then thought it might make a sturdy TV series. You must remember, at this time TV drama was mostly live. To set a series out on the streets of L.A.—well, it was revolutionary. I picked oldster Barton Yarborough as my partner. He'd done it on radio, too, and when he died suddenly I picked Ben

Alexander, whose credits go all the way back to *All Quiet on the Western Front* [1930].

BAWDEN: Did you know what a career-changing enterprise you were getting into?

WEBB: No idea. I mean, portable cameras did not exist. Had to invent them. Getting the crew out there was always a logistical nightmare. The sound technician had to adapt the mikes so as not to pick up all the traffic noise. And then there was the casting. We used every available character actor because we went through so many people every week. I naïvely thought I could write everything, too, but we needed scripts two to three weeks in advance, so we could block out locations. You know, people still ask why both of us [Sergeant Friday and his partner, Officer Smith] slide through that one car door. That's because we had the camera stationed in a fixed position on the car hood. It took a long time at first until we could refine our techniques. It had a ragged edge to it and that was deliberate. Within a few weeks we became the show to watch.

BAWDEN: How do you explain its sudden popularity?

WEBB: Realism. There have been many parodies. Some made me giggle. But we were the first filmed cop show. And I greatly respected these guys. I wanted to show what they went through. We just didn't cover murder cases—everything was dramatized. And there always was a real case in the actual files. And do you know people love watching this show today as we present a view of L.A. which has gone. For one thing, there's very little smog and the traffic was still moderate. Drugs were just starting to make an appearance. Friday had a certain fixed moral interpretation of good versus evil. That is why audiences respected what he was doing.

BAWDEN: After the show left the air, you brought it back in 1967. How did that happen?

WEBB: I pick up the phone and ring Ben Alexander [to offer him a chance to reprise his role] and he comes on the phone giggling and says, "Jack, you don't read the trades [the Hollywood show business trade journals], do you?" I didn't know he was doing *Felony Squad* over at ABC with Howard Duff. So I picked Harry Morgan as my new partner. I'd worked with him way back in 1950 in *Dark City*. And we went just two seasons, due to so-so ratings. You see, the novelty was gone.

BAWDEN: What happened to half-hour TV dramas like *Dragnet*?

WEBB: It became cheaper to make an hour drama rather than two thirty-minuters. Economics. It drives everything.

BAWDEN: I remember another series of yours from that era that seemed so un–Jack Webb: *Noah's Ark,* in 1956.

WEBB (*irritated*): Critics have always been trying to pigeonhole me. It was one of the first all-color shows made for NBC. Very expensive. Jack Webb doing a show about a vet—how strange! Well, it lasted two half seasons, but was so expensive NBC aborted it quickly.

BAWDEN: Your success with *Dragnet* brought you back into movies?

WEBB: *Dragnet* [the movie version] in 1954 was one of the first movie spin-offs of a TV series. Others were comedies: *Our Miss Brooks, Here Come the Nelsons* [*Ozzie and Harriet*]. We brought in Dick Boone from *Medic* [the TV show] as the police captain and peopled it with great character actors like Virginia Gregg and Dennis Weaver. It came and went and made a profit.

BAWDEN: You seemed to concentrate on making movies for a bit.

WEBB: Had a great deal with Warners for using TV techniques for inexpensive films. We started with *Pete Kelly's Blues* in 1955 and I had Janet Leigh in her first film since moving from MGM and it was a huge hit. Peggy Lee got a Supporting Oscar nomination. I also directed *-30-* [1959], which is a fine newspaper yarn. I had Bill Conrad as the city editor. I think it shows how an L.A. paper operated at that time and it was a big hit commercially. And thank you for not mentioning *The Last Time I Saw Archie* [1960], which was my effort to be funny. Also Bob Mitchum's—and it showed we hadn't a funny bone between us.

BAWDEN: It was heavy going when you took over Warners TV.

WEBB: I wasn't the creator, you see. And some of their big hits were sinking fast anyway. Then my show with Jeff Hunter [*Temple Houston*] went to air four weeks after being green-lighted and it was a mess. I admit that.

BAWDEN: Your next show, *Adam-12,* was a sort of *Son of Dragnet,* right?

WEBB: You got it. We started in 1968 and ran to 1975.

BAWDEN: David Janssen has told me he had trouble mouthing your trademark terse dialogue in *O'Hara, U.S. Treasury.*

WEBB [*irritated*]: David Janssen said it was tough mouthing those lines? I mean how much thought goes into saying, "Go to it" or "Yipes"?

BAWDEN: You really scored with *Emergency!,* which started on NBC in 1972 and used the same basic techniques as *Dragnet.*

WEBB: Get the viewer involved, put the camera right into the action, show how paramedics and the E.R. staff work as one. I got so excited I even directed several episodes just to get it going.

BAWDEN: Now tell me about your latest, *Mobile One* [1975].

WEBB: I got Jackie Cooper [a former child star] back into acting and I added Julie Gregg and Mark Wheeler as young and beautiful staffers. I'm casting big parts with TV names: Tom Bosley, Anne Francis, Farley Granger.

BAWDEN: What next?

WEBB: I'll do what I've always done. I'll gather a crew and start creating my next series.

Afterword

Mobile One did not last a full season on ABC. Another Webb-produced series, *Hec Ramsey,* starring Richard Boone as a frontier forensic scientist, was a segment of the *NBC Mystery Movie* series and lasted two seasons (1972–1974). He returned with another series, *Project UFO*, a documentary-style drama about the government's efforts to track down flying saucer reports. It began in mid-season 1978 and lasted a season and a half.

Webb was working on yet another revamping of *Dragnet*, to star Kent McCord (from *Adam-12*) and debut on NBC in September 1983. But he died on December 23, 1982, of an apparent heart attack. He was sixty-two. With Webb's death, L.A. police chief Daryl Gates announced that badge 714—Joe Friday's badge—would be permanently retired.

Webb was married four times, first to actress-singer Julie London, with whom he had a daughter and a son. They were divorced in 1954 but remained friends, and Webb starred her in his later TV series, *Emergency!* He married Dorothy Towne in 1955 and they were divorced two years later. His third wife was former Miss USA Jackie Loughery (1958–1964). He married Opal Wright in 1980 and was still wed to her at the time of his death.

Webb's daughter Stacy collaborated on a biography titled *Just the Facts, Ma'am,* with Daniel Moyer and Eugene Alvarez. But Stacy Webb died in a car crash in 1986 and the book wasn't published until 1999.

Webb's signature creation, *Dragnet,* continued to have a life of its own. In 1987, *Dragnet,* a comic parody of the original series, was released, with Dan Aykroyd playing Joe Friday, a descendant of the original cop played by Webb. Tom Hanks played his partner and Webb's onetime *Dragnet* partner, Harry Morgan, reprised his role as Bill Gannon, now the chief of detectives.

In 1989–1990, a new syndicated version of *Dragnet,* called *The New Dragnet,* was seen, using none of the original characters and an all-new cast. It was teamed in several markets with the revival of another Webb-produced show, known as *The New Adam-12*. Neither show was very successful, but forty-eight episodes of *The New Dragnet* were produced.

In 2003, Dick Wolf, creator of the *Law and Order* franchise of hit crime shows, produced *L.A. Dragnet*, another revival of the series, with Ed O'Neill as Joe Friday. It ran on ABC, but was not a ratings success.

Lawrence Welk

Interview by Ron Miller

Lawrence Welk was unique among the television stars of his era. He was a band leader from the 1940s who played old-fashioned dance music yet became a TV celebrity at the same time the rest of America was being overwhelmed by the rising tide of the rock and roll revolution.

The Lawrence Welk Show debuted on ABC's Saturday night lineup in 1955, immediately capturing the attention of moms and dads whose teenage children were going out to the movies to hear Bill Haley & the Comets rock the screen in *The Blackboard Jungle*. While the teens in Philadelphia, P.A., were rockin' with TV's *American Bandstand*, their parents were watching senior citizens do the polka to Welk's "champagne music" from 9 to 10 p.m.

To be sure, band leaders had been stars on radio and in the movies from the late 1920s through the war years of the 1940s. Paul Whiteman was the star of Universal's spectacular 1930 movie *The King of Jazz*. Glenn Miller, Harry James, Xavier Cugat, Artie Shaw, Benny Goodman, and lots of other baton-wielders were big attractions on-screen, often even appearing as actors in films built around them—such as Kay Kyser, who helmed his own radio shows and was the main star of a whole series of movies at RKO and Columbia.

But the big-band era skidded to a halt in the late 1940s, and many of the name swing bands folded before TV became a national phenomenon. Though some band leaders did survive into the TV era—Tommy and Jimmy Dorsey, for example, hosted their *Stage Show* on CBS from 1954 to 1956, but it wasn't a ratings success and is best remembered today for bringing Elvis Presley to television before Ed Sullivan got hold of him.

But it was the leaders of the so-called sweet bands like Lawrence Welk and Guy Lombardo who seemed to fit the new medium best, along with some of the novelty bands like Harry Owens's Hawaiian band, Spike Jones &

Lawrence Welk. Ron Miller collection.

His City Slickers, and the western band leaders like "Dude" Martin. In the San Francisco Bay Area, where I grew up, Del Courtney's band had a local daytime show and Bob Scobey's Dixieland-style band had a late-night show for a short time.

Perhaps the time was ripe for Lawrence Welk, whose cornball music was the antidote to rock and roll for parents who thought their kids were losing their minds. He was also a master showman who knew how to assemble a very entertaining hour with comedy, music, and pretty girls like the Lennon Sisters and "Champagne Ladies" like Alice Lon and Norma Zimmer, with whom he danced on camera to his own music.

Welk was an accordion player at a time when the accordion was becoming a forsaken instrument. He also had a thick German accent—he grew up in the German-speaking community of Strasburg, North Dakota—that helped make him an unusual character. With his standard "A one and a two" opening as he conducted his orchestra and his ever-present bubble machine that helped purvey the "champagne" theme of his rather bubbly music, he was the perfect target for imitators, most especially the brilliant Stan Freberg, who produced a hit novelty record about what might happen if Welk's bubble machine somehow went berserk during a concert. Later, TV's *Saturday Night Live* did regular parodies of his show.

Welk's show was a mighty success for ABC and ran on Saturday nights from 1955 to 1971, when it was finally canceled because advertisers complained it was "skewing old" and not enough young viewers were watching. Welk refused to abandon his loyal following and took the show into syndication to local stations, where it remained a top attraction from 1971 to 1982. After Welk finally called it quits, the show continued to play in reruns—and still does in some places on the TV landscape.

The TV show made Welk a very rich man because it spurred record sales and drew millions of loyal fans to his live performances, especially at his longtime performance venue—the Aragon Ballroom in Venice Beach, California.

Setting the Scene

The music of Lawrence Welk was not a very vital part of my youthful years. When his recording of "Oh Happy Day" with a droopy vocal by bass singer Larry Hooper hit the charts in 1953, I much preferred the more obscure original 1952 recording of the song by high school student Don Howard. When Welk first began his weekly show on national television, I was a junior in high school and deeply involved with the progressive sounds of Dave Brubeck and Stan Kenton.

But I was finally forced to pay attention to Welk when I started dating the girl who eventually would become my wife. Her dad was a devoted Welk fan and I figured I'd better show some interest if I wanted to marry the man's daughter. I'd say I learned to tolerate "champagne music," but never loved it.

But in 1979 I was offered a chance to interview Welk and realized the man was now an icon of television. Since I was by then a syndicated television columnist, I sincerely wanted to meet him and get to know him. I'd interviewed a few of his musicians over the years and they'd all given me warm appraisals of him, although some seemed unhappy with his notorious dress code for performers, which banned short skirts for women and long hair for men.

The interview took place in Welk's headquarters office atop a high-rise building in Santa Monica, California. He turned out to be a genial, warm-hearted man. He was seventy-five at the time of our interview and looked tanned and fit, dressed neatly but casually in checkered trousers and a lime green sweater. He seemed amazingly unsophisticated and natural. For example, he wanted me to see the remarkable system he had installed to open and close the curtains on his office windows, which surrounded us on three sides and revealed an impressive view of the Santa Monica beachfront. He kept pushing the buttons and making the drapes open and close for me to appreciate the whole process.

He was honest and jovial. His English was notably loaded with fractures; he would say *you-ah* instead of *you* and *me-ah* instead of *me*. When I left he presented me with an autographed LP album and a signed copy of his autobiography, which I ultimately presented to my father-in-law in hopes of raising my status among his sons-in-law.

Today I consider Lawrence Welk to be a genuine American original and I treasure my memory of our single chat together. I might add that I'm now at the age where his music sounds a lot better to me than it did in my teens.

The Interview

WELK [*shaking my hand*]: Well, how are you? You can call me Lawrence. What's your name? I'll just write it down here so I won't forget.

MILLER: You certainly have a wonderful view from here.

WELK: We like it.

MILLER: You seem to have done remarkably well since the network dropped your show.

WELK: We're on 221 stations in the United States and 31 in Canada. That's more stations than when we were on the network.

MILLER: How did all this start? I've read accounts that sound like you were a musical version of Abe Lincoln, growing up in a log cabin and living out the American dream.

WELK [*grinning*]: I was a farm boy, very sickly and very backward because I only went to four years of schooling. I went into the music business at twenty-one years of age. I had waited all my life for it because I loved music more than anything else.

MILLER: The legend is that you were discovered by a man named George Kelly, who heard you playing your accordion at a county fair in your native North Dakota.

WELK: He told me, "Young man, you have great potential." He knew how to get a dance hall for only $3 a night when they were charging $5.

MILLER: So he taught you how to organize your act and how to use a little showmanship to draw a crowd to the dance hall?

WELK: I learned from him. I liked it very much—the show business—and I dedicated myself to it. I was hungry for learning.

MILLER: So you formed a band in the 1920s and started playing very small towns all over the Midwest. What was that like?

WELK: We learned the people loved easy music they could dance to all night. They always had smiling faces.

MILLER: But you weren't exactly hitting the big time?

WELK: At the end of the evening, we also had to fold up all the chairs and clean up the dance hall.

MILLER: The late 1920s were not a happy time for many Americans, especially after the market crash in 1929. Was there a low point for you then?

WELK: In 1929, I thought we were doing well with radio broadcasts and touring, but one night the five members of the band came to me and told me they had made the decision to go out by themselves. The reason they gave me was that I was not a good enough musician and I was holding them back.

MILLER: That had to be a major low point.

WELK: That was possibly the most hurt I'd ever had. It took me about three weeks to snap out of that.

MILLER: Once you did, though, you rebuilt your band, made it bigger, and by 1938 you were doing national radio broadcasts and getting loads of fan mail. When did the "champagne music" thing get going? Were you starting to be so popular that you could afford champagne?

WELK [*laughing*]: No, it came from the mail we were getting. People said our music sounded "bubbly," like champagne. That's when we decided to call it "champagne music" and it has worked for us. I don't touch the stuff myself. Maybe a little Manischewitz now and then.

MILLER: You were making recordings that did well through the 1940s and you started a local television show on station KTLA in Los Angeles that attracted the attention of ABC, which had carried your radio show starting in 1951. They put *The Lawrence Welk Show* on the TV network in the summer of 1955. Some critics tended to label your music "cornball." Did that bother you?

WELK: I didn't mind. I know who my people are. Let me give you an example. Not long ago I was given an honorary degree at a college in Kansas. On the way back, I had my driver stop for a bite to eat in a small town with a population of twelve hundred people. Somehow it leaked out I was there. We were about to leave when the principal of the high school came over and said, "Mr. Welk, it would mean everything to our kids if you could come over to the school and say hello to them." So we drove over to the school and within minutes the principal called a special assembly. I took out my accordion and did a half-hour show. It was the biggest applause I ever had in my whole life! I could do no wrong. I realized for the first time that I had a young audience, too.

MILLER: What do you think of the parodies of you that some TV performers have done?

WELK: I've never been hurt by anything done in good fun. I understand it. Besides, I do a bit of it myself. [He winked at me, put his finger in his mouth, and made a popping sound like a champagne cork.] You see!

MILLER: Some of the entertainers you've worked with over the years have told me they loved working for you, but didn't like your dress code and rules about hair length. They say Alice Lon lost her job as your "Champagne Lady" because she wore her skirts too short. What about those rules of yours?

WELK: The viewers take care of that. If someone's hair is too long, the mail will start pouring in and he'll realize he has to cut his hair.

MILLER: After the enormous success of the show, was it a devastating blow to learn you were being canceled when ratings still were high?

WELK: I'll never forget the day I learned about it. I was playing golf that day and when I came off the course, there was a phone call from a newspaperman I considered a friend. He told me he'd just seen the new ABC fall lineup and I wasn't on it. It was quite a shock. I was thinking of my musical family. I wasn't that worried about myself because when you get up to be sixty or sixty-five, you feel you've pretty much had it anyway.

MILLER: Is it true that your own sponsors wanted to keep you on the network, but ABC wanted to attract different advertisers that appealed to younger viewers?

WELK: Our sponsors promised me they would stand by us if we went to another network.

MILLER: But the other networks were looking for younger viewers, too, so you decided to try syndicating the program to local stations?

WELK: We notified every station in the country and asked them if they'd like to carry our show but be able to put it on at any time they wanted. The next day we had about four hundred wires [telegrams] back from stations that wanted to hear more.

MILLER: Going into syndication was a great move, I guess, since you've never been out of the top ten in syndicated shows ever since. You've outlasted all the "sweet bands" of your era and your orchestra is just about one of a kind today.

WELK: You know why I'm here today? It's because it took me so long to get here.

MILLER: You appear to be a very vigorous fellow. What's your daily routine like?

WELK: I'm still a South Dakota farm boy because my day usually starts at 4:30 or 5 a.m. I get up in the morning and fall into my swimming pool. I do that for about fifteen or twenty minutes. By that time my wife will have breakfast for me and we'll have that together. I leave the house at 7 a.m. and I'm here at the office by 7:15. Then I go over the schedule for my next show and meet with my staff the rest of the day.

MILLER: Still, you're no longer a youngster. Do you ever think of retirement?

WELK: I'm a very fortunate man because I've done what I like to do all through my life. I think it would be very difficult for me to retire. But I would very much like to create an organization that could function by itself.

MILLER: I suppose that's because you care about all the people who depend on you for their livelihood today.

WELK: We have about fifty full-time staff members. As for the band, there's always pressure on the young musicians to go out on their own to do their own thing.

Afterword

Welk finally retired from touring with his band after the show ended in 1982. He did return for TV Christmas specials in 1985 and 1986, but retired from all public appearances in 1992.

Welk was married only once, to Fern Renner in 1931. They had three children. Welk died from bronchial pneumonia at his home in Santa Monica on May 17, 1992. He was eighty-nine.

In his years as a TV star, Welk invested heavily in real estate and operated several resorts and businesses. His programs have been repackaged for continual television showings and are still widely seen.

Jonathan Winters

Interview by Ron Miller

If ever there was a comedy star whose career was perfectly made for the TV medium, it surely was Jonathan Winters, whose unique talents flowered on TV in the 1950s and helped him become a legendary star who remained in demand for nearly half a century.

Born in Ohio in 1925, Winters began to invent his own imaginary characters in his childhood, perhaps to people his world with folks he could tailor-make for a make-believe social order where he could more easily fit in. Often a lonely kid whose parents divorced in his youth, Winters worked his way to popularity by entertaining his fellow students at school with his native ability to imitate not only other people, but almost any kind of machine or object.

In the early 1950s, Winters began to appear in stand-up comedy gigs in New York City and made his initial attempt to get on television as a losing contestant on *Arthur Godfrey's Talent Scouts*. He was more successful gaining the support of late-night *Tonight Show* hosts, first Steve Allen and then Jack Paar, who used him frequently.

Winters's success with comedy albums also was an important factor in his phenomenal rise in popularity. He began to record comedy albums for Verve Records in the 1960s. Altogether, he earned eleven Grammy nominations in his career and won twice.

Winters's first regular appearances in prime-time television were on *And Here's the Show*, a 1955 summer replacement series for comedian George Gobel's NBC sitcom. He was the costar of that series with comedian Ransom Sherman, and it was on this series that viewers first got to meet his full range of characters, including fussy old woman Maudie Frickert and country rube Elwood P. Suggins.

This led NBC to showcase him on *The NBC Comedy Hour* (1956) and finally to give him his own series, *The Jonathan Winters Show*, which ran for fifteen minutes after the evening news broadcast.

Winters's manic style of performing was dazzling. He had a special gift for improvisation. In his many guest spots on television, he often was asked to create visual and vocal impressions spontaneously. He frequently seemed to dare program hosts to try to stump him. It never happened.

Though Winters did star in his own series on more than one occasion, including his own syndicated series called *The Wacky World of Jonathan Winters* (1972–1974), his frenzied style sometimes could wear the viewer out and the conventional wisdom suggested he was better off doing a guest spot than tackling a whole program on his own.

For that reason, perhaps, Winters was featured in a great number of television shows of different types as a regular performer, panelist, or voice actor, among them *Shirley Temple's Storybook* (ABC), *The Andy Williams Show* (ABC), *Masquerade Party* (CBS), *Hee-Haw* (syndicated version), and *The Mouse Factory* (syndicated). He was the voice of Mayor Cod on CBS's *Fish Police* cartoon series.

In 1981–1982, Winters played the role of Mearth, the adult infant fathered by Robin Williams in ABC's *Mork and Mindy* series. The fact that Winters had inspired the comedy style of Williams, then played Williams's son, hatched out of a giant egg, was one of the monumental "in-jokes" of TV history.

In 1991–1992, Winters won a Supporting Actor Emmy Award for his role in the series *Davis Rules*, which ran on ABC before moving to CBS.

Winters did make some impressive appearances in feature films— including *It's a Mad, Mad, Mad, Mad World* (1963), Stanley Kramer's big-screen comedy star extravaganza; Tony Richardson's 1965 *The Loved One;* and Norman Jewison's 1966 *The Russians Are Coming! The Russians Are Coming!* but his appearances in these films were mostly like his TV guest spots— limited and hilarious. He didn't seem suited to play the main character in any film.

Through his most successful years, Winters was plagued with emotional problems that sometimes led to breakdowns, and he was hospitalized for treatment on a couple of occasions when his behavior caused public disruptions.

Randy Quaid with Jonathan Winters (*right*) in *Davis Rules*, 1991. Courtesy of ABC publicity.

Setting the Scene

I discovered Jonathan Winters in my high school years when my favorite weekly comedy series, *The George Gobel Show*, was replaced for the summer by *And Here's the Show*, featuring Ransom Sherman and Jonathan Winters. I remember being blown away by Winters's crazy brand of comedy, especially his "sail cat" routine about finding a dead cat, flattened on the highway by a truck and dried out by the sun, which he picked up and sailed out like a

Frisbee over a nearby canyon—complete with his uncanny special vocal effects. I became an instant devotee.

My only personal meeting with Winters came many years later, in May 1979, when he was filming a TV special at the Great America amusement park in Santa Clara, California, located close to the newspaper where I worked as a TV columnist—the *San José Mercury News*. He agreed to meet me for lunch in the amusement park's cafeteria.

I'm not sure the cafeteria staff fully appreciated the show Winters put on for me. He was trying to display his usual penchant for improvisation by pretending to see an imaginary "critter" in the imaginary hamburger being eaten by a diner at the table next to us. "What's that on your bun?" he asked loudly. "Looks like some kind of bug. Look at that little critter go!" Pretty soon all the other diners were laughing out loud as Winters unleashed his bag of vocal effects to create the image of a diner becoming aware he was eating a bug-infested hamburger.

Though Winters was affable and friendly enough, I felt he was a rather sad sort of man who wasn't able to relax totally. Maybe that's because he'd been a public figure for so long that he always knew everybody was watching him. I think part of him relished the attention, but possibly another part wished there wasn't any.

The Interview

MILLER: You've just demonstrated that you're a comedian who can convulse a crowd of perfect strangers in the middle of their lunch break.

WINTERS: See, I've got everybody laughing and I haven't told a joke yet. Reality is still the hottest property around. Jokes are a bummer.

MILLER: You're only fifty-three, which is young for a comedian in the era of Jack Benny, Bob Hope, and George Burns. But the rumor is you're not going to do stand-up comedy in clubs anymore. Is this true?

WINTERS: Yes. I finally got tired of working in front of drunks and hecklers, so I'm more or less pulling out of the nightclub circuit. I really don't want to do any more situation comedies or variety hours either.

MILLER: Can you be having what they call a midlife crisis?

WINTERS: My ego is such that I don't want to be working at seventy-five and having kids in college saying, "God, is he still there?" Maybe it's because it's getting near the end, because I'm in the fourth quarter. But I'd like to do some movies, a couple of serious roles, maybe some good satire before I pack it in.

MILLER: You're really thinking about picking up all your marbles and leaving the game?

WINTERS: Well, why not? Everybody knows I've got a few [marbles] missing anyway.

MILLER: Some critics feel your tremendous early success may have made you a victim of overexposure, that the ratings for your TV shows began fading for that reason. Does that make any sense to you?

WINTERS: If you have something special, you really have to protect it. You can't keep relying on one character. Look at Geraldine. She ate up Flip Wilson. That's why I said good-bye to Maudie Frickert.

MILLER: Do you think that might happen to the new comic who's most often compared to you—Robin Williams of *Mork and Mindy*?

WINTERS: If the public tires of Mork, they may tire of Robin, too. They may see them as one and the same. [This was before Winters and Williams joined forces on Williams's TV series.]

MILLER: I've heard you're very critical of the way decisions are made in television by constantly checking the ratings.

WINTERS: Now a show has to make the grade in just three to five weeks. That's like taking a three- to five-week college course. What can you learn in that time? You certainly can't learn your craft!

MILLER: I've seen you work with absolutely no script, improvising on the spot, and still getting big laughs. Is that your special gift?

WINTERS: That's the way I like to work. I'm doing it my way now, just like Sinatra says in his song.

Afterword

Though he was talking about slowing down when we talked in 1979, Winters continued to find new ways to expand his career for years after we met. In 1988, for instance, he wrote a book of short fiction, *Winters' Tales*, which revealed yet another immense layer of his talent. In 1999, he won the distinguished Mark Twain Prize for his achievements in American humor. After we met, he created the Mearth character on TV's *Mork and Mindy*, bonding with Robin Williams in what would become a firm friendship.

He continued to create new characters, often in voice work in animated television shows and feature films. One of his last was the Grandpa Smurf character in *The Smurfs* (2011) animated feature film. One of his last completed works was doing that vocal characterization for *Smurfs II* (2013).

Winters died from natural causes on April 11, 2013, at his home in Montecito, California. He was eighty-seven. He was married only once, to wife Eileen, with whom he had two children. She died before him in 2009.

Efrem Zimbalist Jr.

Interview by James Bawden

Efrem Zimbalist Jr. was born in New York City in 1918, the son of parents already renowned in the world of music. His father, Efrem Zimbalist Sr., was a Russian-born concert musician and composer. His mother was the Romanian-born operatic soprano Alma Gluck. Even his subsequent stepmother, Mary Louise Curtis Bok, had deep roots in music and was the founder of the Curtis Institute of Music.

Naturally, Zimbalist Jr. was expected to pursue a career in music. But after attending Yale University in the 1930s and serving in the US Army for five years during World War II, he began to veer toward a career in acting.

Though he was accomplished in music and had modest success as an actor on the stage and in movies, Zimbalist is best remembered for his roles in the genre of law enforcement in two very popular television series: *77 Sunset Strip*, playing private eye Stu Bailey, and *The FBI*, in which he played Inspector Lewis Erskine.

Setting the Scene

I first met and interviewed Efrem Zimbalist Jr. at CBC Radio headquarters on Jarvis Street in Toronto in 1977. The always affable Zimbalist was in town as CBC Radio saluted him with a full orchestra performing many of his musical compositions.

Zimbalist was most excited to hear that music genius Glenn Gould was also in the building making a radio documentary, and it was arranged that the reclusive Gould would accidentally on purpose bump into him in the winding corridors of the decrepit Victorian mansion, which for decades had been a private girls' school. But Gould failed to appear as I walked up and down with Zimbalist before we hit the cafeteria for a long afternoon of talk and reminiscences.

321

Efrem Zimbalist Jr. in *77 Sunset Strip*, circa 1958. Courtesy of Warner Bros. publicity and the James Bawden collection.

My final chat with Zimbalist was done on the telephone after he replaced Anne Baxter as the star of the *Hotel* television series.

I've combined my separate interviews for this presentation.

The Interview

BAWDEN: Growing up in luxury in Connecticut, with two music legends as parents, was there any tendency to continue the line in music?

ZIMBALIST: Well, yes. It was expected of me. And that's the reason I'm in Toronto this week as CBC Radio performs some of my classical compositions. I was always writing musical pieces, since I could walk. Father was an immensely successful concert pianist. Mother was born in Romania as Reib Feinsohn, although she took the stage name Alma Gluck, which she later admitted hating. When I told my father I wanted to act he said merrily, "What name are you going to use?" He thought Efrem Zimbalist Jr. too long for the marquee, but I didn't want to change it. I started out at the Yale School of Drama and was expelled for bad marks, so I enlisted in the army and fought in Europe.

Then I didn't know what to do and a pal, Garson Kanin, gave me a part in a Broadway play he was producing—Robert Sherwood's *The Rugged Path*. It starred Spencer Tracy in his first Broadway appearance in years.

BAWDEN: And?

ZIMBALIST: It ran for only sixty-six performances. A bad play. Spence was wasted much of the time from drinking and suffered from stage fright for the first time in his career. Kate Hepburn was behind the curtain to prod him on because he couldn't remember his lines. They shouted a lot at each other. Finally, Spence said to hell with this and left for Hollywood and never ventured back to Broadway ever again. But I had sold the business to myself. I wanted to be in a hit next time.

BAWDEN: Then what happened?

ZIMBALIST: I got a bigger part in a 1948 production of *Hedda Gabler* opposite Eva Le Gallienne. We ran for fifteen whole performances. A real stinker. Nobody came. But I met my wife, Emily McNair.

BAWDEN: Then you had your first TV acting gig.

ZIMBALIST: I got a film part in Joe Mankiewicz's *House of Strangers* [1949]. I was the nastiest of the bunch and I got noticed. Emily died of cancer and I had two little niblets to look after so I just stopped looking for acting jobs. My dad made me assistant curator at his Curtis Institute of Music in Philadelphia. Then I got a job in the new NBC daily TV soap opera *Concerning Miss Marlowe*, which starred Louise Albritton and ran exactly a year, from July 1954 to July 1955. It was fifteen minutes and was live and I can't remember a single plot line. Procter & Gamble made it for NBC.

BAWDEN: I've never heard of that soap at all.

ZIMBALIST: Nobody has.

BAWDEN: How did you get into films for good, then?

ZIMBALIST: Well, I was in Noël Coward's *Fallen Angels* on Broadway and director Josh Logan saw me and got Jack Warner to sign me up as a male ingénue. That was 1957 and I was already thirty-nine. I was a southerner in *Band of Angels* [1957] with Clark Gable, who wore a tight corset, and Yvonne De Carlo, who was supposed to be a half-breed. It was awful. Then I was in *The Deep Six* [1958] with Alan Ladd. *Home Before Dark* [1958] was actually good, with Jean Simmons as a housewife who has a breakdown. This is among my favorite parts. In *Bombers B-52* [1957] I was Natalie Wood's squeeze. She was twenty, I was forty, and her mother was played by Marsha Hunt, who was thirty-nine and just winked every time I had to embrace Nat.

Then I did *Girl on the Run* [1958], which was the pilot for the series *77 Sunset Strip*. I fought not to do it, but Jack Warner said to trust him and he was right. I loved doing TV because I could get home at night and look after my kids and there was no location work. Most movies were being shot far from the San Fernando Valley where we lived.

BAWDEN: Then *77 Sunset Strip* became a hit series that ran six seasons starting in 1958. Why did it succeed?

ZIMBALIST: Beats me. Warners just did that kind of hour-long mystery better than anybody else. Sitcoms? Warners wasn't into that kind of thing. You know, Jack Warner tested the market with TV versions of three hit movies: *Cheyenne, Casablanca,* and *Kings Row,* and only *Cheyenne* made it. Jack came to the quick conclusion that what worked in the movies didn't work on TV and he was right.

Bill Orr was the Warners VP of TV and he knew how to sell a show. He also was Jack's son-in-law. Orr sold this one to ABC, which was going after a younger viewership than NBC or CBS. I think I was making around $800 weekly when we started. We shot mainly on the old standing sets on the Burbank back lot. It took more than five shooting days to make an hour episode, so there were two crews shooting—one for me, the other for costar Roger Smith. I'd visit his episode for one scene and vice versa. It was the only way to stay ahead and make those thirty-nine new episodes a season.

We were treated as second-class Warners citizens at the beginning. There was even a debate about allowing us to eat in the studio commissary along with the movie people. But since TV was keeping Warners going, Jack Warner said, "Why not?" You know, Roy Huggins created it, based on characters from his 1947 movie *I Love Trouble* with Franchot Tone, and he originally favored a harder-edged story line, which was softened during the first year on orders of ABC. We were peddling a lifestyle, no doubt about it.

We shot fast, about seven pages a day. Edd Byrnes and his "Kookie" character took off with the kids and established us as must-see TV. There were very few retakes so you had to be ready on the first take. Sometimes we used multiple cameras if we were behind in the schedule. The most important thing for a new series is the time slot. ABC put us on Fridays at 9 opposite *Desilu Playhouse* on CBS and NBC's *Bell Telephone Hour* and we mowed down the competition. Kids could stay up later on Friday nights and they were all watching us. In 1962, they put us a half hour later at 9:30, and ratings drooped significantly.

BAWDEN: On hiatus you made movies.

ZIMBALIST: Jack sold my rights to United Artists for $100,000 for *By Love Possessed* [1961], a hugely budgeted soap that starred Lana Turner, but it only did fair business. That same year I made *A Fever in the Blood* for old pro Vincent Sherman at Warners opposite Angie Dickinson, who was being built up by the studio. It was filmed in nineteen days using TV techniques.

BAWDEN: I have a thesis: every time you contemplate flying, you phone up Dana Andrews first.

ZIMBALIST (*laughing*): Oh, you are so right. In *The Crowded Sky* [1960] I was piloting a single-engine plane that crashed into a commercial flight captained by Dana Andrews. In *Airport 1975* I was piloting a jumbo jet only to be hit by—wait for it—a single-engine plane piloted by Dana Andrews. So yes, we do get nervous when we fly. I always peer out the window trying to spot Dana in the clouds.

BAWDEN: In 1965 you jumped into another TV hit, *The FBI*, which ran for nine years. Again on ABC.

ZIMBALIST: People still believed in the FBI. I had a few talks with J. Edgar Hoover at the beginning. He was very concerned with the agency's reputation. Hoover insisted the FBI never be shown mucking up in a case. They had to get their killer at the end and I always had to be dressed well, but not overdressed, considering the salary for an agent. I was told he read all the scripts the first year but after that lost interest. This one just ran and ran.

And on my hiatus I was back at Warners doing an elongated bit as Audrey Hepburn's husband in *Wait Until Dark* [1967]. I even got to spoof the agency in *Hot Shots* [1991], but I wasn't as funny as Les Nielsen might have been, I confess.

BAWDEN: You're back in yet another series, *Hotel* [1986]?

ZIMBALIST: Why not! First Bette Davis played the owner, but she retired after the pilot because of breast cancer followed by a stroke. Then her replacement Anne Baxter left us very quickly. [Baxter died from a brain aneurysm.] Producer Aaron Spelling asked me to step in and over a weekend I did wardrobe and was on the sets Monday morning, and I'll do at least nine of these and then we'll see. And I've been on daughter Stephanie's series [*Remington Steele*] and I'm guessing I'll go on as long as they'll have me. Dad lived to be ninety-five. Maybe I can top him.

Afterword

Efrem Zimbalist Jr. continued to work for several more years after *Hotel*. He played the father of Zorro in the first season of *The New Zorro* (1990) television series and had a recurring role in the science fiction series *Babylon 5* in the 1990s. He lived as long as his father, dying of natural causes in Solvang, California, at ninety-five on May 2, 2014. He was survived by his son, Efrem III, a lawyer, and actress daughter Stephanie Zimbalist, who followed in his steps as a popular television star. She is best remembered for her costarring role in the hit detective series *Remington Steele*.

Acknowledgments

Though nearly all of the interviews in this volume were originally conducted by the authors for the newspapers they formerly worked for as columnists, none of the interviews are reprints of the original articles they wrote for those publications. Using their original notes and tape recordings, the authors have revised and enlarged the first published versions and added biographical material, personal commentary, and updated information.

The authors conducted no interviews together, but have merged the separate interviews they did with some performers to create enhanced interviews that include information gathered by both authors.

All the interviews done by Ron Miller in this collection were conducted for the *San José Mercury News*, and most of those interviews also appeared in newspapers throughout the United States and Canada via the Knight Ridder News syndicate. An earlier version of Miller's interview with James Arness also was translated into German and published in a German periodical.

James Bawden's interview with Ed Sullivan was conducted for the *Toronto Globe and Mail*. His interviews with Lucille Ball, George Burns, Vivian Vance, Efrem Zimbalist Jr., and Annette Funicello were conducted for the *Spectator* of Hamilton, Ontario. Bawden's interviews with Bea Arthur, Harry Morgan, Donna Reed, Robert Stack, Robert Vaughn, Macdonald Carey, John Forsythe, Julie Harris, and Ricardo Montalban were conducted for the *Toronto Star*. Bawden's interview with Ann Sothern was conducted for *Filmograph* magazine. Several Bawden interviews were conducted with the same stars for different newspapers at different stages in his career and merged for this collection. The interviews with Eve Arden, Buddy Ebsen, Mike Connors, Susan Douglas, and Lorne Greene were conducted for both the *Spectator* and the *Toronto Star*.

In addition, some of the quotes from the interviews in this book also were used by both Bawden and Miller in obituaries and memorial articles written for the website TheColumnists.com, for which both authors wrote from 1999 to 2013.

ACKNOWLEDGMENTS

The authors also would like to acknowledge the many network publicists and independent press agents who helped them secure the interviews contained in this volume. The photos used to illustrate the interviews were provided by the networks, the agencies representing the stars, newspaper photographers, or photo archive services.

Finally, the authors would like to acknowledge the guidance of Anne Dean Dotson, acquisitions editor at the University Press of Kentucky, and the superb staff members of the publisher, who helped make this collection special.

About the Authors

James Bawden and Ron Miller, friends for more than forty years, share a love of television and classic films that has led to their collaboration on a series of books for the University Press of Kentucky that collect their interviews with legendary stars and filmmakers. This book is the third in the series that began with *Conversations with Classic Film Stars* (2016) and continued with *You Ain't Heard Nothin' Yet* (2017).

Bawden is one of Canada's most respected writers on the subjects of movies and television. He has bachelor's degrees in history from the University of Toronto (1968) and in journalism from Carleton University (1970). He also has a master's degree in history and politics from Laurier University (1975). He was the television columnist for the *Hamilton Spectator* in Ontario, then moved on as television columnist for Canada's largest newspaper, the *Toronto Star*. He has written for most of the top film journals, including *Films in Review*. He lives in Toronto.

Miller has a bachelor's degree in journalism from San José State College (1961). He was the nationally syndicated television columnist for the *San José Mercury News* from 1977 to 1999 and is a National Headliner Award winner for his columns. He is a former national president of the Television Critics Association and former TV columnist for *Mystery Scene* magazine. He is currently a lecturer on movies and television at the Academy of Lifelong Learning at Western Washington University in Bellingham, Washington. He has written articles and fiction for scores of national magazines, including *TV Guide*. In addition to his books with Bawden, Miller was coauthor of *Masterpiece Theatre* (1995) with Terrence O'Flaherty, and sole author of *Mystery! A Celebration* (1996) and *Mystery Classics on Film* (2017). He lives in Blaine, Washington, with his wife, Darla.

Index

Page numbers in italics refer to photographs. Release dates are provided for films with shared titles.

331

Index

Screen Classics

Screen Classics is a series of critical biographies, film histories, and analytical studies focusing on neglected filmmakers and important screen artists and subjects, from the era of silent cinema through the golden age of Hollywood to the international generation of today. Books in the Screen Classics series are intended for scholars and general readers alike. The contributing authors are established figures in their respective fields. This series also serves the purpose of advancing scholarship on film personalities and themes with ties to Kentucky.

Series Editor

Patrick McGilligan

Books in the Series

Olivia de Havilland: Lady Triumphant
Victoria Amador

Mae Murray: The Girl with the Bee-Stung Lips
Michael G. Ankerich

Hedy Lamarr: The Most Beautiful Woman in Film
Ruth Barton

Rex Ingram: Visionary Director of the Silent Screen
Ruth Barton

Conversations with Classic Film Stars: Interviews from Hollywood's Golden Era
James Bawden and Ron Miller

Conversations with Legendary Television Stars: Interviews from the First Fifty Years
James Bawden and Ron Miller

You Ain't Heard Nothin' Yet: Interviews with Stars from Hollywood's Golden Era
James Bawden and Ron Miller

Von Sternberg
John Baxter

Hitchcock's Partner in Suspense: The Life of Screenwriter Charles Bennett
Charles Bennett, edited by John Charles Bennett

Hitchcock and the Censors
John Billheimer

A Uniquely American Epic: Intimacy and Action, Tenderness and Violence in Sam Peckinpah's The Wild Bunch
Edited by Michael Bliss

Sidney J. Furie: Life and Films
Daniel Kremer

Albert Capellani: Pioneer of the Silent Screen
Christine Leteux

Ridley Scott: A Biography
Vincent LoBrutto

Mamoulian: Life on Stage and Screen
David Luhrssen

Maureen O'Hara: The Biography
Aubrey Malone

My Life as a Mankiewicz: An Insider's Journey through Hollywood
Tom Mankiewicz and Robert Crane

Hawks on Hawks
Joseph McBride

Showman of the Screen: Joseph E. Levine and His Revolutions in Film Promotion
A. T. McKenna

William Wyler: The Life and Films of Hollywood's Most Celebrated Director
Gabriel Miller

Raoul Walsh: The True Adventures of Hollywood's Legendary Director
Marilyn Ann Moss

Veit Harlan: The Life and Work of a Nazi Filmmaker
Frank Noack

Harry Langdon: King of Silent Comedy
Gabriella Oldham and Mabel Langdon

Charles Walters: The Director Who Made Hollywood Dance
Brent Phillips

Some Like It Wilder: The Life and Controversial Films of Billy Wilder
Gene D. Phillips

Ann Dvorak: Hollywood's Forgotten Rebel
Christina Rice

Lewis Milestone: Life and Films
Harlow Robinson

Michael Curtiz: A Life in Film
Alan K. Rode

Arthur Penn: American Director
Nat Segaloff

Film's First Family: The Untold Story of the Costellos
Terry Chester Shulman

Claude Rains: An Actor's Voice
David J. Skal with Jessica Rains

Barbara La Marr: The Girl Who Was Too Beautiful for Hollywood
Sherri Snyder

Buzz: The Life and Art of Busby Berkeley
Jeffrey Spivak

Victor Fleming: An American Movie Master
Michael Sragow

Hollywood Presents Jules Verne: The Father of Science Fiction on Screen
Brian Taves

Thomas Ince: Hollywood's Independent Pioneer
Brian Taves

Carl Theodor Dreyer and Ordet: *My Summer with the Danish Filmmaker*
Jan Wahl

Clarence Brown: Hollywood's Forgotten Master
Gwenda Young